Cluniac Monasticism
in the Central Middle Ages

Cluniac Monasticism in the Central Middle Ages

Edited by
NOREEN HUNT

ARCHON BOOKS
1971

ISBN 0 208 01247 8

*This edition first published in
the United States of America, 1971
by Archon Books
Hamden, Connecticut 06514*

Printed in Great Britain

Contents

Preface

The aim of the series in which this book appears is to present to undergraduates examples of new approaches to research and some of the important contributions to key medieval themes or controversies which have generated a scholarly literature of their own. This literature can be difficult to obtain. Not only is it written in several languages but some of it appears in publications not always to be found in the largest libraries.

Cluniac monasticism is still a key controversial theme in medieval history. The following introduction makes clear that by confining the articles to Cluniac topics no attempt is being made to equate Cluniac monasticism with all monasticism in the central middle ages. It merely seemed that a more coherent collection could be made with Cluny rather than monasticism in general in mind. In any case, Cluny cannot be studied in isolation and the articles included in this book reflect the greater precision with which the term Cluniac is now being used.

In the matter of translating the main text of each article (as distinct from the footnotes) two facts have been kept in mind. One is that Latin is no longer required of history students in many British universities. The other consideration is the appearance of an increasing number of combined courses in some universities, whereby students of other disciplines may find themselves dabbling in medieval history. Therefore it seemed necessary to prepare a main text which could be read without tears, Latin or any other language save English. Here I must commend those continental scholars whose original articles contained treasured Latin quotations for the magnanimity with which they have acceded to this policy. The Latin has been kept, but in the footnotes, which cater on the whole for the initiated.

Dame Frideswide Sandeman, O.S.B., and Dame Maria Boulding, O.S.B., both of Stanbrook Abbey, translated the main texts of all save three of the articles and I am grateful to them for the care they have taken. Dame Frideswide also translated the excerpts from St Odo's *Occupatio* which appear in Professor Morghen's article. These, and most of the other medieval texts translated in the book appear in English for the first time. Dr Schwarzmaier's article on Polirone was translated by Mrs Joan Edwards, whom I would like to thank.

Acknowledgements are due to the following editors and publishers for permissions to translate and to reproduce material originally published by them: Professor Philippe Wolff and other editors and publishers of the *Annales du Midi* (Toulouse) for the articles on the crusading idea and on monasticism in the east Pyrenees; Professor W. Cramer, editor of 'Studia Anselmiana', Rome, for Dom Hourlier's article; the publishers Aubier (éditions montaigne), Paris, for permission to reproduce, with modifications, the article on Aldebald the scribe; Professor K. Hauck and the publishers Gruyter, Berlin, for permission to reproduce Dr Wollasch's article; Professor J. Fleckenstein, editor of the *Festschrift* dedicated to Professor G. Tellenbach, and the publishers Herder, Freiburg/Basel/Vienna, for allowing me to reproduce Dr Schwarzmaier's article. Full details of the origin of each article and further acknowledgements are given in the first footnote of each article.

My main thanks are due to the scholars who have so kindly consented to have their work translated and reproduced in this volume: they have been patient and generous in what must have been for them at times the painful process of preparing their work for the English edition: Professor Raffaello Morghen, President of the Italian Institute of Medieval History, Rome; Dom Kassius Hallinger, O.S.B., of Fulda and Sant'Anselmo, Rome; Dom Jacques Hourlier, O.S.B., Solesmes; Rev. Bernard de Vregille, S.J., of the Institut des Sources Chrétiennes, Lyons; Professor Anscari M. Mundó of Barcelona University; Dr Hansmartin Schwarzmaier of the Karlsruhe Public Record Office; Dr Joachim Wollasch of the University of Freiburg in Breisgau; Canon E. Delaruelle of the Institut Catholique, Toulouse; Dom Jean Leclercq, O.S.B., Clervaux and Sant'Anselmo, Rome. I am particularly grateful to Professor Kenneth J. Conant of the Mediaeval Academy of America for writing an article specially for this book.

NOREEN HUNT

London
September 1970

Abbreviations

AA SS	*Acta Sanctorum Bollandiana*
AA SS OSB	*Acta Sanctorum Ordinis S. Benedicti*, ed. Mabillon.
B	Bernard of Cluny, *Ordo Cluniacensis*, in Herrgott, *Vetus Disciplina Monastica*, pp. 133–364; quoted by book, chapter and page.
BB	A. Bernard and A. Bruel, *Recueil des Chartes de l'Abbaye de Cluny*, quoted by volume and number of charter.
BHL	*Bibliotheca hagiographica latina* (Brussels, 1838–1911).
Bibl. Cl.	*Bibliotheca Cluniacensis*, ed. Marrier, quoted by column.
Cart.	Charter or cartulary.
CF	*Consuetudines Farfensis*, in B. Albers, *Consuetudines Monasticae*, 1 (Stuttgart, 1900), quoted by book and chapter.
Coll.	Odo, *Collationes*: *Bibl. Cl.* cols 517 ff.
Congrès	*Congrès scientifique de Cluny en l'honneur des Saints Abbés Odon et Odilon* (Société des Amis de Cluny, Dijon, 1950).
CSEL	*Corpus Scriptorum Ecclesiaticorum Latinorum* (Vienna–Prague–Leipzig, 1866 ff.).
DA	*Deutsches Archiv für Erforschung des Mittelalters*
DHGE	*Dictionnaire d'Histoire et de Géographie ecclésiastique.*
GC	*Gallia Christiana*, ed. Benedictines of St Maur, quoted by volume and column.
JL	*Regesta Pontificum Romanorum*, ed. Jaffé, vol. 1, 2nd ed. (Leipzig, 1885), quoted by number of entry.
JS	John of Salerno, *Vita Odonis*: *PL* 133, 13 ff.; also trans. and ed. Dom Gerard Sitwell, *John of Salerno, Life of St Odo of Cluny* (London, 1958).
MGH	*Monumenta Germaniae Historica*, ed. Pertz and others, *Scriptores, Zeitschrift*, etc.; quoted by volume and page.
NF	*Neue Forschungen über Cluny und die Cluniacenser*, ed. G. Tellenbach (Freiburg, 1959).

Occupatio	Odo, *Occupatio*, ed. A. Svoboda (Leipzig, 1900), quoted by book and verse.
PL	*Patrologia Latina*, ed. Migne, quoted by volume and column.
QFIAB	*Quellen und Forschungen aus italienischen Archiven und Bibliotheken*.
RB	*Revue Bénédictine* (Maredsous).
RHE	*Revue d'Histoire ecclésiastique* (Louvain).
RHF	*Receuil des historiens des Gaules et de la France*, ed. M. Bouquet (Paris, 1738–1904).
RM	*Revue Mabillon* (Ligugé).
Spiritualità	*Spiritualità cluniacense. Convegni del Centro di Studi sulla Spiritualità medievale*, 2 (Todi, 1960).
U	Ulrich, *Consuetudines Cluniacensis*: *PL* 149, 643–778; quoted by book, chapter and column.
VG	*Vita Geraldi*, by St Odo, in *Bibl. Cl.* 639 ff., quoted by book, chapter and column. Also available in English: Sitwell, op. cit.

1 Cluniac Monasticism

NOREEN HUNT

Cluny continues to hold her own as an important field of study for historians, especially for medievalists concerned with the central middle ages. These ages approximately coincide with what has been called the heroic period of Cluniac history: the tenth, eleventh and – to a lesser extent – the twelfth centuries: that is, from Cluny's foundation in 910 to the end of the abbacy of Peter the Venerable in 1156. Thereafter, until 1790 when the monks finally left the great abbey, which was soon despoiled, Cluny played a minor historical role, though even its later history is not without interest.

By any reckoning Cluny was a major European institution. Historians accept that the central middle ages were marked by a noticeable religious movement, that monasticism was one of the principal expressions and agents of that phenomenon, and that Cluny was one of the main centres. Formerly there was a tendency to exaggerate the influence of Cluny and equate it with the whole of the reform movement. It is now recognised that there were other independent and very influential centres, of which Gorze was probably the most impressive, but neither the reform movement as a whole, nor monasticism in particular, can be studied without reference to Cluny, whose history, in one way or another, is bound up with the general history of Europe during this period.

Despite the dispersal of the Cluniac archives during the French Revolution, the Cluniac sources form one of the most valuable collections for the central middle ages. Recently this collection has been enhanced by the discovery of the necrology of Marcigny-sur-Loire, the community of nuns founded by Abbot Hugh in 1055.[1] This necrology, containing *c.* 10,000 names of monks and nuns of the Cluniac congregation and of other persons closely associated with the abbey, is the most important medieval necrology we now possess and it provides the key to a better knowledge of Cluny and the Cluniacs.

[1] See Wollasch, 'A Cluniac Necrology', pp. 143 ff. below.

There is no richer assembly of medieval charters than those which belonged to Cluny.[1] Literary sources are more limited, but the lives, letters and restricted writings of the abbots have a significance that is not confined to Cluny's own history.[2] The surviving customaries are essential documents in the history of the monastic tradition.[3] The site of Cluny has provided scope for systematic study and excavations over forty years: the results illuminate the history of art and architecture and make possible the judgement that the main basilica, 'Cluny III', 'represented the monastic achievement in building better than any other edifice'.[4]

Given Cluny's size and influence, and the survival of so many sources, it is not surprising that Cluniac monasticism has generated an international historical literature of its own, which shows no signs of abating. New methods and fashions in history find the Cluniac field provides scope for exercise and it is there that the first trials sometimes take place, as is happening now, for example, with the discovery of how much we can learn from medieval necrologies. Far from exaggerating Cluny's role in history, more research is leading to greater precision and reducing, in some aspects, the place formerly ascribed to Cluny. The problems in Cluniac history have become more apparent, and some of them are controversial.

One of the biggest gaps in our knowledge of Cluny is the absence of a complete list of affiliated houses. It is not known how many monasteries were dependent on Cluny though numbers ranging between 200 and 2000 have been quoted with a confidence that has no historical basis. The term 'Cluniac' was used loosely in the past. Sometimes it was applied to houses which were never juridically linked with Cluny but which were related in other ways: either by adopting Cluniac customs (as happened at Fleury) or by electing a Cluniac abbot (as did Reading) or by sending monks to Cluny for a time, who would return to share their Cluniac experience with their own communities (Hirsau sent monks in this way; Sancho, king of Navarre sent Paternus to Cluny in 1025 and made him abbot

[1] See below, Select Bibliography, p. 239 f.
[2] Ibid. p. 239.   [3] Ibid. p. 240.
[4] K. J. Conant, *Carolingian and Romanesque Architecture* (London, 1959) p. 115. See also below, p. 239.

of San Juan de la Peña when he returned). In the tenth and first half of the eleventh centuries relations between Cluny and dependent houses were tenuous and erratic. After that the juridical links were firmer, but the earliest list of affiliated houses was not made until the thirteenth century. By that time several houses had broken away. Partial lists are found in papal bulls, and charters are a main source for establishing whether or not monasteries were dependent on Cluny. The difficulties in the way of making a complete list of Cluniac dependencies are formidable, especially if the list is to indicate in what year monasteries became dependent and when their relations with Cluny were modified. It is doubtful if such a work could be done within a single lifetime, but gradually regional lists are appearing and the cases of individual houses are being settled.[1]

This gap is partly responsible for the vagueness and exaggeration which has characterised some writing of Cluniac history. The confusion and ignorance concerning which monasteries and monks were or were not Cluniac has also aggravated some of the controversies concerning Cluny. The relation of Cluny to the papal reform in the eleventh century, mainly the work of monks, and the question of whether Pope Gregory VII was a Cluniac or not are notable examples of problems which have been clarified by a finer understanding of the term 'Cluniac' and a more accurate knowledge of Cluniac monasteries.[2] Once it is established that membership of the congregation meant that Cluny recognised the monk as having made monastic profession within the congregation, if not at Cluny itself, we are given a reliable yardstick with which to measure the description 'Cluniac'.[3] And if the massive research programme for necrologies, initiated by Dr Wollasch, is ever fully implemented, we shall be provided with a list, not only of Cluniac houses, but of the names of their inhabitants and close associates.[4] We shall then have arrived at what can fairly be described as an exact

---

[1] See N. Hunt, *Cluny under St Hugh* (London, 1967) pp. 5 ff. and 124 ff., and p. 422 below.

[2] See Dom A. Stacpoole, 'Hildebrand, Cluny and the Papacy', in *Downside Review*, LXXXI (1963) 142–64; 254–72. H. E. J. Cowdrey, *The Cluniacs and the Gregorian Reform* (Oxford, 1970) appeared just as the present volume was going to press.

[3] See Hunt, op. cit. pp. 157 f.   [4] See below, p. 143 ff.

minimal knowledge of the general ambience of the Cluniac congregation. We are within sight of establishing this as regards the abbey of Cluny itself. It is already known, for example, that at least 76 bishops in the eleventh century can safely be described as Cluniac: it is very probable that the actual number of Cluniac bishops was nearer 100. On the other hand, it has also been established that though Cluny undoubtedly helped to prepare the way for papal reform, many of the leading ecclesiastics in the second half of the eleventh century were not Cluniac in any sense of the word.

The same kind of research has helped to distinguish and elevate the relative spheres of influence of other monastic centres, notably Gorze.[1] The assertion of differences between Cluny and Gorze has been a natural reaction against what has been called the 'panclunism' of earlier historians. It is likely, however, that there was more eclecticism and interaction than was ever documented. All the monasteries had inherited the Rule of St Benedict, and with it a powerful body of common monastic tradition, not necessarily written, so that the term 'Benedictine' must be used of monasticism at this time in a very loose sense. The differences concerned customs and emphases rather than basic modes of monastic thought.

It has been said, for example, that Lotharingian and Burgundian monasticism differed in their approach to culture. This is true in some respects. Some of the German monasteries become notable centres of the kind of learning for which there was literally little time at Cluny owing to a lengthier liturgy. But to suggest that Cluny was disinterested in culture, a thesis that threatened to prevail at one stage, is to approach the question in a very narrow sense. Too great a stress on assessing culture by literary output, an occupational hazard of monastic historians, can mean the ignoring of deep-rooted characteristics of the culture shared by both kinds of monasticism. Above all, the formative influence of the liturgy must be recognised. Its proper performance implied a literate community. Dom Jean Leclercq rightly reminds us of the monastic achievement in educating its own men. In one sense the monks can be said to have practised a religion of the Book. Not only were the

[1] See especially K. Hallinger, *Gorze–Kluny* ('Studia Anselmiana', xxii–xxv, Rome, 1950).

Scriptures known from constant and comprehensive reading (and that is no small education): commentaries were also read to help deepen the understanding. The Book of the Gospels was carried in processions and otherwise remained night and day on the main altar. The liturgy also involved a musical education in the rigorous medieval sense. The numerate element of monastic culture can easily be overlooked, and it is unrealistic to forget that monastic churches stood not only for religion but for sound geometry.

Defining Cluny's place in relation to previous monastic tradition has proved almost as difficult and controversial a question as determining its relation to contemporary medieval monasticism. The phenomenal development of Cluny and the obvious new vitality of other centres of reform led historians to contrast the whole movement with the previous state of monasticism. Only gradually has it been appreciated how much Cluny owed to the Carolingian tradition, in much the same way as it has been realised that the Cistercians were more rooted in traditional monasticism than was formerly thought. Nevertheless, though we know now that there was less material interruption of the Carolingian tradition than used to be thought (Berno, founder of Cluny, brought more from Baume than historians were wont to recognise) the Cluniac and allied movements did mark a new development. Cluny enjoyed an independence foreign to Carolingian monasticism though native to the more ancient tradition.

All these problems have led to a deeper and wider enquiry into the nature of Cluniac monasticism: into what it was all about. Modern Cluniac historiography reflects a lively interest in Cluny's ideology, and in one way or another the articles assembled in this book reflect that interest.

As it stands, however, there is one serious gap in the following collection, which is not, therefore, fully representative of all schools of Cluniac study. I refer to the absence of any article written from the Marxist point of view. It has already been indicated that the Cluniac field is a meeting ground for historians using a variety of methods and approaches. Some of them are represented in this book. But Cluniac studies have undoubtedly received an impetus from the seriousness with which Marxist historians have entered the field. Professor Ernst

Werner's inaugural lecture at Leipzig in 1952 was devoted to the social basis of eleventh-century monastic reform: he concluded that monasticism had helped to initiate a new phase in the development of feudalism.[1] Unfortunately the published paper is too long to have been included here. There seemed no other article suitable in length and sufficiently central to our theme until, alas too late, I came across Dr Bernard Töpfer's article on the cult of relics and the pilgrimage movement during the period of monastic reform in the Burgundian and Aquitanian regions.[2] As it has not been possible to include this article here and as this school of historians has perhaps influenced contemporary monastic historical writing more than may be apparent (Professor Morghen suggests that Dom Hallinger is occasionally reacting too strongly against the work of East German historians; one also wonders if Canon Delaruelle is in part replying to their theses, though he does not actually say so), it will not be out of place to summarise Dr Töpfer's conclusions here.

For him, one of the outstanding problems of the middle ages is the relation between the church (curiously undefined) and the lower classes. It is recognised that in the end the church managed to influence and bring the lower classes under her control. The tenth and eleventh centuries were a crucial period in this process and the vital question is, by what means were the people attracted? The parish priest, thinks Dr Töpfer, may have contributed to the movement but there were too many complaints about clerical deficiencies for it to be held that the priests were effective. Nor does he attribute much importance to the bishops. Who, then, had the opportunity to work on the people? The monasteries. What means did they use? Relics: 'the chief instrument of propaganda', still far from having been studied exhaustively.[3]

Relics were, of course, an ancient Christian cult, as he points

[1] E. Werner, *Die gesellschaftlichen Grundlagen der Klosterreform im 11 Jht* (Berlin, 1953).

[2] B. Töpfer, 'Reliquienkult und Pilgerbewegung zur Zeit der Klosterreform im burgundisch-aquitanischen Gebiet', in *Vom Mittelalter zur Neuzeit*, ed. H. Sproemberg and H. Kretzschmar (Berlin, 1956) pp. 420–39.

[3] Ibid. p. 438: 'Die Reliquien sind . . . damals das wirksamte Mittel der kirchlichen „Propaganda" gewesen.'

out, for each church was expected to have the relics of at least one saint. The synod of Frankfurt, 794, forwarded the cult by decreeing that wherever there were relics a chapel had to be built.[1] The tenth and eleventh centuries witnessed a veritable boom in relics and Dr Töpfer thinks it would not be hard to show how energetic were the tenth-century abbots in trying to procure relics of note.

The logic is inexorable: relics attract local pilgrimages, shrines are built from gold, silver and other precious metals. The invention and translation of relics provide occasions for involving the people, who thereafter are held by expositions, venerations, feast days: all occasions for pilgrimages to draw the people in. There is a spate of lives of saints and miracle stories of wonders worked at their tombs, together with stories of vengeance visited on the cynics. All this made for bigger and better shrines and pilgrimages. Next there was a boom in church building, especially after A.D. 1000 and the whole development of romanesque is explained in terms of the veneration of relics.[2]

The pilgrimages which have attracted the attention of historians – Santiago and Jerusalem (Rome is not mentioned) – are merely prominent examples of what was happening on a smaller scale all over Europe. The examples of Fleury, St Martin's shrine at Tours, St Philibert at Tournus, St Foy at Conques, St Sernin in Toulouse, St Gilles at Autun, Aurillac, Figeac, Paray-le-Monial are cited. In 994 an altar was erected on the spot where St Mayeul, abbot of Cluny, had died at Souvigny. In 1018 there was a fearful accident at Limoges where a building fell and killed 52 pilgrims. In 1010 the news went round that the head of St John the Baptist was at St Jean d'Angély. Quite a stir followed and people flocked to the place.[3] In 1037 the monastery of Vézelay announced that they were in possession of St Mary Magdalene's relics.

[1] Ibid. p. 422, n. 9: Synodus Francofurtensis c. 15: MG Capit. 1, p. 76: 'De monasterio, ubi corpora sanctorum sunt ut habeat oratorium intra claustra ubi peculiare officium et diuturnum fiat.'

[2] Ibid. p. 432, where L. Hourticq is quoted: 'Der ganze romanische Baustil ist die Frucht der Reliquenverehrung.'

[3] Ibid. p. 430: Adémar de Chabannes, p. 179: 'Omnis Aquitania et Gallia, Italia et Hispania ad famam commota ibi occurrere certatim festinat.'

Thus the ordinary people were increasingly drawn to the churches: there are frequent references to this very fact in the documents. Dr Töpfer considers that the movement was stronger in Italy, England and France (he speaks of the methodical influencing of the people there) than in Germany, where the movement was less marked. This he adduces as evidence of a more conservative, aristocratic church, unconcerned with the people. We are left in some doubt as to which policy is to be judged the worse, and one may also be permitted to wonder if Germany really needed much more than the (unmentioned) three kings and St Ursula's eleven thousand virgins at Cologne.

Gradually the monasteries became increasingly involved in the formation of the laity and so the problem which historians have been debating concerning the relation and attitudes of monasticism to the world is solved: patently the monasteries were deeply involved in manipulating relics and the lower classes. Since so many Cluniac dependencies were centres of pilgrimage, Cluny cannot be said to have held aloof from this movement.

It is doubtful if any historian would say that Cluny was uninvolved with the pilgrimage movement and did not at times benefit and also suffer from it. Cluny became famous as a place dedicated to St Peter and some people regarded it as an integral part of the Roman pilgrimage or as an alternative to Rome when the roads to Italy proved too dangerous. William de Warenne, for example, found he could not complete his pilgrimage to Rome because of political disturbances, so he turned aside to Cluny to fulfil his vow and to pay homage to St Peter. Lewes in England was founded as a result of this visit.[1]

It is also unlikely that any historian would deny the medieval interest in relics: indeed most medievalists have a repertoire of tales on the subject. This is not to say that historians do not take seriously the influence of this aspect of medieval religion. It has been shown how Pope Leo IX used to advantage the bones of St Remigius to win favour with the populace of Rheims when he opened his council there in 1049: he translated the relics

----

[1] BB IV 3561.

amid great pomp and laid them on the high altar so that the council proceedings 'were carried out in the presence of St Remigius . . . and worldly bargaining was given no chance'.[1] St Hugh, abbot of Cluny, was chosen to preach to this assembly.

It seems an oversimplification, however, to explain the religious movement of the tenth and eleventh centuries, even in its outward manifestations, in terms of one factor, be it relics or anything else. I confess that in a previous analysis of the causes operating in the expansion of Cluny I failed entirely to examine whether and how far relics were the possible explanation of that remarkable phenomenon.[2] I would grant that Cluny and relics, the cult of the saints and commemoration of the dead would make a fascinating and valuable subject for a thesis, but I would still submit that a complexity of religious, political, social and economic factors contributed to Cluny's increase. On the other hand, we have long been aware that one of the factors in Cluny's decline was the loss of simplicity and the adverse effects on the liturgy and horarium of certain particular developments in the sphere of the veneration of saints and commemoration of the dead, so it may yet be shown that relics, far from assisting in the development of Cluny, may have impeded it.

These and similar questions bear not only on the external history of Cluny but on the nature of its monasticism. There probably never was a time when monasticism was not regarded by some as an enigmatic institution, condemned, ignored, suspected, or uncritically elevated. It is interesting to note that the first criticisms are usually made by monks themselves and are to be found, indeed, within some of the greatest monastic documents. The Rule of St Benedict distinguishes four kinds of monks: two kinds are condemned, one is regarded with reservations and only the cenobites are unreservedly approved. St Odilo, 994–1049, condemned some of his monks for being too ambitious in acquiring control of other monasteries. St Hugh reacted firmly, almost fiercely, against those who looked on him as a saint and tried to procure relics in his lifetime. It seems clear, too, that not all his disciples shared the same ideals and detachment when it came to evaluating invitations to become involved in worldly and ecclesiastical affairs.

[1] See C. Brooke, *Europe in the Central Middle Ages* (London, 1964) pp. 258–9.
[2] Hunt, op. cit. pp. 131 ff.

It must not be thought, however, that all monastic criticism sprang from zeal for reform, though it may be expressed as such and may contain a measure of valid condemnation. Equally it may reflect a certain pluralism or tension within monasticism itself, of which one illustration is an ambivalent attitude towards the material, so fiercely debated in the Cistercian–Cluniac controversy.

The historian has to take account of this complexity within monasticism and to be aware, too, of the way historiography (including the historiography of monastic historians) has influenced the writing of monastic history. He must not be surprised if, despite the way modern methods and approaches are being brought to bear on many aspects and levels of Cluniac history to advance our knowledge and understanding of that institution, the question is being asked yet again: was it all a mere façade?

Some historians would say that this question goes beyond the province proper to the historian. Other historians have no such hesitations. Certainly any historian may ask what the Cluniacs themselves believed they stood for, and he can seek to gain as many insights as possible into their way of life and modes of thought. It is hoped that the following articles may serve that purpose.

2 Monastic Reform and Cluniac Spirituality[1]

RAFFAELLO MORGHEN

Although there is a vast amount of literature on monastic reform in the tenth century, it can justifiably be claimed, as has been stated recently, that the movement has not been depicted in its true light in the general history of the period.

The pre-eminence given to political history by certain schools of historians has had the effect, as regards the tenth century, of drawing the main attention of scholars to the problems of the so-called feudal process and to the fortunes of the 'imperial popes' of the Saxon period rather than to the remarkable development of the spiritual movement at work in the heart of European civilisation, determining its historical progress in a decisive way. Even if one wishes to trace the history of the spiritual movement which stemmed from Cluny one finds that it has been interpreted either as a history internal to monasticism itself or as a history which at most had rather feeble ties with civil history and was scarcely related to the movement of church reform promoted by Pope Gregory VII.[2]

[1] [Translated from 'Riforma monastica e Spiritualità cluniacense', in *Spiritualità Cluniacense, Convegni del Centro di Studi sulla spiritualità medievale, 1958* (Todi, 1960) pp. 33–56. Ed.]

[2] Among recent historical work on the origins of Cluniac monasticism particular mention may be made of two accounts: J. F. Lemarignier, 'Structures monastiques et structures politiques dans la France, de la fin du Xe et du début de XIe siècle', and Dom K. Hallinger, 'Progressi e problemi della ricerca sulla riforma pre-gregoriana', both papers printed in *Il Monachesimo nell'Alto Medioevo e la formazione della civiltà occidentale, Settimana di studio del C.I. St. sull'A. medioevo*, IV (Spoleto, 1957) 357 ff. and 257 ff. See also the article by Dom Hallinger [translated below, pp. 29 ff. Ed.], which gives valuable and extensive information. Notwithstanding Lemarignier's important contribution to the problem, the underlying research still appears to be too rigidly orientated towards the possibility of political interpretations of spiritual phenomena, whereas the variety of developments reveals a complexity of determining causes. Dom Hallingers by contrast, makes acute observations on the concept of monastic reform, though he tends to limit

Even Fliche, who treated monastic reform as the prehistory of the Gregorian reform, denied that Cluny had had a noticeable effect on the reform of the church; he judged that Cluny's tendency to emphasise the importance of prayer and liturgy at the expense of practical deeds prevented the formulation of a concrete plan to raise the church from its state of subjection to the laity. Such a programme he attributed to Waso of Liège, seeing in it the 'true originality' of Waso's thought.[1]

Research carried out over recent years in the field of medieval spirituality now permits the historian of civilisation to form a more appropriate and accurate idea of the monastic movement of the tenth century and of its important place in the whole historical framework of that period. The spiritual movement which began with Cluny at the beginning of the tenth century not only promoted new forms of religious life within the monasteries and contributed to the vigorous affirmation of the religious ideals of the church of Pope Gregory VII. It also inspired new expressions of art in architecture and liturgical singing. Indirectly it assisted the revival of economic life by bringing about the cultivation of waste land, causing houses, churches and villages to rise where previously there stretched forests and swamps as far as the eye could see, increasing the number of monasteries, free settlements, artisans and merchants, so that Cluniac houses often became centres of intense social life whose influence spread beyond the confines of the monastery. Moreover, monastic reform reflected the spiritual needs of the common people, eager at the beginning of the second millenium for a freer life and a more personal religion. At the same time,

---

them to a critique of the Marxist interpretation of Cluniac monasticism propounded by E. Werner. Dom Philibert Schmitz has emphasised, with considerable scholarship, the undoubted influence of Benedict of Aniane on the reform of the monastic order, especially as regards the introduction of certain liturgical innovations subsequently accepted as part of the Benedictine tradition. I would not be prepared to subscribe, as I think Dom Philibert Schmitz does, to the thesis of Naberhaus in his biography *Benedikt von Aniane, Werke und Persönlichkeit* (Münster, 1930), where he attributes a radical, decisive importance to the reform of 817 as regards the 'whole destiny of western monasticism'.

[1] A. Fliche, *La Réforme gregorienne* (Louvain and Paris, 1924, 1925, 1937) 1 46. See also R. Morghen, 'Questioni Gregoriani', in *Archivio della R. Deputazione Romana di St. patria*, LXV, vol. VIII (1942).

monasticism raised within itself an aristocracy of great spirits who, to a large extent, influenced and dominated the whole of religious life and, directly and indirectly, social and political life in the tenth and eleventh centuries. Such men were Berno and Odo of Cluny, Odilo and Peter the Venerable, St Romuald and St Peter Damian, Humbert of Silva Candida and Hildebrand of Soana.

In order to define clearly the historical problem of the tenth-century monastic revival it seems necessary to start from two premises which have the value of being inescapable statements of fact. One is the basic unity of inspiration in the movement of the tenth and eleventh centuries; the other is the spontaneity of its origins and its fundamental difference from Benedict of Aniane's reform in the ninth century.

Certainly the simple identification of Cluny with all movements of monastic reform in the tenth, eleventh and twelfth centuries, implicitly stated by Sackur in his well-known history of the Cluniac congregation, does not entirely correspond to historical reality.[1] But to say that there is a unity in the monastic movement of the tenth century is not to deny *a priori* the specific differences between the various reforms so much as to claim that the different reforms started from the single need for a revival of religious consciousness. In the work of Odo of Cluny, and in the tradition initiated by him, this need found its most important and most complete fulfilment.

Seen from this angle, the monastic revival of the tenth century represents the most obvious expression of the powerful spiritual stimuli which were at the root of the revival of the whole of European life at the beginning of the new millenium: hence the independence of the monastic movement of the tenth century from that promoted by Benedict of Aniane, which was a true and proper reform, launched in the Synod of Aachen in 817, promulgated by decree and enforced by imperial authority, as a new, centralised structure of the monastic order over which the same imperial power assumed control. As we shall see, the reform of monastic life in the tenth century had diverse origins

[1] E. Sackur, *Die Cluniacenser in ihrer kirchlichen und allgemeingeschichtlichen Wirksamkeit*, 2 vols (Halle, 1892–4); Hallinger, 'Progressi e problemi' (see above, n. 2) p. 258.

which cannot be explained by postulating a prearranged programme and a deliberate act of authority without distorting
the very essence of its history.

For those who believe in the efficacy of religious factors in
determining the course of human fortunes, the rise and sudden
expansion of the monastic revival, fostered and spread by Odo
of Cluny in the first half of the tenth century, is an outstanding
and significant example. When in 910 Count William of
Aquitaine founded the monastery of Cluny, entrusting the
direction of the monastery to Abbot Berno and placing it in
immediate dependence on the holy see, one can truly say that
this was the beginning of a new period in the history of European
civilisation. The great force with which the Cluniac monastic
ideal rapidly spread throughout the western world from the
seed planted by William of Aquitaine can hardly be explained
by the exceptional value of the pious count's donation, since the
entire history of the middle ages is full of examples of donations
and the founding of churches and monasteries on the part of
kings, nobles and knights. The placing of the monastery directly
under the papacy was very significant for the development of
Cluny, but even in this matter the tendency of monasticism
to escape from direct dependence on the diocesan bishop in
order to put itself under the protection of Rome is clearly
discernible as a recurrent motif throughout the history of
medieval monasticism. Therefore, the origins of the vigorous
impulse which marked the first diffusion of Cluniac monasticism
must lie in a new spirit, capable of infusing fresh vitality into the
tradition. Such was the spirit which Berno and his successors
were able to bring to monastic life, interpreting in the light of
their tradition the signs and spiritual needs of contemporary
society. Only in this way is it possible to understand how the
new ideal was affirmed throughout the west, especially during
Odo's abbatial rule in the fifteen years from 927 to 942: at
Aurillac in Aquitaine; at Romainmoutier in Burgundy; at
Jumièges in Normandy; at Fleury-sur-Loire; at St Paul's without the Walls and St Mary's on the Aventine in Rome; at
Subiaco and St Elia at Nepi; at Einsiedeln in Germany.
Simultaneously with, or shortly after, the foundation of Cluny
other centres radiating the new monasticism sprang up, pro-
ducing monastic institutions which, in the context of a com-

munity intent on religious revival, nevertheless evolved with complete freedom of inspiration.

In 950 the monastery of Gorze was founded and the reform spread through the work of Gerard of Brogne in Lower Lorraine and Flanders, in the monasteries of St Bavo, St Bertin, St Amand, St Omer and St Vaast.

During the abbacy of Mayeul the wave of Cluniac reform reached Lérins and Valence and once more flowed into Italy through the monasteries of Santa Maria e Salvatore in Pavia and of S. Apollinare in Classe in Ravenna. Towards the end of the century William of Volpiano brought the spirit of reform from St Bénigne at Dijon, another important monastic centre, to Bernay in Normandy, together with the early type of Cluniac architecture. Abbot Odilo spread the influence of Cluny in southern Italy, while the centenarian St Romuald, that restless and indefatigable pilgrim, having brought his ideal of repentance and asceticism to all Europe, took steps to found the monastery of Camaldoli, in which was to be affirmed, in contrast to the cenobitic ideal of Cluny, the other ideal of European reformed monasticism, the eremitic ideal, which was to be particularly characteristic of the new Italian orders of the Camoldolesians and the Vallombrosans.

Scarcely a century after the abbacy of Odo, Cluny had attained its apogee in the time of Abbot Hugh. The huge Cluniac family was gathered into a single congregation of all the monasteries united in the community dependent on the mother house. The abbots had succeeded to the abbatial seat at Cluny almost by adoption, constituting a dynasty wherein choice of the master and the loyalty of the disciple to his master's spiritual programme replaced the laws of natural inheritance.

Many monasteries of the congregation had grown up in walled towns and held extensive landed properties with vassals, artisans, merchants, soldiers, servants: all laymen united to the monastery by all kinds of ties, offices, business and dependence. The abbots of Cluny were among the most powerful seigneurs in Europe. The Cluniac monks, freed from manual work and giving themselves mainly to the liturgical office and prayer, seemed to be the representatives of a new spiritual aristocracy, whose sense of propriety and dignity, characteristic of the Cluniac spirit, showed, even in external forms, the interior impulse from which the monastic revival of the tenth century had started.

If, in the course of time, Cluniac monasticism became part of the political establishment, necessarily linked to the ruling powers of the society in which it arose, it is certain that this happened as a result of tendencies lying at the heart of the movement, disposing it to adapt and develop in response to the demands or scope of the conditions in which individual monasteries found themselves. In this connection it is significant that the Cluniac reform did not attempt to formulate its own code, as was the case with the reform of Benedict of Aniane, but found its gradual expression in the definition of customs which grew as the new monastery developed. The plan of reform was not, therefore, prearranged, but appeared as the autonomous development of new forms of monastic life, prompted by new spiritual needs.

Nor, as Lemarignier has shown, did the formation of feudal structures have a determining influence on the new structural forms in which Cluniac monasticism was defined. Connections with the feudal world there were, and strong ones, since the feudal world constituted the very structure of the new European society after the collapse of the Carolingian empire. The connections were, however, either in opposition to or in defence against bishops and nobles who wanted to make monasteries the instruments of their power (hence the significance of Cluniac liberty) or were the friendly and protective relations between devoted seigneurs, sincerely inspired by feelings of religious piety but also interested in promoting the growth of individual monastic institutions with which they were associated by familiar ties or by practical involvement as benefactors.

It is well known, on the other hand, how in the Carolingian period the monasteries were the bases of royal power. The king regarded even the goods of the monastery as property of the royal treasury and disposed of this wealth and gave concessions to laymen, just at the time when the foundations of the feudal order were being laid. The abbot therefore almost assumed the figure of a public servant and subsequently of a vassal of the king, to whom he owed donations and military service.

How could such firm bonds, which for centuries had linked

the monastic institutions to the sovereign and the great seigneurs,
be broken? It was precisely from these links that there originated
the interminable series of concessions and grants of landed
property on the part of popes, emperors and princes, who
occupy the charters and fill the registers of all the medieval
monasteries. In order to exist, the monastery needed landed
properties and these could be granted only by the sovereign and
the seigneurs. Only in the thirteenth century was the ideal of the
mendicant cenobite established. In the tenth century there was
no mobile wealth available to support the new monastic institutions. Wealth still rested in the ownership of land, and land was
in the hands of the feudal classes. In this respect Odo of Cluny
thought it obvious and natural that the wealthy should sustain
the church.[1]

This does not mean to say that one can conclude that the new
Cluniac monasticism owed its fortune to the complex combination of donations and the liberal conferring of wealth on
individual monasteries by sovereigns and seigneurs, though
historians have often attributed Cluny's success to such factors.
Nor must it be thought that the donations and grants of the
sovereigns and seigneurs to monasteries indicate that those
sovereigns and seigneurs were committed to the programme of
spiritual reawakening promoted by Cluny. It is particularly
necessary to remember this when considering the support given
by Alberic to Odo's spiritual work in the monasteries of Rome
and Italy. It is certain that other interests apart from religious
ones inspired Alberic's actions in favour of monastic reform at
Subiaco, which he wanted to dominate instead of Hugh of
Provence, who had conceded privileges to Subiaco in 942
precisely at the time when his declared enemy was gaining
power in Rome. The history of the monastic revival in the tenth
century cannot therefore be identified with, still less explained
by, the series of donations and monetary grants made by
sovereigns and seigneurs to the new religious institutions.
Otherwise all the popes and sovereigns of the time would have
to be included in the history of the movement: Pope John X
and Rudolph of Burgundy, who conferred possessions and
privileges, Pope John XI, Alberic's brother, and Hugh of

[1] Odo, *Occupatio*, ed. A. Svoboda (Leipzig, 1900) lib. VI, v. 745: 'Nam
liquet aecclesiam regum lactare mamillam.'

Provence, who were also liberal in their assurances and donations; Hugh and Lothair, who conceded to Cluny the free
election of the abbot; Pope John XIX, who was the friend and
protector of Odilo. Such a history of the monastic movement
of the tenth century would gain in wealth of detail but not
necessarily in clarity of description.

John of Salerno, the monk converted to the ideals of monastic
reform by Odo and subsequently his fervent disciple and
biographer, clearly shows the spiritual motives of Odo's reform
activity and the disinterestedness of the holy abbot as regards
increasing the patrimony of the monastery as opposed to the
effectiveness of its spiritual action. 'Why concern yourself with
anything else save winning souls? Other abbots can involve
themselves in affairs and please men. You, however, relying on
devotion and works of mercy, should attend to pleasing God
alone, for the good of souls.'[1]

The 'winning of souls' not 'involvement in affairs' was, then,
the principal aim which drove Odo to undertake four very
exhausting journeys to Rome between 933 and 940, to mediate
peace between Hugh of Provence and Alberic and to spread
in the monasteries of Rome and Italy concern for the spiritual
renewal which preoccupied him. For him, the winning of souls
meant encouraging by word and example the renewal of the
inner man, that *metanoia* which is at once an essential mark of
Christian behaviour and a necessary condition of every religious
revival.

The special character of the spiritual activity practised by
Odo and his successors shows us clearly how Cluniac reform
was based above all on the personal and direct work of
exceptional men, united and agreed on a common programme
of revival, and how they were able to maintain control over the
whole of monasticism. For more than a century they handed on,
one after another, the supreme abbatial power without a break
in continuity, placing at the head of the monasteries, whether
founded or reformed, abbots or priors who were chosen from
among their followers and their most faithful disciples: men

---

[1] John of Salerno, *Vita Odonis*: *PL* 133, 59: 'Numquid tibi aliud curae fuit
nisi de animabus lucrandi? Nam ceteri abbates hoc qualiter *rebus possint
abundare*, et hominibus placere. Tu vero pietate misericordiaque fretus, soli
Deo placere satagis, propter lucrum animarum'.

such as the Frenchman Baldwin, who either simultaneously or within the space of a very few years was placed by Odo at the head of the monasteries of St Paul without the Walls, St Mary on the Aventine and Monte Cassino; John, a canon converted to the ideals of reform by Odo and made prior of St Paul's; the Frank Teodard, made prior of the reformed monastery of St Elia, Nepi.

The centralised structure which resulted from the personal nature of the work done by the great abbots of the tenth century was first acknowledged in the title, albeit honorary, of *archimandrite* of all the Roman monasteries, the title with which Alberic is said to have honoured Odo. Such centralisation then became, as is known, one of the peculiar characteristics of Cluniac monasticism.

It is not possible to appreciate fully the significance of the nature of the revival in the tenth century if in the final analysis one fails to realise that the monastic movement also represented the vigorous reaction of the highest circles of monastic and secular spirituality to a certain type of religiosity which had been establishing itself towards the end of the first millenium and which, nourished and fostered by a mixture of worldly and spiritual values, fruits of the temporal power acquired by the church, had brought both to the threshold of the so-called 'iron age'. The most obvious and disconcerting signs of this were a materialist and almost magical religiosity in which spiritual values were reduced to terms of hierarchy and worldly power. Interiority was not appreciated and even the investiture of charismatic power was almost entirely based on procedural and juridical criteria of validity. The essence of religious life was reduced to a mere outward show of ritual and ceremony.

Falco and other historians have referred to the tenth-century crisis as a crisis of authority.[1] This crisis was not only political, through the failure of that order which Charlemagne had attempted to give the west as it emerged from the atrophy which followed the barbarian invasions. It also had an essential spiritual aspect, in the failure and sterility of motivating ideals, always necessary if authority is to have vigour and prestige in

[1] G. Falco, 'La crisi dell'autorità e lo sforzo della ricostruzione in Italia', in *I problemi comuni dell'Europa post-carolingia, Settimana di studio del C.I. St. sull'A. medioevo*, II (Spoleto, 1955) 39.

the judgement of the common conscience, and which had certainly marked the work of the great emperor. But when force sufficed to obtain the anointing of king or emperor, when purchase of the office with a sum of money was enough to become a bishop or an abbot, when to climb the ladder of the holy see no more was needed than to be a brother or son of a Roman noble or to have powerful support from Italy or beyond the Alps, the prestige of authority declined fatally and the unrelenting struggle of bold, ambitious and ruthless men was let loose round every seat of authority.

The monastic revival of the tenth century aimed, therefore, to embody a reaction to that explosion of personal forces which had made the churches and monasteries instruments of struggle and power. It attempted to stand for the recognition of an authority still founded on the empire and on the church, conceived as the unshakeable foundations of Christian society. But above all it tried to be a spiritual reaction to the prevalence of those worldly and external interests which had weakened and almost destroyed the sense of inner Christian values.

Most research so far undertaken to identify the essential aspects of monastic reform has been concerned with the spirituality which inspired the Cluniac revival of the tenth century. Dom Hallinger's detailed picture of this has already been mentioned and may make it unnecessary to define further the spiritual attitudes of monasticism in general, since he refers to them extensively and they were particularly strongly represented in the Cluniac revival.[1] This is especially true of the concept of monastic life as the ideal state for flight from the world, for attainment of total commitment to Christ, and as the earthly anticipation of eternal bliss.

Here it is better to speak of those impulses which appear to be most original in Cluniac spirituality, or which were at least given new expression and which affected more directly the spiritual forces at work in the heart of Christian society in the tenth century. With regard to such motivating themes, a testimony of singular perception survives in the *Occupatio* of Odo, an epic-didactic poem, as Svoboda described it in 1900

[1] See below, pp. 29 ff.

when he prepared the critical edition.[1] It is in seven books and 5580 hexameters, and it is still far from having been exhaustively studied.

The *occupatio* intended is *occupatio mentis*: that is to say, meditation. Almost at the end of the poem the author himself justifies the title in verses which, to be honest, are not particularly elegant:

> With heart relaxed on these events so muse,
> That thought thereon may stay the vagrant mind,
> And each man deem his judgement close at hand.[2]

So the poem consists of a series of meditations on the great drama of humanity, from original sin to the redemption, written with a view to ascetic edification and in dread of the imminent coming of Antichrist prophesied in the Johannine Apocalypse.

'Now is the time of Antichrist', Odo had warned in his first writings.[3] But in the *Occupatio* the eschatological expectation is tinged with gloomy reflections on a catastrophe already taking place. The knowledge that humanity has now reached the end of time pervades the whole of the seventh book and of itself justifies the author's insistent call to penitence or to the renewal of the inner man in sight of the judgement of God.

Before the image of the passing world, the figure of the supreme judge, terrible in majesty looms in the mind of the poet:

> How fleeting here is all that seems to please,
> While everlasting the reward for passing acts;
> Soon will this whole world's aspect fade away,
> Our Judge shine forth resplendent in the flesh;
> His towering majesty and might revealed,
> When shaken cosmic power shall homage pay.[4]

---

[1] See above, p. 17 n.

[2] *Occupatio*, lib. VII, vv. 649–51:
> Talia sunt cordi fluido et tractanda perinde
> Figat ut instabilem talis meditatio mentem,
> Et sibi iuditium penset tam quisque propinquum.

[3] See Sackur, op. cit. I, p. 118, n. 4: 'Instante iam tempore Antichristi'.

[4] *Occupatio*, lib. VII, vv. 579–84:
> Quamque fugax totum, quod hic esse uidetur amenum!
> Sicque momentaneis perpes retributio factis,

The first book deals with the creation of the angels and the fall of the unfaithful angels; the second with the condition of man and original sin; the third with the expulsion from earthly paradise and the subsequent corruption of human nature; the fourth with the patriarchs of the Old Testament and with natural and Mosaic law; the fifth with the mystery of the incarnation and the coming of Christ on earth; the sixth is dedicated to the institution of the eucharist and the triumph of Christ; the seventh, as already stated, is concerned with the coming of Antichrist, the imminent end of the world, the vices which have led mankind astray, the punishment which awaits the wicked and the rewards of the good and penitent.

The work of Odo belongs to the cultural tradition of the Carolingian period but contains some original and careful research, especially in etymology. Many words are formed from Greek or Hebrew and a new vocabulary is invented by the author, who has a taste all his own for hermeneutic allegory.[1] Even apart from this, it is a highly cultural work, aimed at limited spiritual circles. This is very significant for, to speak in modern terms, it is evidence of the aristocratic, and to a certain extent conservative, nature of the Cluniac reform.

It is not necessary at this point to explain in great detail the degrees of medieval asceticism comprehensively treated by Odo, or his bitter complaints about the vices and widespread sins of the society of his time, complaints which form the main argument of the other work by Odo, the *Collationes*, and of the *De pressuris ecclesiasticis* of Atto of Vercelli, the *Preloquia* of Rathiev of Verona, and later the *Liber Gomorrhianus* of Peter Damian.

As has been indicated, Odo was essentially a conservative. Not only was he bound to the socio-political order of the Carolingian period as regards ideals, including a clear distinction between the duties of the priesthood, fulfilling a high function in the world, and the tasks of Caesar, who had the duty of protecting and guarding the church ('Under the power of

Post modicum cunctam mundi transire figuram,
Quod ueniet subitus iudex in carne choruscus
Magnaque maiestas parebit et alta potestas,
Adstat ad obsequium uirtus commota polorum.

[1] On the lexicography of Odo, see Svoboda's preface to his edition of the *Occupatio*, especially pp. xix–xxii.

Caesar the pope purges the centuries', sang Leo of Vercelli). Odo was also conservative in the way his spirituality was nourished by the most venerable and ancient stream of Christian tradition.

A particular devotee of St Martin of Tours (a public servant and later bishop of the fourth century who might almost be called the *consul Dei* of Christian Gaul, monk and founder of the monastery of Marmoutier, forced to break away from the silence of the monastery, as happened later to Pope Gregory the Great, and to assume by the unanimous will of the people the bishopric of his town), Odo discerned the spiritual needs of his time and strongly revived the essential elements of the Christian experience of St Paul and St Augustine, adapting it to the religious understanding of tenth-century man.

There were three supreme forces at work in his spirituality: contempt for earthly values, especially those of the appetites of the flesh and the influence of worldly power; commitment to Christ, truly and ontologically achieved through the eucharist; acknowledgement of an intimate connection between the eucharistic rite and the Pauline concept of the church, the mystical body, of whom Christ himself is the head.

For Odo, the sins which above all others have brought man to perdition are pride and lust – but especially lust. The libido is the root of all other sins: 'Evil passion rages throughout the world.'[1] Odo's understanding of the libido implies not only immoderate abuse which leads to all kinds of sexual aberrations, described in great detail and deplored by Odo himself and by the other reformers of his time. It also implies a primeval sinful instinct which adversely affects even conjugal intercourse, so that, as is said in the *Collationes*, the child is born already defiled by the stain of original sin. Odo sees therefore an unchaste woman, one 'held fast by the bonds of the flesh', as the prime instrument of the devil. He eventually admits candidly that he would like to be able to convert to chastity at least the women of his own region and says equally bluntly that if men could see the mixture of fluids, membranes and bones that lie beneath the skin of a beautiful woman they would not be able to suppress

---

[1] *Occupatio*, lib. VII, v. 117: 'In toto furit orbe maligna libido.'

the most profound disgust. He would have men be like the lynx of Thrace, whose glance could penetrate to the very heart of all objects.

This concept of woman and of sex reflects a remote but obvious Augustinian influence and is reminiscent of the Pelagian controversy. The whole of humanity is seen as a single doomed mass – condemned to the service of concupiscence, present even in the eagerness with which the suckling clings to its mother's breast. Such views substantially influenced judgements of the excesses which clerical concubinage, widespread in the tenth century, had brought into the heart of the church and even into monastic institutions. The Augustinian tradition took on new vigour in Odo's mind in the light of the conditions and demands of his time and added to all the other forces aiming at the purification of the church. When, therefore, at the beginning of the eleventh century there appeared in different parts of Europe groups of heretics who condemned sexual intercourse even within marriage, it was hardly necessary for them to invoke ancient manichaean doctrines, since already in the previous century a great mind like Odo's had vindicated the ideal of virginity and continence as the foremost virtue of the Christian and as an essential requirement for the renewal of the inner man.

Munditia is the term Odo uses to describe such virtue: purity, of the heart as well as of the body, a necessary condition of being able to detach oneself from the world and adhere to Christ, to draw near to the eucharist, to become part of the mystical body of Christ, which is the church.[1] It is precisely the eucharist and the intimate connection between the eucharistic rite and the unity of the church which are the two most original mainsprings of Odo's religious understanding. To the eucharistic rite and the concept of the mystical body Odo dedicated, as has been said, the whole of the sixth book of his work. In it he decisively departs from any spiritual interpretations of the eucharistic rite, to affirm that sacramental realism which had already been expressed by Pascasius Radbertus about a century before and which, in the midst of the struggle to reform the church at the

[1] Ibid. vv. 107–8:
> Munditiae donum quiddam quasi vileque produnt,
> Cum sine ea nullus Dominum est omnino visurus.

time of Hildebrand, was to receive definitive formulation in the work of Humbert of Silva Candida and find its conclusion in the condemnation of Berengar.

The transubstantiation of the elements of bread and wine into the body and blood of Christ was exalted by Odo as the concrete reality in which were fulfilled the highest aspirations of the believer, adherence to Christ and participation in the life of his own body, the church:

> Delightful gift, by which from many grains
> One wine, one loaf are fashioned through the font,
> And seven churches filled therewith like one.
> Here Head and body come together and unite.
> Joy here for one and all, and endless life;
> — So easy, beauteous, simple, full of God.[1]

In explaining transubstantiation Odo finds no need to use the rational distinction between substance and accident that St Thomas Aquinas introduced. The reality of the miracle is guaranteed through the word of God. He said: 'This is my body and this is my blood', and his word has become natural law:

> Here nature's law must cede to God's command,
> And transformation follow as He bids,
> Miraculously at His sovereign will.
> At once then nature leaves her wonted way;
> The bread is turned to flesh, the wine to blood.[2]

The church, for Odo, is nothing but the Pauline body of

---

[1] Ibid. lib. VI, vv. 47–52:
> Hinc placet hoc munus, quo fit de pluribus unum
> Aut liquor aut panis mixto baptismate granis,
> Aecclesie septem uelut una replentur ut isdem;
> Corpus hinc capiti, caput inde coheret et illi.
> Hoc genus, hoc unum placet, hoc durabit in euum;
> Hoc facile est, nitidum, simplex deitateque plenum.

[2] Ibid. vv. 68–72:
> Lex ea nature est uerti, in quod iusserit auctor;
> Imperium sequitur de se mox transit in illud,
>   Quod iubet omnipotens, res in miracula uertens.
> Protinus ergo uicem mutat natura suetam:
> Mox caro fit panis, uinum mox denique sanguis.

Christ to which Christ himself 'coheres' as head, and of which the faithful are the members. This concept of the church is felt to be the central experience of the religious tradition and all other aspects characteristic of Odo's spirituality are corollaries of it: the necessity of purity if one is to draw near to the eucharist, abstinence even in conjugal relationship, the moral incompatibility of the priesthood and clerical concubinage. Priests, he thinks, cannot consecrate the body of Christ with hands which have touched the body of a concubine, without thereby ceasing to be part of the body of Christ. Even though Odo himself seems unaware of the ultimate consequences to which similar attitudes could lead, as with the followers of the Patarini, he does realise that the unworthiness of the priest may lead the people to doubt the validity of the sacrament:

> Sublime the office but in disrepute,
> For scandalous example meets the eye
> Of those who, though uncultured, are aware
> No sacred minister should be defiled.
> Whoever joins a whore, Christ's body leaves;
> These folk conclude; he is unchaste, unfit.
> The king, who sees the wedding guests, demands:
> 'How cam'st thou, friend, without a nuptial-robe?'
> Confounded, into darkness he is cast.[1]

Such are the dominant themes of Odo's spirituality as we find them expressed not only in his writings but infused into and actualised in Cluniac monasticism of the tenth century. At the end of the following century this monasticism seemed to Robert of Molesme to have been weakened by its own success and to stand in need of a return to its primitive strictness. It had not,

---

[1] Ibid. lib. VII, vv. 210–18:
> Maiestas cause populo uilescit inde;
> Pluribus exemplum prebetur agendo piaclum,
> Qui licet insulsi facile discernere possint,
> Officia altaris non esse gerenda prophanis.
> Quam meretrici heret, se aufert a corpore Christi;
> Hii uideant: corpus si scorti est, ergo prophanus.
> Conuiuas thalami uisens rex talia dicit:
> 'Tu peplo sponsale carens hic, amice, quid intras?'
> Obmuttit, tenebras uinclatus it exteriores.

however, lost the sense of spiritual values from which it had
been born.

About two centuries after the death of Odo of Cluny the
spiritual drama of Héloïse and Abélard was drawing to its
epilogue. Like the herald who comes onto the stage in ancient
tragedies to narrate the death of the hero (this is Gilson's happy
image) there rose up between those two unhappy people the
noble figure of Peter the Venerable, abbot of Cluny. He had
known and esteemed Héloïse from the time she was a girl and
had followed with human understanding the vicissitudes of the
two lovers, divining with unusual insight their relationship and
deepest psychological and spiritual reactions. He had admired
the strength of soul, the nobility, the wisdom, the rigorous
penance of the abbess of the Paraclete.

He was also an admirer of Abélard. When, worn down by
anguish and exhausted by the incessant struggles which he had
had to sustain against rivals and enemies, the old master
knocked at the door of the monastery of Cluny, Peter welcomed
him with love, surrounded him with solicitude, reconciled him
with St Bernard, obtained for him absolution from Pope
Innocent II and permission to be able to end his tempestuous
life in peace in the monastery. With profoundly human words
the abbot commended Abélard in a famous letter to the pope:
'Deign to direct that he should finish the last days of his life and
of his old age, which may not be very numerous, in your house
at Cluny and that no command may drive him away and force
him to leave this place, where this wandering sparrow is so
happy to have found a nest. For the honour with which all good
men surround you and for the love in which you held him, may
your apostolic protection deign to cover him with your shield.'

No better figure than Peter the Venerable, no finer episode
than his intervention in favour of Abélard lends itself to
illustrating the essential characteristics of Cluniac spirituality
still alive in the great abbot two centuries after the foundation
of Cluny.

Perhaps Peter the Venerable did not live in the same eschatological expectation with the dramatic intensity of Odo. Nor,
perhaps, did he consider earthly love as a sign of the slavery of
man to the devil. But in him had remained unchanged the sense
of the church as a society of chosen souls, united in total

adherence to Christ and to his law, which had already inspired the reform of Cluny. The concept of the mystical body was expressed, instead, in Peter the Venerable by a sense of humanity: serene, detached, but nonetheless warm, as of one who has overcome evil and transcended the interests of earthly life, in a vision of a higher world of eternal values, which can be reached by many different routes, not excluding those of sorrow and error.

In comparison with him, St Bernard seems in some ways to personify better the continuity of the spiritual tradition of Odo. But Bernard's concept of the church, no longer only a mystical body but a concrete and living reality under the firm control of the hierarchy, together with his ideal of the soldier of Christ (no longer simply an athlete of Christ in the struggle against the temptations of the devil, but a knight armed for the defence of the church and for the Christian conquest of the world, even in the field of earthly power) revealed the distance which now separated two spiritual worlds and two ages.

In the religious vision of St Bernard the tradition of Pope Gregory VII was alive and present: the influence of a theocratic concept. Even when presented as yet uncontaminated by ambitions of earthly power, it nevertheless tended to be interpreted in terms of political domination over the world. Cluny, by contrast, had succeeded in dominating solely by spiritual force, thus fully vindicating the pre-eminent and single-minded ideal of Christian inwardness against the ephemeral triumphs of earthly power.

3 The Spiritual Life of Cluny in the Early Days[1]

KASSIUS HALLINGER

I. INTRODUCTION

In 1942 G. Schreiber declared that the problem of Cluny had not yet been solved, and this surprising judgement still holds good.[2] In spite of E. Sackur's monumental work and mounting piles of literature on the subject we have still not nearly fathomed the phenomenon of Cluny in all its depths.[3] We do not even possess an adequate list of all its affiliated houses, and as for Cluny's own inward life, it remains for us a thing practically unknown.[4] Sackur's tendency to exaggerate the importance of Cluny meets with growing opposition, and recent research has not only modified our former conception of Cluny: it has even detached from it altogether the vast area of reform in Lorraine.[5]

Now that scholars have accepted this new, more restricted

---

[1] This article appeared first in *DA* 10 (1954) 417–45. The [French] edition was an abridged and modified version of the original, made at the request of Dom J. Leclercq and translated by Dom H. Rochais. To these two confrères I wish to express my gratitude. [It is from the French edition, 'Le climat spirituel des premiers temps de Cluny', in *RM* 46 (1956) 117–40, that the present translation has been made. Ed.]

[2] G. Schreiber, *Gemeinschaften des Mittelalters* (Münster, 1948) pp. 81–8.

[3] E. Sackur, *Die Cluniacenser in ihrer kirchlichen und allgemeingeschichtlichen Wirksamkeit*, 2 vols (Halle, 1892–4). A bibliography of later work is given by K. Hallinger in *Enciclopedia cattolica*, III (1949) cols 1883–98.

[4] On the question of Cluniac houses, the two publications of J. Bouton, in *Bernard de Clairvaux, Comm. d'Histoire de l'Ordre de Cîteaux* (1953) pp. 193–249, need some revision. The most useful lists are in G. de Valous, *Le monachisme clunisien* (Paris, 1935) II 179–270 and J. Evans, *Romanesque Architecture of the Order of Cluny* (Cambridge, 1938) pp. 153–218. [See also N. Hunt, *Cluny under St Hugh* (London, 1967) pp. 5 ff. and 124 ff. Ed.]

[5] See P. E. Schramm, in *Göttingische Gelehrte Anzeigen*, 207 (1953) 80 ff., and T. Schieffer, in *DA* 1 (1937) 352 ff. On reform in Lorraine, see K. Hallinger, *Gorze–Kluny* ('Studia Anselmiana', XXII–XXV, Rome, 1950–1).

idea[1] it is possible to concentrate more precisely on the inward, monastic aspect of Cluny. We have gradually become better informed about the government of the order, as for instance its attitude towards priories, customs and liturgy. These new insights inevitably raise the question of the spirituality of Cluny. But this in itself is a subject with too many aspects to be covered by a single comprehensive answer. This present study will therefore be restricted to the early years of Cluny. What impression do we get of Cluny at the beginning? Had it an ideal, and if so, what was it? What were its spiritual foundations?

A glance at studies already undertaken shows that these questions have not been overlooked. The answers have followed five main lines.

1. LITURGICAL SPIRIT

The liturgical aspect is obviously what strikes some. For them, the monks at Cluny solemnise the liturgy and say the office of the dead. All else is beyond their purview.[2]

2. OPENNESS TO THE WORLD

Other investigators have been struck by the considerable increase in landed property, the way the great abbots travelled about and their relations with princes and popes. The judgement of these historians is diametrically opposed to that of the above. In this case the history of Cluny is seen as inseparable from that of the role it played in the world – a role interpreted as one of deliberate political activity.[3]

[1] The main conclusions are summarised in Bruno Gebhardt, *Handbuch der deutschen Geschichte*, 1: *Frühzeit und Mittelalter* (1954) pp. 215–18. [See also p. 117, n. 9 of the French edition of the present article for a lengthy bibliography in which the sole English publication is that of H. Dauphin in *Downside Review*, 7 (1952). Ed.]

[2] See F. Heer, *Aufgang Europas*, 1 (1949) pp. 387, 407; Schreiber, op. cit. pp. 102 ff, For a better understanding, see the detailed treatment in the German original of the present article in *DA* 10 (1954) 418 ff.

[3] See A. Brackmann, *Hist. Zeitschrift*, 139 (1929) 34 ff. See also the following notes.

3. FLIGHT FROM THE WORLD

A. Fliche and G. Tellenbach had no difficulty in opposing the above thesis, showing that life at Cluny rested on the firm ascetic foundation of strict separation from the world.[1]

4. FEUDALISM

Those who approach the subject from its sociological aspect take up another, quite different attitude. In 1949 F. Heer tried to explain the whole Cluniac world merely from the sociological point of view. According to him, this world reflected from the outset the low standard of culture of a closed group of men belonging to the nobility. Cluny was fatally affected by this indescribable insensitivity, relieved by no uplifting idea of any sort.[2] Werner's work, which came out in 1953 in East Germany, shows how far this type of criticism can go.[3] The author approaches history from the Marxist point of view, and so generalises and emphasises beyond all proportion the feudal elements which certainly form one feature of the image of Cluny.

Unlike F. Heer, Werner admits that Cluny was animated by an ideal, but he denies the objective validity of that ideal.[4] According to him the whole spiritual world of Cluny was nothing more than an artificial façade covering up the essential and decisive reality of class warfare. Adoration of the cross, devotion to our Lady, suffrages for the dead, solemn liturgy – all that went to make up the spiritual life of Cluny – were in fact simply means employed by feudal overlords to maintain their supremacy over lower classes of society then on the brink of emancipation.[5] P. E. Schramm rightly condemns this way of

---

[1] G. Tellenbach, *Church, State and Christian Society at the Time of the Investiture Contest* (Oxford, 1940) pp. 189 ff.; A. Fliche, *La réforme grégorienne*, 1 (Louvain, 1924) pp. 39–60. Most important is the short study by C. H. Talbot, 'Cluniac Spirituality', in *The Life of the Spirit*, 2 (1945) 97–101.

[2] Heer, op. cit. 1 387–424, esp. pp. 394, 405 ff., 410 ff., 417, 592.

[3] E. Werner, *Die Gesellschaftlichen Grundlagen der Klosterreform im 11. Jahrhundert* (dissertation, Leipzig, 1952; publ. Berlin, 1953).

[4] Ibid. *passim*, but esp. pp. 3 and 22.

[5] Ibid. pp. 33 ff., 70 and *passim*.

writing history: 'E. Werner speaks of spiritual and religious values as a blind man might speak of colours.'[1]

5. MONASTIC ROOTS

In 1949 Dom J. Leclercq pointed out the essentially monastic features of Cluny.[2] Knowing nothing about his study of the subject, I had already that same year published an article tracing the life-force of Cluny back to the same spiritual sources.[3]

Here we shall first describe the monastic ideal of Cluny in its early days, as reflected in the main documents of the time of St Odo, and then in another section consider how far this ideal was actually put into practice.

II. THE MONASTIC IDEAL OF ST ODO'S DAY

To form an opinion of a man's ideas it is not enough to look at one particular thing that he has done; all his work must be taken into consideration. Anyone who has concentrated on another type of literature about Cluny will read Odo's writings with increasing astonishment.[4] The ideas they express are any-

---

[1] P. E. Schramm, *Geschichte in Wissenschaft und Unterricht*, 11–12 (1954) 754. To his opinion can be added the observation that E. Werner has not achieved his object: Marian devotion, an increase in the number of Masses, the cult of the cross are something quite other than a sociological phenomenon. At Cluny, prayer for the dead had roots that were deeper than superficial economic considerations. In short, Werner has yet to prove that the whole interior and external life of Cluny was merely a façade.

[2] J. Leclercq, 'L'Idéal monastique de St Odon d'après ses œuvres', in *Congrès*, pp. 227–32.

[3] See above, p. 29, n. 3.

[4] Such was the reaction of C. Schmitt, *Encicl. cattol.* IX (1952) cols 65–7. See also A. Hessel, in *Hist. Zeitschrift*, 128 (1923) 1–25; W. Williams, in *Monastic Studies* (1938) 24–8; J. Laporte, in *Congrès*, pp. 138–43; A. Nitschke, 'Die Welt Gregors VII' (diss. Göttingen, 1950). Compare the discussions of P. E. Schramm, in *Göttingische Gelehrte Anzeigen* 207 (1953) 72 and K. Voormann, 'Studien zu Odo von Kluny' (diss. Bonn, 1951). I am grateful to Professor W. Holtzmann for having allowed me to examine the last named work. For the works of Odo of Cluny, see M. Manitius, *Geschichte der latein. Literatur des Mittelalters* (Munich, 1923) II 20–7.

thing but elementary platitudes: they show a deep understanding of the monastic life remarkable in the tenth century
and, as far as essentials are concerned, valid for monasticism in
every age.

These ideas deserve careful consideration on account of their
historical significance. Such monastic values not only moulded
a great number of monks in the tenth and eleventh centuries
but their influence extended beyond the monasteries to the
contemporary secular world itself.[1]

What were the fundamental ideas on which monastic life at
Cluny was originally based?

1. To Be a Monk Is to Make Present the Pentecostal Church

This is no vague fanciful idea. Odo was profoundly convinced of its validity, and expounds it in his *Occupatio*, which
appeared shortly after 924.[2] This gives a vast scheme of the
history of salvation and shows exactly where monasticism fits in.
All through the seven books the reader learns from Odo to
avoid following extraordinary paths of his own fancy and rather
to find security in identifying himself with concrete historical
events. The essential evolutionary stages are the creation, the
fall and the incarnation. The culminating point is pentecost,
when the Holy Spirit created the ideal community. Monasticism
fulfils this final evolutionary stage; in it the pentecostal Spirit

---

[1] The success of the reform movement in which Cluny took the lead can
only be explained by Cluny's monastic values. This fact is mentioned several
times in 'Gorze–Kluny', pp. 10, 445, 449, 458, 516, 587, n. 171, 715, 742 ff.,
748 ff. and 1019 (index). If, in spite of such affirmations, F. Weigle can speak
of a picture contrasted with Gorze (*DA* 9, 585), he has not quite understood
the gist of the book. T. Schieffer, on the other hand (in *Arch. f. mittelrhein.
Kirchenges.* 4, 35 and 39), is obviously sympathetic towards Gorze but without
detracting from the main conclusions; similarly T. Mayer, *Hist. Zeitschr.*
174, 574, asserts that such sympathy has not led to unscientific partiality.
U. Engelmann reaches the same conclusion in *Benediktin. Monatschrift*, 28,
497. Dom H. Dauphin, loc. cit. n. 9, has made clarifications which will have
to be taken into consideration.

[2] *Odonis abbatis Cluniacensis Occupatio*, ed. A. Svoboda (Leipzig, 1900). See
Manitius, op. cit. II 22 and L. Kolmer, *Beilage z. Jahresber. d.H. Gymn. Metten*
(1912) pp. 31 ff.

brings about a state of community of soul (*animus socialis*). The divine fire unites the hearts of all so closely that the rift caused by the selfishness of original sin seems at last to be healed and transcended. As in the community at pentecost everything is held in common: this is 'the beautiful form of the Church at her birth', says St Odo.[1] Since the time of St Basil and St Augustine monasticism has drawn life from this ideal, so Odo was certainly following tradition.[2] But he was not content to bear tradition along as a dead weight; he reflected on all its aspects and really made it his own.

2. TO BE A MONK IS TO TRANSCEND THE WORLD

A still stronger influence on the formation of the spirit of Cluny was that of St Gregory the Great (d. 604). Considering the high regard in which he was held in the monastic world it is not astonishing that Cluny should from the start have adopted some of the favourite ideas of this monk-pope. The fact that he felt such a desire to withdraw from the world was not entirely due to an innate love of solitude; unhappy personal experiences were also involved, and the effect of his own inner aspirations on his disciples was all the deeper and more spontaneous on that account.[3] Odo's biographer states of him that in his mature years he had already, while still alive, forgotten the world.[4] It is only too easy to pass over such a saying lightly and overlook what Odo was really demanding of himself and his disciples. But if we stop to examine the words closely we shall see that they are deliberately chosen. According to Odo, monks make

---

[1] *Ecclesiae nascentis honesta forma*, or, as Odo's text has it: 'Ecclesiae formam docet hoc nascentis honestam': *Occupatio*, lib. VI, v. 572.

[2] St Basil, *Regula ad Monachos*, 3, *PL* 103, 496; St Augustine, *Enarratio in Ps. 132*: *PL* 37, 1729 ff. See A. Zumkeller, *Das Mönchtum des hl. Augustinus* (1950) pp. 129 ff.

[3] For St Gregory's influence on St Odo, see Laporte, loc. cit. pp. 138 ff. Statements by St Gregory in favour of the eremitic life may be found in *Dialogues*, 2, ed. U. Moricca, *Fonti per la Storia d'Italia*, 4 (1924) p. 14 and in *Regist. Epist*. 1, 5; *MGH Epist*, 1 5. See also O. Porcel, 'La doctrina monastica de San Gregorio M.' (diss. Washington, 1950).

[4] JS III 12, col. 84. On John of Salerno, see A. Chigny in *Congrès*, pp. 121–129.

'profession of a sublime resolve'; that is to say, their life with all
its endeavour reaches beyond this world.[1] They must not 'lick
the ground', as it is vividly expressed in the life of Gerard of
Aurillac, but must transcend all earthly things.[2] This exodus
takes place by degrees. First comes indifference towards worldly
goods; next the right of ownership itself is renounced.[3] Ardent
love of God is then awakened and leads finally through ascetic
exercises and constant bearing of one's daily cross far beyond
the familiar realm of ordinary experience.[4] In this way a man
is stripped of himself and, as Odo puts it, reaches the summit,
or rather mounts even higher than the topmost peaks of the
earth.[5] Again we must emphasise the danger of looking at
history merely from the outside and so underestimating the
significance of ideas such as these. To understand what influence
they had in practice we can turn to John of Salerno, a witness
by no means to be despised.

We discover, for instance, that when travelling Odo loved

---

[1] *VG* II 16, col. 94. For the authenticity of this life, see A. Poncelet, in
Anal. Boll. 14 (1895) 89–107 and A. Zimmermann, *Lexicon f. Theol. u. Kirche*,
4 (1932) 406 ff. In the *Collationes* Odo places the monks among the ranks of
celestial beings: they lose their kingdom when they are led astray through
earthly things. See below, n. 5 for further references.

[2] *Terram lingere*: *VG* II 1, col. 88, where Gerald is described as already
monastically mature.

[3] *VG* II 2, 8, cols 88, 91; *Coll.* 2, 34, 36, cols 89, 213, 215; JS I 11, 18, 22,
cols 48, 51, 53.

[4] *VG* II 8; *Coll.* 1, 10, cols 91, 168: 'ad desiderium conditoris incalescere'.
VG 2, praef., col. 87. See also the homily for the feast of St Martin, *Bibl. Cl.*
126, and *Coll.* 2, 11, col. 196 (*conditio portandae crucis*: daily martyrdom).
Stress is frequently laid on austerity: see, for example, *Coll.* 2, 8, cols 167 ff.
The necessity of struggling against the vices is expressed in *VG* 2, 1, col. 88.
For the previous history of the theme of monastic martyrdom, see E. Malone,
'The monk and the martyr' (diss. Washington, 1950) and J. Leclercq, *La vie
parfaite* (Paris, 1953) ch. 5, pp. 125–60.

[5] *Coll.* 2, 1, col. 88: 'in rerum uertice situs, iam super altitudines terrae
eminebat'. Odo mostly refers to contemplation as raising a man high above
the earth; he who forsakes these heights is flung headlong into the abyss.
See *VG* I 6 ff., col. 70, where the comparison is taken from St Gregory the
Great, *Moralia*, 35, 10, n. 36: *PL* 76, 543. For the concept of asceticism as a
soaring above the world, see St Ambrose, *De uirginibus*, 1, 3, n. 11: *PL* 16,
202 and M. Frickl 'Das sittliche Verhältnis von Seele, Materie äusserer
Welt und Leib in des hl. Ambrosius *De Isaac et anima*' (diss. S. Anselmo,
Rome, 1951).

to give everything away and make no provision for the following day. He offered money to his would-be murderer and, rather than break the night silence, his monks allowed their horses to be stolen before their very eyes.[1] Men like that really are not of this world.

3. To Be a Monk Is to Return to the State of Innocence

To St Odo transcending created things does not mean becoming insensitive. In his eyes the self-stripping involved in asceticism is a return to our original state. Seeing things in this new light, Odo is able to incorporate into his own thought that desire for a return to paradise which is a key idea of the Fathers.[2] Seen in this perspective, all history appears as the restoration of a lost ideal. Not only Origen (d. *c.* 254) but even St Ignatius of Antioch (d. *c.* 110) already lived by such ideas.[3] It is interesting to notice how these ideas gained ground precisely in the tenth century, that century of iron. Strange to say, it was St Gregory the Great who passed on this ancient ideal: his homily on the Magi in particular represents rigorous asceticism and whole-hearted self-renunciation as a salutary way of restoring that state of original justice forfeited by self-centred weakness.[4] Compunction quenches the seductive allurements of original sin, and conversely selfish consent to sin casts a man out again

---

[1] JS ii 7–10, cols 63–7.

[2] A valuable introduction to this concept of the patristic age is given by J. Daniélou, *Sacramentum futuri* (1950) pp. 3–52. For the fathers a life free from marriage was equivalent to a return to paradise (*reditus in paradisum*): see D. Dumm, 'St Jerome's theory of virginity' (diss. S. Anselmo, Rome, 1950).

[3] G. Bürke, 'Die Origenes Lehre vom Urstand des Menschen', in *Zeitschrift f. Kathol. Theol.* (1950) 20 ff. and E. Peterson, 'Der Stand der Vollkommenheit in der Urkirche', in *Acta et documenta Congressus generalis de statibus perfectionis*, i (1950) 476–9.

[4] St Gregory the Great, *Hom. 10 in Matt. ii*: *PL* 76, cols 11, 1113–14: 'regio quippe nostra paradisus est'. Odo takes up this idea many times: for example, in *Coll.* 2, 12, col. 196, where *reditus* is once again assured to all men; similarly 3, 49, col. 258. Odo refers to his hero Gerald as *cedrus paradisi futurus*: *VG* i 9, col. 172. The role of Mary in the *reditus* is indicated in the sermon for the feast of St Mary Magdalene: *Bibl. Cl.* 138.

from paradise regained.[1] If this holds good of all Christians, it applies even more to monks, who actually achieve this state of paradise.[2] Every renunciation they make is seen as effacing original sin, destroying its effects and at the same time restoring the original order of obedience.[3] This re-established order extends even to the animal world, from which fear vanishes, as in the case of the wolf which obligingly ministers to St Odo.[4] Far from being the severe figure he is usually taken to be, Odo induces street urchins to sing and pays them for it; habitually brimming over with joy himself, he even makes his monks laugh.[5] Who would have expected to find such Franciscan characteristics in the tenth century? Once again we see how necessary it is to go back to the sources to get a correct and realistic idea of the origins of Cluny.

4. To Be a Monk Is to Anticipate the Life to Come

The life of ancient Cluny was nourished at depth from a fourth source – that of eschatology, the realm towards which all becoming moves, where time's threefold measure no longer functions. In eschatological perspective past and future become present. One can see this in St Augustine's attitude to the Greek idea of complete restoration. According to him people in the

---

[1] *Coll.* 2, 12, col. 196: 'qua ad paradisum reditur . . . quem locum totiens deserimus, quotiens peccamus'.

[2] JS 1 14, col. 49. Austerity is presented as a road that leads to the *paradisi gaudia*.

[3] Odo often evokes the original state of man. According to him the saints recover this original condition: *VG* 1 3, col. 68; the original fall is repeated every time a concession is made to degrading selfishness: *Coll.* 2, 18, col. 201; every renunciation reduces the *praesumptio* of original sin and re-establishes the original order: *VG* praef. and 1 15, cols 87 and 76. Such ideas, which are prominent in Odo's thought, were common in the patristic era: see Tertullian, *De ieiunio*, 3–7: CSEL 20, pp. 277–83, where ascetic behaviour is understood as a *renouatio status primordialis*: CSEL 20, p. 279.

[4] JS 1 14, col. 50. On the peace which exists between the 'perfect' and the wild beasts, see A. Stolz, *Theologie der Mystik* (1936) pp. 26 ff.

[5] JS 11 5, col. 63. Thus, the picture of Odo solely as a stern guardian of discipline (Heer, op. cit. 1 396) must be modified.

east tend to look back too much to the past, regarding
asceticism as the restoration of a bygone state. But that is only
one aspect of it. The real idea of restoration should rather be
that of a new creation, the building up of that great tomorrow
when we shall take our place among the ranks of the angels.[1]
Yet even this concept of the future is incomplete. The labour of
asceticism does not only anticipate what is to come; it trans-
forms the past as well as the future into the present. We find
this idea of our eschatological present especially emphasised by
the best minds of the African church.[2] It is not a little surprising
to find such ideas recurring at basic level in the early days of
Cluny. It was certainly not just a matter of an occasional
echo from the past. Odo inherited this way of thinking and
appears to have been profoundly influenced by it. He obviously
delights in bringing out the anticipatory side of monastic asceticism. The following examples should make this clear.

5. To Be a Monk Is to Attain Eternal Peace

Private possession, source of so much lamentable discord, is a
problem solved, at any rate in principle, by the church at
pentecost and by monasticism fashioned after its pattern. The
evil is cut away at its root, for the Holy Spirit has united the
hearts of men and in so doing inaugurated a state of peace, the
final stage of the world's history. Monastic renunciation of
property assumes from this fact an eschatological significance,
and prefigures a state which will only become universal at the
end of time.[3]

[1] *De Genesi ad litteram*, VI 24: CSEL 28, I 196. Numerous references to other
sources are given by G. Ladner, *Mitt. des Inst. Österr. Geschichtsforsch.* 60
(1952) 41–8, esp. n. 82.

[2] Tertullian, *De carnis resurrectione*, 61: *PL* 2, 932. Here, asceticism is a
means of anticipating the final and eternal silence: 'uirtutis futurae linia-
menta'. Similarly St Cyprian, *De oratione*, 36, CSEL 3, 1, p. 294, 11:
'imitemur, quod futuri sumus'; and St Augustine, *Enarratio in Ps. 132*, n. 13:
PL 37, 1736: 'corde praecede, quo sequaris corpore'. Others also, outside
Africa, had the same ideas: e.g. St Jerome, *Epistolae*, 22, 41: CSEL 54, 210:
'esse incipe, quod futura es', and earlier Origen, *Exp. in Eph. 5*: 'qui similes
angelis futuri sumus, iam nunc incipiamus esse': text in Fr W. B. Bornemann,
In investigatione monachatus origine (1885) p. 24.

[3] Leclercq, loc. cit. p. 229, where references are given.

6. To Be a Monk Is to Anticipate the Silence of Eternity

One of the main aims of a monk has always been to find peace through silence.[1] Primitive Cluny was convinced of this. Silence was regarded as one of the essential features of conversion.[2] A whole battery of arguments, biblical, typological and moral, were kept ready to be used when required to defend the rule of silence. To keep silence is to remain in the presence of the Son of Man. Silent adoration in his presence, far removed from secondary occupations, fully and unquestionably justified the practice of silence as far as primitive Cluny was concerned.[3] Odo in his turn added depth to this thought. He liked to refer to days of complete silence, observed on the greatest feasts and during octaves, as 'participation in eternal silence'.[4] The traditional basis of this interpretation must be sought very far back indeed. Eternal silence meant to the gnostic as well as to St Ignatius of Antioch the innermost depths of the Godhead, of that infinite silence from which the Logos came forth.[5] In the Apocalypse the opening of the seventh seal ushers in a permanent state. A great silence reigns, the silence of every creature before

---

[1] Pachomius, *Regula*, 60, ed. A. Boon, *Pachomiana latina* (Louvain, 1952) p. 32; St Basil, *Regula*, praef.: *PL* 103, 487; St Benedict, *Regula*, cap. 6, ed. C. Butler (1935) pp. 28 ff.

[2] Proved by the resistance shown in the time of St Odo to this aspect of the Cluniac programme: see JS II 23, 12, cols 74, 63.

[3] Ibid. II 10–13, cols 66–9. In II 13 and 68 the stress is laid on adoration, as also in *VG* II 15, col. 94.

[4] The information supplied by JS I 32, col. 57 is confirmed by the customaries of Cluny edited by B. Albers, *Consuetudines monasticae*, II (1905) p. 22: see *Gorze–Kluny*, II 872 ff. and 925–33. G. Brugnoli, 'La biblioteca dell'abbazia di Farfa', in *Benedictina*, 5 (1951) 10 ff. betrays a total ignorance of Cluniac customs and tradition. The list of books given in the *Consuetudines Farfenses* belongs to Cluny: see A. Wilmart in *RM* (1921) 89–126.

[5] I. Cechetti, 'Tibi silentium laus', in *Miscellanea Mohlberg* (Rome, 1949) pp. 521–70, esp. pp. 522 ff., which contains studies on gnostic, biblical, christological, ascetic, mystical and liturgical silence. He does not deal with monastic silence. On this see D. P. Salmon, 'Le silence religieux', in *Mélanges bénédictins* (Paris, 1947) pp. 11–57. St Odo knew St Gregory the Great's *Moralia*, 30 xvi, n. 53: *PL* 76, 533, where apocalyptic silence is treated. It is hardly likely that Odo depended directly on St Ignatius of Antioch.

the Son of Man.[1] There is no need for us to decide here from which of these traditional streams of thought Odo drew his inspiration. In each case his interpretation of ascetic silence is dominated by the thought of the eschatological present: that is to say, even now before the end of time the man of silence is drawn into the infinite depths of the eternal silence of God.

7. To Be a Monk Is to Take Part in the Eternal Feast

Regarded in this light, silence is practised especially on the greatest feasts of the liturgical year. This leads on to another way in which Odo sees the next life prefigured. To him the labour of asceticism is itself a participation in the feast of eternity. He compares a monk like Gerard who had sustained the struggle against sin and was now ripe for monastic life to a mountain peak already bathed in the light of eternal dawn.[2] This vivid simile recalls the way in which ancient Alexandrian thought defined the life of the ascetic in terms of perpetual adoration. Those who deliberately deny themselves belong no longer to this world, but to the court of heaven with its delights.[3]

8. Monasticism Is an Angelic Life

St Odo gives two reasons for this foretaste of the heavenly banquet. First of all there is the monk's renunciation of marriage, which anticipates the time when the married state will no longer exist, for, as our Lord says, 'all will be like the angels'.[4] Those who live like this, says Odo, not only deserve to be numbered amongst the blessed spirits hereafter, but even now in the flesh they live an angelic life.[5] The monk's other title to a

---

[1] Rev. 8: 1 ff.   [2] *VG* II 1, col. 88.

[3] G. Bekès, *De continua oratione Clementis Alexandrini doctrina* ('Studia Anselmiana', Rome, 1942). See also n. 5 below.

[4] Matt. 22: 30.

[5] *Occupatio*, lib. VII, vv. 542–50 (*uita angelica* and sexual abstinence); similarly in *VG* II 8, col. 91: 'monachi perfecti beatis angelis assimilantur'. Monasticism is for St Odo *caelestis disciplina, caelestis militiae tyrocinium*: see his sermon on St Benedict, *Bibl. Cl.* 138, 141, where Benedict is described as an angel: col. 141. When speaking of St Odo, John of Salerno can think of no

place amongst the angels while yet on earth is based on the liturgy.[1] The words of the psalms are altogether on a different plane from the merely human: Odo expresses this in Vergil's majestic phrase 'uttering no human sound'.[2] This exactly expresses the mentality of primitive Cluny. When he quotes it Odo means that just as the Sybil of Cumae could no longer utter any human sound, so in the same way the liturgical community is possessed by the Godhead. To such a community the oracles of God have really been entrusted. For that reason, says Odo, a longing for this world is no longer legitimate for those whose voices already blend with the great chorus of eternal praise in which all creatures will join at the end of time.[3] A monk has his place in the choir of angels because he has renounced marriage and shares in eternal praise. The perfect monk has his place, and the fallen one has his, for Odo reckons the latter amongst the fallen angels. In either case the monk's position is eschatological.[4] But it is in a monk's special intimacy with Christ that anticipation of the future is fully realised.

9. MONASTICISM MEANS UNENDING INTIMACY WITH CHRIST

This is the last of Cluny's own definitions of itself. It is generally believed that pre-romanesque art presented an image of Christ that was hieratic, sublime and aloof, exclusive of intimacy. Christ was seen above all as king of heaven and lord of hosts. The psalter was made up of the songs of the warriors of God.

better expression than *angelicus uidelicet et humanus*. On patristic references to the *uita angelica*, see Leclercq, *La vie parfaite*, pp. 19–56; L. Bouyer, *Le sens de la vie monastique* (Paris, 1950) pp. 43–68; J. Daniélou, 'Terre et paradis chez les Pères de l'Église', in *Eranosjahrbuch*, 22 (1953) 433–73.

[1] Perfect chastity gives the right to sing the 'new canticle' and places the monk among the royalty of heaven: *super aethera reges*: see *Occupatio*, lib. VII, vv. 555–9.

[2] *nil mortale sonans*.

[3] E. Norden, *P. V. Maro Aeneis Buch VI 2* (1916) p. 52 (there, *nec mortale sonans*). The liturgical application of this quotation from Vergil shows how highly Odo esteemed the liturgy. Similarly *Coll.* 2, 6, col. 190: 'quibus eloquia Dei credita sunt'; ibid. the condemnation of *terrenis inhiare*.

[4] *VG* II 8, col. 91.

In the majestic and triumphal nave of the romanesque basilica reigned the fear of God.[1] According to I. Herwegen, even on the cross the saviour was represented until after the Carolingian era in a regal attitude and only towards the thirteenth century did the head come to be shown bowed in suffering.[2] F. Heer attributed such ideas to Cluny, but in the light of the sources it seems most unlikely that they ever prevailed there.[3] Primitive Cluny had quite a different idea of Christ. For St Odo he was not only king but shepherd; the lowly God, despised, insulted, crowned with thorns, drinking bitter gall and carrying his cross, the Lamb who accepts immolation. He is, in a manner quite contrary to the feudal ideal, Christ the poor man.

In the realm of metaphysics Odo sees Christ as the Truth. His Christology is imbued with palpable warmth, and that is something not to be overlooked. There is already a hint of later mysticism in which Christ reveals himself as the intimate indweller, the hidden treasure of the heart, a sweet presence pouring torrents of joy into the soul.[4] The force of intimate love

[1] Thus F. Heer and W. Weisbach (*terror Dei*): see n. 3 below.

[2] See following note.

[3] Heer, op. cit. 1 402, 393, 396, 398, 410; W. Weisbach, *Religiöse Reform und mittelalterliche Kunst* (1945) pp. 37–41; I. Herwegen, *Kirche und Seele* (1928) pp. 22 ff. It seems however to be during the Carolingian era that Christ the king began to be represented in ways which highlighted his humanity rather than his divinity. So, in the following era, the tenth century, it was necessary to re-emphasise his divinity.

[4] *humilis Deus; dulcedo praesens; cordis secretum.* In Cluny's early years Christ is sometimes presented as a king: e.g. *De S. Bened.: Bibl. Cl.* 142; *Coll.* 1, 31, col. 179 and *passim.* But this is neither the only nor the main concept: *Coll.* 1, 19, col. 172 (shepherd); cols 170, 182 (*humilis rex, humilis Deus*); cols 214, 261 (the one who is scourged, crowned with thorns, given gall to drink); *VG* 2, praef. cols 13 and 87 (carrying his cross); ibid. col. 88 (*agnus*); ibid. col. 75 (*pauper*); *Coll.* 2, 30, col. 210 (*sacerdos*); *VG* 1 15, and *Coll.* 1, 18, cols 76 and 172 (*veritas*), and *passim.* In the primitive church the concept of Christ the king was not predominant in the liturgy, as is shown by A. Dumon, 'Grondleggers der Middeleeuwse vroomheid', in *Sacris Erudiri*, 1 (1948) 206–24. The same has been proved of the writings of St Ambrose: K. Baus, *Das Gebet zu Christus beim hl. Ambrosius* (Trier). My pupil M. Balsavich has shown that the same is true of Gregory the Great: 'The testimony of St Gregory the Great on the place of Christ in prayer' (diss. S. Anselmo, Rome, 1955). On the affective character of Cluniac devotion to Christ, see *VG* 1 6, col. 70 (*cordis secretum, refectio, riuos dei*); ibid. cols 71, 73, 76 (the interior

for God existed well before St Bernard. It is incredible that anyone should deny this and affirm that Odo's notion of charity
did not include love for God but was wholly concerned with
good works.[1] Monks have an especially intimate relationship
with Christ. He is the 'loving Jesus' in their midst, binding
them together. They meet him everywhere – in the office, in
sacred reading, in the poor, but above all in their own hearts.

The prosaic asceticism of daily life, according to Odo,
consists in going to meet Christ, drawing near to him, clothing
oneself with him: in a word, prefiguring in the present the
intimate familiarity of everlasting life.[2]

III. THE IDEAL IN PRACTICE

Such in broad outline was the ideal which inspired Cluny from
the first, an ideal that implies a whole complex of basic notions
which contributed to the making of Cluny and which should not
be dismissed without careful analysis. So far no one has paid
much attention to the subject. People do not seem to have
realised how intent the tenth century was on reading a meaning
into monastic life. In the twentieth century we are even less
likely to understand the ideas which went to shape Cluny and
were themselves rooted in the patristic age. Whatever people
may think, Cluny undoubtedly had its own monastic ideal from
the beginning. As we have seen, it was an exacting ideal and
anything but elementary. However, it was realised. It formed a
monastic way of life with a structure of its own and a well-
defined purpose, a way of life which, independent of other

---

guest); ibid. cols 70, 72, 79, 91 (*dulcedo praesens*); col. 94 (*in Christo delectatione*);
col. 74 (*suauis amplexus sponsi*); sermon for the feast of St Benedict, *Coll.* 2,
6, 11; *VG* I 12, cols 143, 191, 195, 74 and *passim* (*Christus = sponsus*); *Coll.* 2,
23, col. 203 (*puer Jesus*); *Coll.* 2, 16 and 3, 37, cols 199 and 246 (*benignus
iudex*) and *VG* I, praef. col. 60 (*benefactor populi*).

[1] Contrary to Heer, op. cit. I 394, it must be recognised that St Odo
speaks very often about the pure love of God: e.g. *Coll.* 1, 10, col. 168; *De
S. Bened.: Bibl. Cl.* 141, 144; *VG* II 2, I 26, cols 89 and 79.

[2] JS I 14, col. 49 (*bonus Jesus*); *VG* II 9, col. 91 (presence in prayer); ibid. I 6,
col. 70 (presence in Scripture); ibid. I 14, col. 75 (present in the poor); ibid.
II 1 and *Coll.* 2, 8, cols 88 and 192 (putting on Christ).

traditions, established itself as a norm.[1] It was this noble super-
natural ideal which both served as the foundation of the Cluniac
edifice and shaped its superstructure. But it was not to be confined within the bounds of monasticism: it released forces which
were to have a powerful effect on history in general. In the
following pages we can do no more than sketch the outstanding
characteristics of the spiritual world of Cluny in its early days.

1. RITUALISM

One of the most expressive of these characteristics is what
Rose Graham calls ritualism.[2] The liturgy has always held a
privileged place in monastic life. After a time zealous souls
were not content with the seven canonical hours; they aspired to
unending praise (*laus perennis*). They wanted – as often as
possible and the longer the better – to associate themselves
with the ranks of the heavenly spirits and so anticipate eternity;
in fact they wished to be wholly monks. At Cluny they were
aware that the words of God (*eloquia Dei*) had been entrusted
to monks.[3] So they added still further to the liturgical accretions
initiated by Benedict of Aniane (d. 821). The number of psalms
and supplementary offices went on increasing and psalms were

[1] On the contrast between Cluny and the monasteries of the empire, see
Gorze–Kluny, I 417 ff. The difference between the two monastic branches
does not, however, signify an iron curtain between Burgundy and Lorraine,
as Dom H. Dauphin suggests (see above, p. 30 n.); nor did it amount to lasting
ill-feeling, and I would not agree with Weigle, according to whom the two
groups would have nothing to do with each other (*DA* 9, 584). Some hostile
reactions did indeed result from the reform. Later the two sides came to
collaborate, regarding each other at times with indifference, at times with
admiration. On this subject, see what is said about Fleury and the development of the young reform movement at Gorze, about the modifying of
customs, about personalities such as Richard of Verdun, Herrand of
Halberstadt, Bern of Reichenau, Eckard of Tegernsee-Aura (see the index
of *Gorze–Kluny*). It is from such research on common problems that I
approach the question of the independence or dependence of the two types
of monastic observance (ibid. pp. 663, 983 and *passim*). On Richard's
reform I would refer, in spite of some differences of opinion, to the valuable
and penetrating work of Dom H. Dauphin, *Le Bienheureux Richard, Abbé de
St-Vanne de Verdun* (Louvain, 1946).

[2] See *Gorze–Kluny*, II 1036 (index) for references to ritualism.

[3] See above, p. 41, n. 3.

prescribed for every occasion. There were psalms to be said
setting out on a journey and there were even psalms for
shaving.[1] From the time of St Odo 138 psalms were said daily,
which far exceeded the measure (*pensum*) enjoined by the Rule.
They were in fact not a little proud of achieving in one day the
task of a whole week.[2] In an article which is well worth reading
Stephan Hilpisch has shown how this increase in quantity was
accompanied by a corresponding heightening of solemnity:
they kept on adding to the decorations, lights and festive
ceremonies.[3]

We must however hasten to add that these two tendencies by
no means account for all Cluniac ritualism; this was ridden
with burdensome impositions which have so far escaped
attention.

Moreover, as far as the early days of Cluny are concerned,
there can be no question of an objective form of piety inspired
by the liturgy as Heer unequivocally states.[4] The ritualism of
primitive Cluny never excluded an aliturgical approach. We
can already recognise the first traces of individualistic affective
devotion. Odo certainly manifests profound reverence for
liturgical worship, but it is significant that he himself obviously
prefers private prayer, which, as he says, is all the sweeter for
being hidden.[5] One would not expect to hear such a decidedly
subjective point of view expressed by an abbot of Cluny.
Considering the ritualistic background it is equally surprising
to find Odo taking up the same attitude with regard to the
frequency with which Mass is solemnised: up to his time this
had gone on increasing, but he himself is convinced that it is
not conducive to true devotion to have too many solemnities;
it is more helpful to have only a few.[6] Still more astonishing is
his categorical refusal to enhance the splendour of their liturgy.
He objects to ostentatious singing and personally prefers to

---

[1] See above, n. 2 and JS ii 5, 19, cols 63, 71: 'Psallendo iter peragere';
U iii xvi 760.

[2] JS i 32, col. 57; *Regula S. Benedicti*, cap. 18.

[3] 'Chorgebet und Frömmigkeit im Spätmittelalter', in *Heilige Ueberlieferung*
(Münster, 1938) pp. 263–84.

[4] Heer, op. cit. i 401.

[5] *VG* ii 9, 16, 26, cols 92, 95, 99: 'Tanto dulcius quanto secretius'.

[6] *Coll.* 2, 28, col. 207: 'quanto rarius, tanto religiosius'.

have a glass chalice and wicker basket for the eucharist. All outward show is vain where purity of intention is lacking, and the whole thing would be simply foolish piety were there no interior life.[1] Even where devotion to Christ is concerned Odo, as we have seen, does not emphasise the majestic aspect presented by the liturgy so much as Christ's abiding presence in the heart as its guest and mystic bridegroom. Odo insists on the fact that it is the interior life alone which can ensure the validity of liturgical worship.[2] So the spread of devotion to the 'abode of the heart' dates from the tenth century. Odo speaks of the 'precious soul', and long before St Teresa he refers to the 'interior castle' of the spiritual life. He even worked out an idea about the 'cultivation of the soul'.[3] Long before St Bernard, St Odo is already loudly and emphatically proclaiming how necessary it is to lead an interior life.

It follows that we must no longer, as has hitherto been done, make a hard and fast distinction in the history of spirituality between the period of Cluniac concentration on the liturgy and that of St Bernard's subjective devotion. Such generalisations cut across the organic development of history and do violence to the interwoven complexity of countless influences. The attitude of early Cluny towards ritualism was more broadminded than many people are inclined to admit. It allowed for both objective and subjective elements, embracing as it did not only the liturgy but also an inward spirituality completely stripped of ritual expression.

[1] *pomposa vox; stulta devotio*: ibid. 2, 34, col. 213. Talbot, loc. cit. p. 98 suggests, without supporting evidence, that certain demands of the interior life were at the root of such insights of Odo.

[2] *Coll.* 2, 28, col. 208. For Odo's devotion to Christ, see above, p. 42 f.

[3] *Coll.* 2, 25, col. 205: *pretiosa anima*; *VG* I 16, cols 193 and 76: *cultus animae*; *VG* I 9, col. 71: *arx pietatis in corde*. An example of the affective aspect of private devotion is Odo's veneration of Mary as *Mater Misericordiae*. On this subject, see P. Cousin in *Congrès*, pp. 210–18, and H. Barré, 'Marie et l'Église du Vénérable Bède a S. Albert le Grand', in *Marie et l'Église* (Société française d'études mariales, Paris, 1951) p. 78, n. 190. Long before Bernard, Odo evoked the theme of mystic marriage: see above, p. 42 n. Contrary to what Heer puts forward, op. cit. I 401, Odo, before Mayeul, insisted on the idea of Christ as head of the mystical body. See his sermon for the feast of St Peter, *Bibl. Cl.* 129 and 200 ff. Also prior to Mayeul, he placed the accent on contemplation: see JS III 12, col. 84; *VG* II 9, col. 92: 'suspensus in contemplatione' and *passim*.

2. Desire for Reform

The second unfailing mark of valid monasticism is a desire for reform, and it is significant that this has been so since the time of St Odo. It is true that other kinds of monasticism have been devoted to reform, but none on anything like the same scale. Tirelessly Odo pursued his great aim of restoring monasteries throughout the world. According to his biographer he literally burned with impatient zeal to be asked to do it, and the ecclesiastical authorities did in fact entrust the task to him. And so, as John of Salerno puts it, 'the family of our father sprang up everywhere': communities subject to the Cluniac observance.[1] Such ardent zeal for reform could germinate only in truly religious soil; or, more exactly, in a monastic and eschatological spirituality.[2] E. Sackur has already dealt with these basic spiritual attitudes, and has claimed to show that the Cluniac reform concerned only the matter of inward spirituality within the monasteries. Modern writers on the subject have tended to follow him.[3] But the sources do not bear out such a restricted interpretation of the scope of the reform.

According to his biographer John, Odo's especial concern was concord between kings and this part of his programme certainly exceeded the bounds of the cloister.[4] Moreover, it was for the sake of reforming the feudal order of knights that St Odo wrote his life of St Gerard, presented as a pattern of nobility in the hope of dissuading the nobles from unseemly behaviour.[5]

Monasteries, according to St Odo, do not exist for their own sakes: they must be the source of floods of grace to the neighbourhood.[6] Though ready to find fault as a reformer, he raises no

---

[1] *restauratio coenobiorum; familia patris nostri*: JS II 16, 19, cols 69 and 71.

[2] See the original German article in *DA* 10 (1954) 435 ff. for further material.

[3] Sackur, op. cit. II 445 ff.; W. Schwarz in *Zeitschrift f. Kirchengesch.* 42 (1923) 257; Fliche, op. cit. I 39 ff. See also the bibliography in Tellenbach, *Church, State and Society*.

[4] *Concordia regum*: JS I 14, II 19, cols 49 and 71.

[5] C. Erdmann, *Die Entstehung des Kreuzzugsgedankens* (1935), insists on this. See also T. Schieffer, in *Archiv f. mittelrhein. Kirchengeshich.* 4 (1952) 37. See above, p. 35, n. 1, for the authenticity of *VG*.

[6] JS I 14, col. 49.

objection to the monk preacher of Aurillac.[1] Odo's zeal for reform extends also to the clergy.[2] These facts cannot be reconciled with the idea that his sole concern was with internal monastic affairs.

In championing liberty St Odo strikes at the very root of the social order of his era. But we must deal with this point at greater length.

3. THE IDEAL OF FREEDOM

This zeal for the monastic cause and effort to ensure the total independence of such a life account for another characteristic mark of Cluny: its insistence on freedom.

Long before G. Tellenbach showed that freedom was a spiritual goal pursued by Pope Gregory VII, relations between Cluny and the Gregorian reform were a matter for discussion. The sociological aspect of the question could not escape attention, and the following opinions emerged. Historians today do not believe that the Gregorian movement had been prepared long before by Cluny. The way Gregory acts is too much like an explosion due from the first to the natural make-up of his personality, whereas Cluny fades almost completely into the background. Contemporary sources contain nothing about preparations at Cluny for a struggle between the church and particular churches; they are silent about a clash with the feudal world. Cluny never broke down social barriers, and never thought of reducing the emperor to the status of a layman. Its history is rather that of a remarkable alliance with the nobility. The idea of a long period of preparation is therefore out of the question. The most that can be admitted is that Cluny created an atmosphere favourable to the reform of Gregory VII.[3]

Once again we must turn to the sources and find out what they have to tell us about Cluny's stand for freedom: the form it took, the interests at stake, and finally whether it did have any influ-

---

[1] *VG* I 49, col. 85. See *Coll.* 3, 7, col. 225.

[2] The *Collationes* are aimed at removing the vices of contemporary priests: see praef. col. 225.

[3] See above, p. 47, n. 3, and Schieffer, loc. cit. pp 4 and 36 ff.

ence on Gregory VII. Let us begin with some relatively late facts.

For disciplinary reasons Cluny wished to be a large monastic community. Ulrich of Cluny points out that a community of some size is better able to ward off the encroachments of secular lords.[1] Such a remark is in itself sufficient to show to what extent the Cluny of feudal times was prepared to withstand the great lords when monastic values were at stake. If it is objected that the earliest evidence on the subject goes back to the period before the investiture contest, then we can quote still earlier witnesses who make the social position of Cluny perfectly clear and throw light on the so-called conformism which is supposed to have feudalised it all too soon.

Bishop Adalbero of Laon (d. 1030), unlike modern historians, did not at all look on the Cluniacs as promoters of the feudal hierarchy: their activity, as he saw it, constituted a danger to the aristocratic French church. Owing to the powerful influence of the monks all sorts of people from the lower classes – shepherds, deckhands and the like – were being advanced to offices and honours. Ralph Glaber (d. 1045) unwittingly confirmed from a totally different angle this criticism voiced by those most concerned.[2] This shows how careful one must be in assessing the spiritual atmosphere of Cluny. In its early years Cluny's deep sympathy with the aristocratic mentality was not nearly as complete as is generally assumed.

Cluniac customs with regard to an abbatial election testify to the same thing, and they certainly date from before the Gregorian age. Bernard of Cluny says that seculars were excluded from the abbatial election.[3] This gesture of independence can scarcely be considered a sign of involvement with the aristocracy, still less a token of goodwill towards the feudal company which according to the traditions of feudalised

---

[1] U *Epistolae nuncupatoriae*, 638: example given from La Charité-sur-Loire and recommended to Hirsau. From the disciplinary point of view, see col. 636. See also *Gorze–Kluny*, p. 1010, 'Grosskonvente'.

[2] See his satire in *PL* 141, 771–86, esp. vv. 33–46. Ralph Glaber, *Historiarum*, III ii: *PL* 141, 793. The success of the Cluniac efforts is shown in v. 55: 'ecclesiae fu(l)gor pauco sub tempore uerget'.

[3] B I i 135. On the chronology of the customaries, see R. Philippeau in *RM* 44 (1954) 141–51 and the basic study of M. Rothenhaeusler in *Stud. Mitt. OSB* 33 (1912) 605–20. [See also Hunt, op. cit. pp. 11 ff. Ed.]

monasticism used to assist at such elections.[1] To this must be
added the fact that the great abbots, not so much for the sake
of following the Rule of the Master as for other obvious reasons,
generally tried to name their own successors: Odo was nominated
in this way by the aged Abbot Berno.[2]

The independence with regard to abbatial investiture enjoyed by Cluny and other monasteries under its influence was
staunchly upheld and shows, at least from the beginning of
the eleventh century and as far as the evidence goes, a resolute
intention to exclude feudal ecclesiastical lords from monastic
affairs.[3] The system of priories shows the same aloof stance.
From the tenth century, too, dates the whole centralising
system, with its obvious precautions against the danger posed
by clans and the gentle but firm attraction it held for churches
of lower feudal rank.[4] Ever since the reform of St Maur-des-
Fossés in about 989 the Cluniacs had been accused of making
it their chief aim to turn all monastic communities into
priories.[5] It is certain that Cluny knew well enough what a

---

[1] At the beginning of the twelfth century Peterhausen, following the
principles of Cluny, still had to oppose the intrusion of laymen: *MGH* SS xx
660 ff. Only in 1102 did Ottobeuren resolve to seek a fresh abbot who would
promote a new observance: *MGH* SS xxiii 616 ff. Cluny opposed lay intrusion into the churches: for an ample bibliography, see *Gorze–Kluny*, p. 840,
n. 244.

[2] M. Rothenhaeusler, see above, n. 3; De Valous, op. cit. 1 90 ff.;
F. Masai, 'Les antécédents de Cluny', in *Congrès*, pp. 192–202, for similarities
with the *Regula Magistri*.

[3] T. Mayer, *Fürsten und Staat* (1950) pp. 65 ff. See also *Gorze–Kluny*, pp.
564 ff. To stand for freedom in abbatial elections was to oppose the bishops
and also the seigneurs: ibid. pp. 565 ff. (case of St Mihuel in 1076).

[4] On the system of Cluniac priories, see *Gorze–Kluny*, p. 757. The Cluniac
hierarchy was, so to speak, 'afeudal' to the extent that it was hardly
influenced by French feudal vassalage, as is shown by J. F. Lemarignier, in
Revue historique de droit français et étranger, 31 (1953) 171–4. The anti-feudal
aspect of the Cluniac priories had already been indicated by G. Schreiber,
in *Zeitschrift f. Kirchengesch.* 62 (1943) 65 ff. E. Werner, see above, p. 31, n. 3,
does not fail to recognise this partly anti-feudal aspect but he prefers to concentrate on the feudal aspects of the Cluniac structure. See also p. 53, n. below.

[Hunt, op. cit. pp. 124 ff. and esp. pp. 154 ff., gives a description of the
Cluniac structure. Ed.]

[5] Sackur, op. cit. 1 289 ff.; R. Molitor, *Aus der Rechtsgeschichte bened.
Verbände*, 1 (1928) pp. 139–41; *Gorze–Kluny*, p. 860. [See also Hunt, op. cit.
p. 164. Ed.]

powerful attraction this system of priories represented and that she positively endorsed it.[1] Turning to the foundation charter of 910 we find ourselves back in the time of St Odo, who, as far as can be made out from the evidence, drew up this great charter of independence himself.[2] The desire for independence expressed by this charter can only be accounted for by monastic tradition and by the bitter experiences which monks under St Benedict of Aniane had undergone in the face of feudal influences. To Berno and Odo it seemed as though to follow the same course would bring about the end of monasticism altogether.[3] Their spiritual heirs have always appealed to the 'pact of independence of 910', which is a sign of what this typically anti-feudal demand stood for in the minds of the Cluniacs, and an irrefutable proof too that they did not concur, to put it mildly, in the systematic encroachments of the laity on the church.[4] The person one is most surprised to find appealing on various occasions to the 910 charter of independence is Gregory VII. Theodor Mayer has done a masterly piece of textual research which shows that Gregory did so. The fact is all the more astonishing since it is a matter of common knowledge that this great pope used to act in a very independent way himself towards everyone else, including even Cluny at times.[5]

Turning now to Odo's writings we can find much that is enlightening, especially in his 'Conferences'. The reform they call for far exceeds the narrow bounds of the cloister; the kind of demands they make are those expressed by the followers of Turpin of Limoges and Odo of Cluny when vindicating the

[1] Werner, op. cit. pp. 12–25.

[2] *Magna charta libertatis*: BB 1 no. 112. See Sackur, op. cit. 1 48 and Manitius, op. cit. 11 21. [There is some difficulty about establishing the exact date of Cluny's foundation: some scholars give 909. See Hunt, op. cit. p. 19. Ed.]

[3] Details in *Gorze–Kluny*, pp. 581 ff. and 550, and *DA* 10 (1954) 437 ff.

[4] See *Gorze–Kluny*, pp. 581 ff. and 550 ff., for supporting evidence, summarised in *DA* 10 (1954) 438.

[5] T. Mayer, in *Zeitschrift f. Schweiz. Geschichte*, 28 (1948) 145–76, dealing especially with JL 5167 for Schaffhausen and 5134 for Marseilles, and with the refusal to bestow the privilege recommended by Abbot William of Hirsau, who in the pope's eyes was still too inclined to acknowledge the rights of lay seigneurs. On the independence of Pope Gregory VII, see Werner, op. cit. pp. 89 ff.

liberty of the church against lay lords. Was it perhaps just a matter of their dreaming of the possibility of one day making an example of some of these powerful lords by excommunicating them? Not at all: this group of men was convinced that all the disorders of their day and all the decadence of the church came from having abandoned former discipline. In earlier ages the church would simply impose censures on flagrant offenders. The only thing to do was to restore the discipline of the good old days; such was the obvious implication of Odo's 'Conferences'. Even princes could be excommunicated. This possibility, which was still a thing unheard of in the days of Gregory VII, was already envisaged by these reformers in the tenth century, and even recommended as a salutary measure. So we see that rivalry between temporal and spiritual forces is perceptible from the tenth century, and moreover that it was a matter for serious thought. Bishops discussed these subjects with monks, and were anxious to see the resulting considerations set down in writing. So it is not true that these ideas of reform are only concerned with internal monastic affairs or that they are centred on the domain of a single monastery: there is evidence in Odo's writings of a campaign against clerical incontinence and simony, and deliberate opposition to laymen holding ecclesiastical benefices, who are addressed by way of warning with the words 'Take then our liberty'. Still more remarkable is the fact that some of Gregory VII's favourite quotations are to be found in Odo's treatise on excommunication.[1]

In conclusion we can at least say that the age of St Odo prepared the way for the future. All the evidence goes to show that, in the years which followed, the main problem was how to resist the encroachments of lay lords on the spiritual domain and counteract their infringements of ecclesiastical law. Cluny played its part in solving the problem. People who imagine that Cluny can be explained on a purely sociological basis must admit that homogeneous phenomena of that sort are rare. The historical reality of Cluny was shot through with contradictions. In particular, early Cluny's insistence on independence can no

---

[1] 'ergo accipite libertatem nostram': see Hallinger, in *DA* 10 (1954) 440–4.

longer, with the best will in the world, be described as feudal. The fact that even within the artificial shelter of the Cluniac withdrawal from the world it was so impossible to escape feudalism that all anti-feudal growth was eventually stifled, calls for more attention than it has perhaps received so far from those interested in scientific investigation of the subject.[1] Humbert of Moyenmoutier stood out for much more precise demands than Odo had ever attempted to make. Although Cluny in its early days was aware of the danger of laymen intruding in ecclesiastical affairs, it had not yet worked out all the consequences that Humbert and his associates did later. From about the middle of the eleventh century the stand made against lay encroachments within the church was characterised by a proselytising asperity which belongs to a later epoch. The sharp resistance which marked this further stage was entirely due to Gregory VII. So one must neither confuse the terms Cluniac and Gregorian, nor on the other hand underestimate the complex of mutual influences between Cluny and Gregory.[2]

4. CENTRALISATION

A fourth characteristic of Cluny, and one more generally recognised, is centralisation. This has been dealt with by Dom Hourlier in some detail.[3] Here we would only wish to add as

---

[1] So H. Jedin. In justifying a total liberty, the foundation charter of 910 tried to achieve, in the midst of a feudal society, a certain ideal inherited from ancient monasticism: the ideal of an existence *extra mundum* (see *DA* 10 (1954) 437). Here the problem of Cluniac feudalism is barely touched. Final judgements on this subject seem premature. Cluny was neither exclusively feudal nor in every aspect anti-feudal. One finds a basic structure which is feudal and which, at the same time, has characteristics which can be described as strongly anti-feudal. See *Gorze–Kluny*, pp. 755, 774, 1018. I have never, as Werner says (op. cit. p. 33), defined Cluny simply as anti-feudal.

[2] The formula 'Gregorian Cluniacism' used by F. Weigle, in *DA* 9 (1953) 584, takes no account of all the explanations which I have summarised (*Gorze–Kluny*, pp. 544–97, esp. p. 584) by saying that Gregorianism and Cluniac monasticism are, in their ultimate development, very different from each other despite their common sources. A dispassionate appreciation is given by T. Mayer, in *Histor. Zeitschrift*, 174, 573.

[3] J. Hourlier, 'Cluny et la notion d'Ordre religieux', in *Congrès*, pp. 219–26.

evidence from the time of St Odo the fact that he blames the
Cluniacs for swooping down like vultures on every part of the
world to make everything their prey.[1] Obviously criticism of
this sort would be incomprehensible had a tendency to centralisation not already manifested itself. We should note, too, that it
was considerations of a purely monastic kind which gave rise to
the system.[2]

5. LOYALTY TO ROME

The idea of Roman protection goes back further than Cluny.[3]
From its early days Cluny sought for monastic reasons to maintain an especially close connection with Rome. Berno openly
relied more on Rome than on the protection of the state as had
been the case at Aniane.[4] From about the middle of the tenth
century Cluny assumed a supradiocesan character which committed it more than ever to the authority of the pope, who for
his part was accustomed to make use of exempt monasteries to
counteract the powerful individualism of the bishops.[5] And so
it was that common interests had long before prepared the way
for the juridical organisation of papal power such as was
realised by Gregory VII. Even if there were many other
influences at work along the same lines as that of Cluny, as for
instance the emergence of the canonical way of life in the
eleventh century, this fact can only serve to complete the
picture we have in our minds today of the trends of the
Gregorian era.[6]

[1] JS II 23, col. 73.

[2] Molitor, op. cit. I 123; *Gorze–Kluny* pp. 749–53.

[3] A. Blumenstock, *Der päpstliche Schutz im Mittelalter* (1890); L. Taché, in
Revue de l'Université d'Ottowa, 11 (1941) 5 ff. and 149–77; J. F. Lemarignier,
in *Congrès*, pp. 288–40.

[4] In the foundation charter Berno holds at a distance representatives of
public power. On the attitude of St Benedict of Aniane, who is not dealt
with here, see *Gorze–Kluny*, p. 1018, 'Anianische Traditionen'.

[5] T. Schieffer, in *Archiv f. mittelrhein. Kirchengesch.* 4, 73 ff. This judgement
on the papal use of monasteries is made by Werner, op. cit. p. 89.

[6] On the canonical movement and the investiture contest, see G. Ladner,
Theologie und Politik vor dem Investiturstreit (Baden – Vienna, 1936) pp. 42 ff.
On the part played by the canonical movement, see the very balanced view
of C. Dereine in *RHE* 46 (1951) 767–70.

From the second half of the eleventh century Rome and Cluny began imperceptibly to part.[1] That does not mean that they had both taken divergent paths long before this. The rupture of their original alliance coincided with the rise of nationalities, and so came at a time when it was no longer possible, even with the support of the reforming papacy, to maintain Cluny's ideal of withdrawal from the world.[2]

[1] *DA* 10 (1954) 445.
[2] *extra mundum.* Even at the beginning of the twelfth century there were contacts between the two parties. See J. Sydow, *Stud. Mitt. OSB* 63 (1951) 45–66. A. Chagny, *Cluny et son empire* (1949) pp. 275 ff., shows the slow decline of Cluny at the time of its supremacy.

4 St Odilo's Monastery[1]

JACQUES HOURLIER

If we are trying to understand a particular form of monastic life it is very helpful to know the setting in which it was lived, the site, the kind of enclosure and the buildings with their dimensions, appearance and layout. Some knowledge of the ground-plan of the buildings, of whether they were humanly impressive and of how they were appointed, will give us a better appreciation of the prescriptions of the customaries, enabling us to follow the monk's daily life in an environment that is vivid to us. Such knowledge may even be the key to the souls of the men who lived there and reveal some facets of their spirituality. William of St Thierry relates that his friend Bernard after spending a year in the novitiate at Cîteaux still did not know whether the dormitory was vaulted or not or how many windows there were in the apse of the church.[2] Along with the biographer we may be edified by such complete mortification of the curiosity, but to recapture the soul of Clairvaux we shall derive greater profit from a visit to Fontenay, the best example still visible today of a monastery built by St Bernard.

The principle just stated seems trite and obvious. Why then have historians of monasticism attached so little importance to it? Only the archaeologists study monasteries, and they almost exclusively to establish the history of art. Since the romantic revival the picture of cowled ascetics gliding through arched cloisters has been popular, and little effort has been made to set the monks against the background of those buildings which did in fact shelter the monastic life for many generations.[3] On the

[1] [Translated from Le Monastère de Saint Odilon ('Studia Anselmiana', L, Rome, 1962) pp. 5–21. Ed.]

[2] Vita prima Bernardi, I iv 20: PL 185, 238.

[3] The romantic theme deserves a study of its own, like the one concerning Trappists: P. Anselme Dimier, La sombre Trappe (St Wandrille, 1946). Some elementary references may be found in Chateaubriand, especially in his Vie de Rancé, or in Vigny, Le Trappiste. Evidence can also be found in visual art: e.g. the illustration of the abbey of Port-du-Salut in B. Messager, La Mayenne pittoresque (Laval, 1845) pl. 18.

other hand scholars study the history of monasticism, analyse its institutions and even explore its economic and social problems with little or no reference to a factor which is necessarily central to all monastic life, the monastery itself.[1]

In pointing this out I am not publishing a manifesto but simply trying to indicate the orientation I wish to give to this paper. There is on the one hand a proliferation of studies on Cluniac monachism, and on the other the labours of archaeologists who are helping us to envisage many monasteries more clearly. I wish to exploit the findings of the latter to the advantage of the former. The study will however be limited to a particular epoch in the history of the famous abbey, a little before the end of the life of its fifth abbot, St Odilo.

The Farfa customary has preserved for us a precious description of St Odilo's monastery;[2] it may be filled out as to detail by other passages from the same document, by other customaries and by charters. It has served as a guide to archaeologists in their excavations and their efforts at reconstruction,[3] and it will

[1] The English seem to interest themselves more easily in the problem of placing the monastic life in its setting. One recalls the little book by D. H. S. Cranage, *The Home of the Monk* (Cambridge, 1926). A fine work, which provides a series of very illuminating plates concerned solely with the physical setting of the monastic life, is David Knowles and J. K. Joseph, *Monastic Sites from the Air* (Cambridge, 1952). See also F. H. Crossley, *The English Abbey*, 2nd ed. (London, 1942). Of the studies made of the connection between spirituality and monastic architecture, mention may be made, in spite of its inaccuracies, of F. Cali, *Le plus grande aventure du monde. L'Architecture mystique de Cîteaux* (Paris, 1956).

[2] I have already summarised the reasons for concluding that this description is in fact a description of Cluny: 'Saint Odilon bâtisseur', in *RM* 51 (1961) 313. In the same article I have sought to establish the date of the document and suggested that this description belongs approximately to the years 1033–5. It deals both with the already existing buildings and those still to be constructed.

[3] Professor K. J. Conant has been directing archaeological excavations at Cluny since 1927 and has published his researches in *Speculum*. For our subject, see especially *Speculum*, 29 (1954) 1 ff.: 'Mediaeval Academy excavations at Cluny, VIII: Final Stages of the Project'. The conclusions were [first] summarised in K. J. Conant, *Carolingian and Romanesque Architecture, 800–1200* (Harmondsworth, 1959) and in *Bulletin de la Société nationale des antiquaires de France, 1960* (Paris, 1962) pp. 88–91. A and I. Talobre, *La Construction de l'Abbaye de Cluny* (Mâcon, 1936), made great use of the customaries but their historical and archaeological interpretations are not

guide us equally in our tour of Cluny. The relevant part of the text of the customary is therefore reproduced here according to the only known witness.[1] Instead of commenting on it we will then pay a visit to the monastery. Finally we will attempt to assess the value that this whole complex of buildings represented for the monks, and what it meant to them.

I. THE FARFA CUSTOMARY (BOOK II, CHAPTER 1)[2]

The length of the church is 140 ft, its height is 43 ft and it has 160 glazed windows. The chapter-house is 45 ft long by 34 ft wide. There are 4 windows on the east side and 3 on the north. On the west side there are 12 arcades with double pillars. The parlour is 30 ft long, the camera 90 ft.[3] The dormitory is 160 ft long and 34 ft wide. All its windows are glazed; there are 97 of them, their height

Ecclesiae longitudinis CXL pedes, altitudinis XL et tres, fenestrae vitrae CLXta. Capitulum vero XL et V pedes longitudinis, latitudinis XXXta et IIIIor. Ad oriente [m] fenestrae IIIor; contra septentrionem tres. Contra occidentem XIIci balcones, et par unumquemque afixe in e[i]s duo colupmnae (afixe in eis). Audi-

always correct. [The complete report of the Mediaeval Academy of America's excavations has since been presented in a magnificent volume: K. J. Conant, *Cluny. Les Églises et la Maison du Chef d'Ordre*, published by the Mediaeval Academy of America (Mâcon, 1968). See also below, pp. 77 ff. Ed.]

[1] MS. Vatican, lat. 6808. Dom Réginald Grégoire, monk of Clervaux, kindly agreed to collate this manuscript with B. Albers' edition in *Consuetudines monasticae* (Stuttgart, 1900) I 137. The collation is on MS. Vat. lat. 6808. Dom M. Herrgott drew from the same manuscript for his *Vetus disciplina monastica* (Paris, 1726) p. 87. For the *Consuetudines Farfensis* he mostly used a manuscript belonging to St Paul's without the Walls, but as this omitted the description of the monastery he was obliged to have recourse to the other manuscript, known to the Maurists (Mabillon, *Annales OSB* ad. an. 1009).

[2] [Here the Latin text has been translated into English and the folio references omitted. See pp. 7 f. of the original French article for the best Latin edition of the original text, reproduced also in Conant, op. cit. pp. 42 ff. English readers should not be misled by the terms 'foot' and 'feet': it has not been easy to establish what measure this implied at Cluny as more than one measuring system was used at that time. Until the end of the Gothic period the Roman foot was usually used (c. 0.295m. with variations). See Conant, *Cluny*, p. 159 (and *pied* in index). Ed.]

[3] [Camera = long room or hall. See below, p. 65. Ed.]

being equal to the height of a man standing with arms stretched upwards, measuring to his fingertips; the windows are 2¼ ft wide. The walls are 23 ft high. The bathroom is 70 ft long by 23 ft wide and contains 45 lavatories, in each of which there is a little window cut in the wall 2 ft high by half a foot wide; above these runs a connecting structure of wood and above this again there are 17 windows 3 ft high by 1½ ft wide. The calefactory is 25 ft square. The refectory measures 90 ft in length by 25 ft in breadth; its walls are 23 ft high and in each wall there are 8 glazed windows, all 5 ft high by 3 ft wide. The monastic kitchen is 30 ft long by 25 ft broad; the kitchen for the lay folk is of the same dimensions. The storeroom is 70 ft in length and 60 in breadth. The almonry measures 10 ft in breadth but its length is 60 ft, corresponding to the width of the storeroom. The Galilee is 65 ft long and two turrets have been built at its front side; below these is an open forecourt where lay people stand so as not to get in the way of the procession. The distance from the south door to the north door is 280 ft. The sacristy is 58 ft long including the turret which has been built at the end of it. The Lady chapel is 45 ft long by 20 ft wide, its walls being 23 ft high. The first of the infirmary cells is 27 ft wide by 23 ft long; it is provided with 8 beds and the same number of seats in the porch against the outer wall of the infirmary. The passage outside is 12 ft wide. The second, third and fourth infirmary cells are built in the same way; the fifth is to be smaller,[1] and here the sick shall assemble for the rite of the washing of the feet on Saturdays, or it can be used for the laying out of the bodies of dead brethren. A sixth cell is to

torium XXXta pedes longitudinis; camera vero nonaginta pedes longitudinis. Dormitorium longitudinis CtūLXta pedes, latitudinis XXXta et IIIIor. Omnes vero fenestrae vitreae, quae in eo sunt XCta et VIItē et omnes habent in altitudine staturam hominis, quantum se potest extendere usque ad summitatem digiti, latitudinis vero pedes duo et semissem unum; altitudinis murorum XXti et tres pedes. Latrina LXXta pedes longitudinis latitudinis XXti et tres: sellae XL et quinque in ipsa domo ordinatae sunt, et per unamquamque sellam aptata est fenestrula in muro altitudinis pedes duo, latitudinis semissem unum, et super ipsas sellulas compositas strues lignorum, et super ipsas constructionem, lignorum facte sunt fenestrae Xcē et VIItē, altitudinis tres pedes, latitudinis pedem et semissem. Calefactorium XXti et Ve pedes latitudinis, longitudinis eademque mensura. A janua ecclesiae usque ad hostium calefactorii pedes LXXV. Refectorium longitudinis pedes LXXXXta, latitudinis XXV; altitudinem murorum XXti tres, fenestrae vitrae, quae in eo sunt ex utraque parte octo, et omnes habent altitudines pedes V, latitudinis tres. Coquina regularis XXXta pedes longitudine, et latitudine XXti et V. Coquina laicorum eademque mensura. Cellarii vero longitudo LXXta, latitudo LXta pedes. Aelemosynarum quippe cella pedes latitudinis Xcē, longitudinis LXta ad similitudinem latitudinis cellarii. Galilea longitudinis LXta et quinque pedes et duae turrae ipsius

---

[1] [Note the change to the subjunctive tense from this point onwards: the description henceforward concerns plans not at that time implemented. See above, n. 2. Ed.]

*be provided where those who are serving
the sick can wash dishes and other
utensils. Close to the Galilee a guest-
house 135 ft long by 30 ft wide is to be
built for the reception of people who
arrive at the monastery on horseback. In
one section of this guest-house there are
to be 40 beds and the same number of
straw pillows and 40 lavatories; men
only shall be lodged in this part. In
another section there shall be 30 beds
where ladies of rank and other women
of good reputation may stay; it shall be
provided with 30 lavatories and these
guests shall attend to their own needs. In a
central position in the guest-house tables
similar to those in the refectory are to be
set up, and there men and women are to
take their meals together. On the six [?]
great festivals this house is to be decorated
with curtains and hangings and with
bench-covers for the seats. Abutting onto
the guest-house there is to be another
building measuring 45 ft in length by
30 ft in breadth, reaching to the sacristy
at its further end. Here there will be
accommodation for all the tailors and
their sewing assistants to sit and work at
whatever the chamberlain orders them to
do; a table 30 ft long shall be provided
for their use and another table affixed to it,
the width of the two of them being 7 ft.
In the space between this workshop, the
church, the sacristy and the Galilee there
is to be a cemetery for the burial of lay
folk. To the west of the tailors' workshop
there is to be a building 280 ft long from
its northern to its southern door, and 25 ft
wide, in which there will be stables for
horses, divided into separate stalls. Above
this there is to be a storey in which the
serving men may take their meals and
sleep, provided with tables 80 ft long by
4 ft wide. Any visitors whose meals
cannot be served in the guest-house
mentioned earlier may eat here. At the end
of this building there shall be suitable
accommodation for people travelling on*

galileae in fronte constitute; et
subter ipsas atrium est ubi laici
stant, ut non impediant proces-
sionem. a(d) porta meridiana usque
ad portam aquilonarium pedes
CCLXXXta. Sacristiae pedes longitudinis L et VIII cum turre, quae in
capite ejus constituta est. Oratorium
sanctae mariae longitudinis XL et
quinque pedes, latitudinis XXti,
murorum altitudinis XXti et tres
pedes. Prima cellula infirmorum
latitudinem XX et VIIte̅ pedes,
longitudinem XX et tres cum lectis
octo et sellulis totidem in porticum
juxta murum ipsius cellulae de foris,
et claustra praedictae cellulae habet
latitudinis pedes XIIti. Secunda
cellula similiter per omnia est
coaptata. Tertia eodemque modo.
Similiter etiam et quarta. Quinta sit
minori ubi conveniant infirmi ad
lavandum pedes die sabbatorum:
vel illi fratres qui exusti sunt ad
mutandum. Sexta cellula praeparata
sit ubi famuli servientes illis lavent
scutellas, et omnia utensilia. Juxta
galileam constructum debet esse
palatium longitudinis Ctu̅XXXta et
Vq pedes, latitudinis XXXta, ad
recipiendum omnes supervenientes
homines, qui cum equitibus advent-
averint monasterio. Ex una parte
ipsius domus sint praeparata XLta
lecta et totidem pulvilli ex pallio,
ubi requiescant viri tantum, cum
latrinis XLta. Ex alia namque parte
ordinati sunt lectuli XXXta ubi
comitissae vel aliae honestae
mulieres pausent, cum latrinis
XXXta, ubi solae ipsae suas
indigerias procurent. In medio
autem ipsius palatii affixae sint
mense sicuti refectorii tabulae, ubi
aedant tam viri quam mulieres. In
festivitatibus sex [?] magnis sit ipsa
domus adornata cum cortinis et
palliis et bamcalibus in sedilibus

foot, in which they can receive an appropriate gift of food and drink from the brother almoner. 60 ft from the monks' refectory, at the end of the lavatories, there shall be twelve washing troughs and the same number of large jars, and here at the appointed times baths shall be provided for the brethren. Beyond this shall be the novitiate, a four-square building; in one part of it the novices shall study, in the second they shall take their meals, in the third sleep; the fourth side shall contain lavatories. Next to this shall be another workshop where goldsmiths, gem-setters and glaziers may ply their crafts. Between the baths, the novitiate and the goldsmiths' workshop there shall be a house measuring 125 ft in length by 25 ft in width, extending to the bakery; the latter measures 70 ft in length including the turret at the end of the building, and 20 ft in breadth.

Continued—

cella, ubi aurifices vel inclusores seu vitrei magistri conveniant ad faciendam ipsam artem. Inter cryptas et cellas novitiorum atque aurificum habeant domum longitudinis Ctum XXti et quinque pedes, latudinis vero XXti et quinque et ejus longitudo perveniat usque ad pistrinum. Ipsum namque in longitudinem cum turrem, quae in capite ejus constructa est, LXXta pedes, latitudinis XXti.

ipsorum. In fronte ipsius sit alia domus longitudinis pedes XLta et V, latitudinis XXXta. Nam ipsius longitudo pertingant usque ad sacristiam et ibi sedeant omnes sartores atque sutores ad suendum quod camerarius eis praecipit. Et ut praeparatam habeant ibi tabulam longitudinis XXXta pedes, et alia tabula afixa sit cumea, quarum latitudo ambarum tabularum habeat VIIte pedes. Nam inter istam mansionem et sacristiam atque aecclesiam, nec non et galileam sit cemeterim, ubi laici sepeliantur. A[d] porta meridiana usque ad portam VIItemtrionalem contra occidentem sit constructa domus longitudinis CCtū LXXXta pedes, latitudinis XXti et V, et ibi constituantur stabulae equorum per mansiunculas partitas, et desuper sit solarium, ubi famuli aedant atque dormiant, et mensas habeant ibi ordinatas longitudinis LXXXta pedes, latitudinis vero IIIor. Et quotquot ex adventantibus non possunt reficere ad illam mansionem, quam superius diximus, reficiant ad istam. Et in capite istius mansionis sit locus aptitatus, ubi conveniant omnes illi homines, qui absque equitibus deveniunt, et caritatem ex cibo atque potum in quantum convenientia fuerit ibi recipiant ab elemosynario fratre. Extra refectorium namque fratrum LXta pedum in capita latrine sint cryptae XIIcī et totidem dolii praeparati, ubi temporibus constitutis balnea fratribus praeparentur; et post istam positionem construatur cella noviciorum, et sit angulata in quadrimodis, videlicet prima ut meditent, in secunda reficiant, in tertia dormiant, in quarta latrina ex latere. Justa istam sit depositam alia

Continued in left column

The following table will serve as a summary of this description.[1]

Buildings	Parts of Buildings	Dimensions in Feet			Remarks
		length	breadth	height	
Church		140		43	160 windows (sic)
East wing	Chapter-house	45	34		4 windows on east; 3 on north. 12 arcades with double pillars on west.
	Parlour	30			
	Camera	90			
	Dormitory	160	34	23	97 windows
	Bathroom	70	23		45 lavatories, each with a small window. 17 large windows higher up
South wing	Calefactory	25	25		75 ft away from church door
	Refectory	90	25	23	8 windows on each side
West wing	Monastic kitchen	30	25		
	Kitchen for lay folk	30	25		
	Storeroom	70	60		
	Almonry	10	60		
Extension of church	Galilee	65			2 turrets on its façade; open forecourt below
Distance		280			from southern to northern door
North of the church	Sacristy	58			Turret at its end
Infirmary	Lady chapel	45	20	23	
	1st, 2nd, 3rd & 4th infirmary cells	23	27		8 seats outside for each cell; cloister 12 ft wide

[1] [See Conant, *Cluny*, p. 44, where Dom Hourlier's chart is reproduced with a further column giving the metrical equivalents. Ed.] Measurements in feet have been preserved here, but for an idea of what this means in metrical terms, one may think of a foot as being approximately ⅓ of a metre

Buildings	Parts of Buildings	Dimensions in Feet			Remarks
		length	breadth	height	
Infirmary	5th & 6th				smaller than cells 1–4
Near the Galilee	Guest-house	135	30		40 + 30 beds; same number of lavatories
Adjoining guest-house	Tailors' workshop	45	30		reaches to sacristy
	Lay folk's cemetery				situated between tailors' workshop, sacristy, church & Galilee
To the west	Stables, with a floor above	280	25		from southern to northern door; at its end is a place for passing guests
To the south	Baths (12)				60 ft away from refectory, at end of lavatories.
	Novitiate				beyond baths; built four-square
	Workshop				near novitiate
	'House' (workshop?)	125	25		between baths, novitiate and workshop; extends to bakery
	Bakery	70	20		turret at end

(to be precise, 34.1 cm.). In the same way the descriptions given in the customary have been preserved: any necessary explanations have been left to the commentary which follows. [See also p. 58, n. 2 above. Ed.]

II. A TOUR OF THE MONASTERY

Using the description given by the customary and supplement-
ing it from the results of archaeological research, we can now
make a tour of inspection through the various parts of St Odilo's
monastery.

Our guide takes us first to the church but does not linger
there; he confines himself to remarking on its length and height
and on the number of its windows. The windows would appear
to total 160, which seems excessive; probably a misreading has
led to confusion and we should restore the more ordinary
number of 60, or 59.[1] However that may be, the question is not
important, for excavations have made it possible for us to
reconstruct with considerable accuracy the plan of this church
known as 'Cluny II', built by St Mayeul and consecrated on
14 February 981.[2] A nave divided into seven bays by three
round and then four square pillars opens onto a broad transept.
Beyond the transept six chapels increasing in depth are ranged
around the sanctuary and the main apse that marks its end.
We have here a classic example of what has been called 'the
Benedictine layout'.

Passing through the transept, we emerge into the cloister. Its
pillars were procured by St Odilo from the heart of Provence
by way of the river Durance and the Rhône: 'towards the end
of his life he built a cloister wonderfully adorned with marble
pillars brought with much trouble from the furthest regions of

[1] Professor Conant reckons that the church contained 63 windows, of
which 4 were later obstructed by abutments. He proposes the reading
fenestrae vitrae LIXta [instead of *fenestrae vitrae CLXta* as in Hourlier's edition].
It is easy to alter *LIX* to *CLX*; the letters *ta* would not have appeared in the
original manuscript (which would read *novem*) but would be added by a
copyist as a result of his false reading.

[2] 'Cluny I' is Berno's church, consecrated by the bishop of Mâcon at
Odo's request, therefore after 13 January 927, the date of Berno's death, but
soon after his decease because Berno was buried in this church. Professor
Conant describes 'Cluny II' in 'Les églises de Cluny à l'époque de S. Odon
et de S. Odilon', in *Congrès*, p. 37 (with plan and reconstruction). See also
the *Speculum* article quoted above. [See also Conant, *Cluny*, which supersedes
all previous accounts. Ed.]

Provence along the swift rivers Durance and Rhône'.[1] It seems likely that the capitals and bases came with the pillars, all probably obtained from some ancient monument. The ambulatory of the cloister is rectangular in shape, its longer side stretching across the end of the transept, down the nave of the church and reaching across part of the Galilee or narthex. The shorter side of the cloister measures 75 ft, the longer side 115 ft if we follow the description in the customary but 130 ft if we accept the archaeological findings.[2]

On the eastern side of the cloister twelve arcades supported by twin pillars open into the chapter-house. A little further on there is a door giving access to the conventual parlour, and through this we enter a large camera, 90 ft long, where the monks read or work at the appointed times. Alongside these buildings a staircase leads to the dormitory, which extends across the whole of the upper storey. Under the stairs is a tub in which clothes for the wash can be placed.[3] The height of 23 ft given for the walls at the end of the description of the dormitory presumably means 23 ft counting from the ground.[4]

The complex of buildings south of the cloister includes the calefactory and the refectory, and also a passage 15 ft wide. The

---

[1] Jotsald, *De vita et virtutibus sancti Odilonis abbatis* (or *Vita Odilonis*) 1 13: *PL* 142, 908.

[2] Professor Conant has a twofold basis for this conclusion: (1) two soundings (one at the eastern extremity of the cloister, the other in line with its west side); (2) the superimposing of St Odilo's plan on St Hugh's, known from a plan of *c.* 1710 (see J. Virey, 'Un ancien plan de l'abbaye de Cluny', in *Millénaire de Cluny* (Mâcon, 1910) II 230.

[3] *CF* II 48 gives these precise details concerning the granary: 'in arca mittant . . . vestimenta deportent ad gradus . . . in arca(s) effundant operi huic instituta'.

[4] Thus, to the point where the roof begins it is the same height as the building on the east side. This seems high enough for a ground floor and another storey, since for a single dormitory such a height seems rather exaggerated. One could object that the refectory is also 23 ft high without having another storey: it is thus very high compared with the chapter-house; but this height is acceptable because the windows on both sides extend above the cloister roofing. However, Professor Conant prefers to ascribe to the east walk a much greater height than that of the other buildings (see the restorations in *Speculum*, 29 (1954) pls VIb and VIIIa): the proximity of the Lady chapel, adjoining the chapter-house and 23 ft high, determined this solution.

'fountain' used for ablutions was probably situated on this side of the cloister.[1]

The vast roof over the western walk of the cloister shelters the twin kitchens, one for the community and the other for lay folk, as also the storeroom and almonry.

The fourth side of the cloister has come to light during excavations. Here the cloister walk is not right up against the nave of the church but separated from it by the length of one arm of the transept, leaving an open space between cloister and nave. In this space a long narrow building flanks the outer wall of the cloister; this would be the *armarium claustri*. The cupboard for storing books often found in the wall of a cloister has here been turned into an annex which was fairly large for this period, measuring about 42 by 3 ft.

After completing our trip round the cloisters we pass through the chapter-house and enter the Lady chapel close to the infirmary. The latter is situated a little further to the east, probably at an oblique angle to the other buildings, as later infirmaries will also be. Probably its various rooms, so minutely described in the customary, are ranged side by side within a rectangular edifice. It is not difficult to guess the purpose of the four cells for the sick, or of the room for washing crockery and clothes. One last cell is used on Saturdays for the washing of the feet, the 'maundy' of the sick, but a different purpose for it is indicated by the words 'conveniant . . . illi fratres qui exusti sunt ad mutandum' (lit: 'let worn-out brothers come here for changing'). In view of the proximity of the cells for sick brethren this might suggest bloodletting, in which case we should read *ad minuandum* ('for lessening'), but it seems preferable to correct the word *exusti* to *exuti* and assume that this room was also used for laying out dead monks.[2]

By superimposing plans we can reconstruct the buildings to the south of the refectory. The lavatories are built up against the end of the camera, and thus at the end of the dormitory.

---

[1] The customary assumes the existence of this fountain (*CF* 1 14) and charters also refer to it: e.g. BB no. 2009.

[2] The bloodletting seems to have been done in the calefactory (*CF* 11 41). It is not stated precisely where the bodies of the dead should be washed and laid out (see *CF* 11 56) but it seems certain that the ceremony took place in the infirmary, with which these chapters (*CF* 11 41 and 56) are concerned.

The customary gives a detailed description of them, without however making it clear how far they project beyond the side of the long room. Similarly, although the purpose of the twelve baths installed in the place that forms an extension to the lavatories is evident, the dimensions of this place are not given; we know however that it was 60 ft from the refectory.[1] The rest of the indications are insufficient to enable us to determine the exact site of the novitiate, the goldsmiths' workshop and the 'house' measuring 125 by 25 ft 'between the baths, the novitiate and the goldsmiths' workshop'. The novitiate consists of four sections: a study, a refectory, a dormitory and lavatories. This 'four-square' novitiate seems to have been built round a hollow inner court, as suggested by the closing words, 'the fourth side shall contain lavatories'. At a later period however the novitiate was built in a straight line, clearly parallel to the refectory; accordingly the original situation is uncertain.[2] Nor does the customary indicate the site or the dimensions of the goldsmiths' workshop which is said to be near the novitiate. Finally, we are left in the dark as to the purpose and exact situation of the 'house'; it would seem to have been allocated to the craftsmen since it is mentioned immediately after their workshop. The customary mentions only that it extended as far as the bakehouse; hence Professor K. J. Conant has situated it on the terrain later occupied by a building that corresponds to this indication and which ran more or less parallel to the refectory. The nub of the problem is to determine how far St Hugh's architects made use of St Odilo's buildings in this part of the monastery, where extensive alterations were made.

---

[1] On bath fittings, though for a period much later than St Odilo's, see G. Duhem, 'Deux étuves du Moyen Âge conservées en France', in *Bulletin monumental*, 88 (1929) 479.

[2] Professor Conant prefers the solution of a rectangular building. For him, the four parts of the novitiate follow each other on and the workshop is a continuation; the *domus* of 125 ft is almost parallel to the novitiate, from which it is separated by a narrow court. This *domus* was to become the novitiate in St Hugh's day when the old novitiate disappeared as the refectory was enlarged. See *Speculum*, 29 (1954) pls III–X. This restoration, based on the plan of 1710, allows the *domus* and the bakery to be directly connected as indicated in *CF*. In this description of the novitiate one could recognise the text of the 'Rule of St Benedict', cap. 58: 'ubi meditetur, et manducet, et dormiat'.

The 1710 plan shows a bakery which closes the west side of the novitiate quadrangle. Its size and position correspond to the information given by the customary, which suggests that it had not been moved since St Odilo's day. The turret that is mentioned as being at the end of the bakery would no doubt be the solid block of masonry forming the chimney, built up to a considerable height to ensure a good draught. The bakehouse is close to the kitchens and the refectory, and also to the store-room, as would be expected, but between the bakery and the kitchen there is a passage linking the novitiate quadrangle with the outer court of the monastery.

In this outer court two doors 280 ft apart mark the extreme ends of a building used for stables on the ground floor and for servants' lodgings above. At one end of the stables is a place where passing visitors are given food. Probably it abuts onto the later 'Cheese Tower', the base of which seems to date from the eleventh century.[1] It is possible however that the stables themselves extend right up to the tower, which would bring the northern door of this long building more or less into the axis of the church, the southern door being close by the tower.

The façade of the church, or more precisely of the Galilee, rises above the open forecourt where lay people stand while the procession, passing from the cloister into the church, pauses in the Galilee. There is in fact a door here and a passage leading to the cloister.[2] Two turrets frame the façade of the building.

From the forecourt we can walk through to the lay folk's cemetery, bounded on one side by the church and on the other by the sacristy and then the tailors' workshop. The width of the cemetery is that of the north transept of the church or a few feet more.

Following Sir Alfred W. Clapham, archaeologists hold that the sacristy and the workshop are coextensive with the nave of the church as it was before St Mayeul's day, the church called 'Cluny I'.[3] Some difficulty arises however when we look for the exact position of the tower at the end of the building.[4] Even the

[1] According to Professor Conant's restorations.
[2] The porter had to keep this door closed all night: *CF* II 43.
[3] 'On the plan of the early churches at Cluny', in *Archaeologia*, 80 (1933).
[4] The foundations of an important tower are situated not exactly at the end (*in capite*) of the sacristy but a little to the side. Clearly one must not

position of the guest-house is uncertain. This large building for the use of guests who arrived on horseback was situated 'close to the Galilee'. Since the tailors' workshop adjoins the guest-house one might suppose that the latter is an extension of the former; this seems the more likely in that both are of the same width, but the suggestion is conjectural.[1]

So we reach the end of our tour of the monastery, during which we have for the most part been following the claustral prior on his daily round of inspection, but also following the porter or the guestmaster in their allotted tasks.[2]

Our tour has proved that there are a number of details which remain obscure. The reason for this is simple enough: excavations have concentrated on selected areas which provide essential information, and an exhaustive investigation is not feasible. The different plans can be usefully compared only in so far as successive layouts have respected or even made use of earlier foundations, or have left at least some evidence such as new walls or traces in the earth. Such is not necessarily the case with all the buildings, particularly where secondary edifices are concerned. Moreover the description of the monastery provided by the customary seems incomplete in parts, and indeed insufficient. It would appear to have been compiled while some buildings were still unfinished, which would explain why only vague indications are given in certain areas while in other parts

interpret the expression in the customary too literally. One is left with the impression that this tower did not harmonise with the rest of the building, unless one places the sacristy a little further north, which Professor Conant does not do.

[1] This does not entirely correspond with Professor Conant's restorations, which are largely based on successive plans. One can catch a certain nuance in the phrase of the customary, where we find *in fronte ipsius* (*palatii*) whereas normally *in capite* is used for the sacristy tower, for the baths, for the bakery tower, for the place adjoining the stables. The customary describes in detail the fittings of the guest-house: it indicates how it should be decorated on the six principal feasts. The word *sex* is not very legible in the manuscript, but the customary (*CF* 1 139) enumerates the five principal feasts: Christmas, Easter, pentecost, SS Peter and Paul, the assumption. To these must be added St Benedict in March, which has been left out of the list of feasts and their degrees.

[2] See *CF* II 12: 'De priore monasterii vel ... qualiter absconsa deferetur . . .'; II 41: 'De portario monasterii'; II 45: 'De hospitibus'.

of the monastery we have enough data for easy and exact reconstruction.

Fortunately, however, the omissions affect only points of lesser importance. The plan as a whole is quite clear and gives us a very satisfactory knowledge of the monastery, especially of the church and the regular buildings round the cloister. Cluny is in a privileged position in this respect; seldom are we able to trace so exactly and in such detail the lineaments of an entire monastery built before the middle of the eleventh century. Since the customary provides detailed information on the community's observance throughout the day and on the customs peculiar to each period of the year and every feast, it would be easy enough to reconstruct the life of a monk of Cluny in his own setting. Such an undertaking would however take us too far afield, so we will confine our study to its proper object and ask ourselves what can have been the significance of the whole complex of these buildings with which we are so well acquainted.

III. THE MEANING OF ST ODILO'S MONASTERY

Having the plan of St Odilo's monastery, we are in a position to compare it with the plan of Cluny in the time of St Hugh and of Peter the Venerable; we might also search for similar arrangements that may have existed elsewhere, particularly in other Cluniac houses, and so approach the question of whether there was such a thing as specifically Cluniac architecture.[1] This problem, which belongs to the history of architecture, cannot however be studied here since there is not as yet a sufficient supply of preliminary monographs available to attempt a synthesis. We cannot even pause to discuss the fact that the dormitory building does not form an extension to the transept of the church but is situated considerably further east. Our sole

[1] See, for example, H. Reinhardt, *Der karolingische Klosterplan von St Gallen* (St Gall, 1952). Professor K. J. Conant, in *Congrès*, pp. 37 ff., indicates some comparisons, especially for the church. Charlieu, even today, gives quite a good idea of what the chapter-house at Cluny must have been like. It would be particularly interesting to compare the plan of St Odilo's monastery with Cistercian plans.

objective will be to discover how the monks of Cluny regarded their house.

The monastery at Cluny is essentially the home of the monks and of those sharing the daily round of their observance. It is the shelter of this whole population and it provides for the needs, temporal and spiritual, of its inhabitants.

The first point to determine therefore is the numerical strength of the inmates, in order to ascertain their living conditions. The number of the total population of Cluny in Odilo's time is unknown, but we can determine the size of the monastic community proper. The minutes of Odilo's election in January 994 are attested by the signatures of seventy-six monks.[1] The list made out for Lent books in about 1042 includes sixty-four names, obviously representing only those monks actually in residence; there would have been others sent out on various obediences.[2] The community would therefore number about seventy-five monks.

The dimensions of the buildings confirm this estimate. The ninety-seven windows in the dormitory could correspond to ninety-six beds at most, while the length of a hundred and sixty feet would accommodate sixty-four beds ranged in two rows, allowing five feet per person. The forty-five lavatories tally with the indications derived from the dormitory. The refectory contains seating accommodation for about a hundred monks. We should envisage four rows of tables running the length of the room and placed rather close together, each table seating twenty-five persons, which at the rate of three feet per person would allow fifteen feet for passing to and fro. We may note the measurements of the tables: they are given as thirty feet by three and a half for the tailors' workshop and as eighty feet by four for the serving men's refectory. The conventual buildings are therefore designed for anything up to a hundred monks, living if not exactly on top of one another at any rate at fairly close quarters.

The customary gives no measurements for the novitiate, but it describes an infirmary that can take up to thirty-two sick people. The storey above the stables would accommodate at the

[1] BB no. 1957.

[2] Dom A. Wilmart, 'Le couvent et la bibliothèque de Cluny vers le milieu du XIe siècle', in *RM* 11 (1921) 89.

most about a hundred servants and other travellers, judging from the measurements of its tables.

All in all the monastery at Cluny can house a considerable population, perhaps about two hundred and fifty persons. Even if the number fell short of this the house would still not be too large. The inmates would have a sense of well-being but not an impression of great spaciousness; the cenobitic side of Cluniac life has left its mark on the buildings as well as in the details of monastic observance, where it is very clear.

It would not appear however that either St Odilo's monks or Odilo himself were given to singing the praises of this community life in which they realised in practice the psalmist's ideal, 'Behold how good and how pleasant it is, brothers dwelling in harmony!' Nor would it seem that they sang about this earthly dwelling of theirs which they regarded as a type of the heavenly Jerusalem,[1] but they must have been sensitive to the beauty of its proportions since they took the trouble to make them so harmonious.[2] This is why the monastery has characteristic features that must have appealed to their sense of the beautiful as much as they now appeal to ours as we study the art of Cluny.

To the eye of a traveller coming down towards the Grosne valley Cluny would appear as a co-ordinated whole. He could easily pick out the principal buildings ranged round their square courtyards and dominated by the massive main church which exceeded all the others in height. The other buildings were in fact rather low. Only the dormitory wing boasted a real upper storey, since the servants' living quarters over the stables need not have entailed building very high. It is by no means certain that the wing in which the dormitory and chapter-house were situated rose higher than the walls of the refectory, but it had a higher and more imposing roof by reason of the greater size of the building it covered.

All the edifices seem rather narrow: 20, 23 or 25 ft. The guest-

[1] The basilica of St Hugh symbolised this idea of the heavenly Jerusalem both by its dimensions and in its iconography.

[2] Professor Conant has underlined more than once the care taken by the Cluniac architects to respect certain proportions: see particularly 'New Results in the Study of Cluny Monastery', in *Journal of the Society of Architectural Historians*, XVI (Oct. 1957). [See below, pp. 77 ff. Ed.]

house and the dormitory wing, however, are notably wider, being 30 ft and 34 ft wide respectively. The storeroom with its 60 ft is easily the widest but is probably not remarkable for its height. This utilitarian building is designed according to principles different from those of other buildings: it is in effect a covered market.

The comparative narrowness of the various main parts of the buildings accentuates the impression of length in each room, but the length is not really excessive. A refectory measuring 90 ft is large, but hardly too large for a numerous community; similarly the church, though it cannot be called small, is modest enough in comparison with the later one that was soon to replace it.

All things considered, St Odilo's monastery gives an over-riding impression of due measure: it is not excessively large but is sufficiently elaborate; its proportions are harmonious and well adapted to the needs of a community of this size. The characteristic features are order, just measure and equilibrium. Professor K. J. Conant's remark about the church is applicable to all the buildings: 'wise in its restraint, elegant in the living grace of its proportions, and built to last'.[1] This touch of elegance is certainly noticeable in the proportions but is also found in the slender grace of the supports and was a quality studied by all the architects from St Mayeul's time to St Hugh's.[2]

Two other combined characteristics struck the contemporary eye: light and cleanliness. Generous provision is made through-out the monastery for air and light. Not for nothing does the customary take care to tell us the number, position and size of the windows, and also to record a wealth of detail on the lighting of the church at night.[3] There is a whole spirituality springing from light.

It is not only fresh air and light that are admitted in abund-

---

[1] *Congrès*, p. 43.

[2] The finesse is such that one wonders if St Mayeul had anticipated vaulting in his church. In St Hugh's church the delicacy was such as to result in a serious accident in the nave. Even today the transept is astonishing for the extreme thinness of its walls despite their great height.

[3] The number of candles varied according to the degree of feasts, following a carefully established scale.

ance; water is also plentiful in this monastery. It circulates everywhere through a double system of pipes, one set for fresh and the other for used water. The number of lavatories and the care taken to provide them close to each dormitory suggest the importance attached to cleanliness, and a similar care is evinced by the installation of baths for the community, and by the way the infirmary is organised with a special room for the washing of crockery and utensils and another for washing the feet of sick brethren and for the laying out of the dead. Again, a tub is provided for the disposal of soiled linen and the monks are directed to put clothes that need mending in a suitable place.

One last trait strikes us: the beauty of these buildings and the whole harmonious impression they make on the eye. Jotsald, enumerating the various buildings for which Odilo was responsible at Cluny and elsewhere, piles up words to convey his own sense of this – words like glory, nobility, adornment, decoration, and these in their original active sense.[1] The customary prescribes for every extra that can add to the splendour of the church and its furnishings on a feast day: curtains, carpets, candles, lamps, reliquaries and other artistic things. In the refectory cloths lend dignity to the long tables. Yet all this is but accessory and occasional; the essential beauty of Cluny, inadequately described but deeply felt, lies in its lucid simplicity and its proportions. In fine, Cluny is beautiful because certain men created there the ideal setting for their life, and their life was a beautiful thing.

The buildings at Cluny express a humanism that is not indifferent to material beauty or even to a certain degree of comfort. These material concerns however are but a means to an ascent of the spirit from which humanism derives all its value.

We can catch an echo of this humanism, muted in St Odilo but clearer in his biographer Jotsald. In a brief sketch of the history of Cluny Odilo speaks of Berno, who began to build the monastery and spared no pains in his dedication to the task, with admirable results:

... he began the building of the monastery and put his best work into it, until after much laborious effort he had given admirable effect to the loving desires of his pious heart.

[1] *Vita Odilonis,* I 13: *PL* 142, 908.

For through his merits and his example many are converted from the world and seek the tranquil harbour of the
monastery.[1]

This text is an instance of how easy it is to pass from the material
to the spiritual level, but a little further on there is a clearer
example still, when Mayeul's work is mentioned:

Indeed his memory lives on and men hold him blessed as we
remember and still behold the fabric of the heavenly building
raised by him and by his sons in Christ, this edifice that
sprang up and throve and thrives still. If we may make brief
mention of the spiritual craftsmen who laboured over its
fabric, there was one who was outstanding . . . the lord abbot
William. . . . If you would seek to know how honourably the
memory of the blessed Mayeul and his disciples lives on, then
the monasteries they built up from the foundations and those
other houses rescued from decay and restored to good estate,
these shall be your answer.[2]

After enumerating the monasteries built or restored by St
Odilo, Jotsald pleads in his own justification that the account
he has given is in no way superfluous, for, he says, the very
buildings are signs of Odilo's holiness and deserve an eternal
reward:

If enemies deride me or friends reprove me for having set
down all this unnecessarily, let them know that all these
things are signs of the holiness of his soul, and that for works
such as these he both merited the patronage of the saints and
has already received in reward a crown of happiness from
the Lord.[3]

This external activity matches his inner qualities and so is
glorious, as Jotsald observes in the same passage:

In addition to these virtues of his interior life his outward
conduct was marked by glorious zeal for the building and
restoration of holy places and for embellishing them with
ornaments which he obtained from anywhere he could.

[1] Odilo, *Vita Maioli*: *PL* 142, 946.   [2] Ibid. 954.   [3] Ibid. 908.

St Odilo was happy to boast that he had left a cloister of marble where he had found a cloister of wood.[1] The page on which Jotsald details the building projects directed by his abbot closes the chapter on temperance, that virtue which inclines us to keep due measure and order in what we say or do. Jotsald provides examples of how St Odilo showed his balance and moderation, and adds that since all the virtues were in him united he showed himself to be affable and kindly towards his subjects; he was beautiful and seemly in all his undertakings:

> He showed himself to be approachable and kindly towards his subjects ... there was an elegance and a beautiful order about all he did in the sight of God and men.[2]

Beauty of form, well disposed, fair to behold, expressive of order and due moderation: all these phrases describe St Odilo. Would they not be equally applicable to his work, the monastery of Cluny?

[1] Ibid: 'de quo solitus erat gloriari, ut jucundi erat habitus, invenisse se ligneum et relinquere marmoreum, ad exemplum Octaviani Caesaris . . .'.

[2] Ibid: 'affabilem se et benevolum subjectis exhibebat . . . in omnibus suis actibus vel actionibus euformis et compositus coram Deo et hominibus apparebat'.

5 Observations on the Practical Talents and Technology of the Medieval Benedictines[1]

KENNETH J. CONANT

In medieval history we learn a great deal about the Rule, the Customs of the monks and their devotion. It is far less easy to find evidence of the more human aspects of life within the communities, where warm personalities and the special capabilities of individuals enriched the monastic existence. The fact that Benedictinism created a veritable commonwealth of peace always made an appeal to choice spirits of every sort, and the development of their talents often had broad consequences for good because the Benedictine world extended everywhere in western Europe.

It is good to remember, too, that even when the world was most distressed, there were always monasteries with high ideals, which drew on an élite. Baume is a case in point: its pure Benedictinism in 908 attracted Odo, a musician, former canon and precentor of St Martin's at Tours, who had essayed an eremitical existence previously. As the austere but warm-hearted second abbot of Cluny, he became one of the most influential ecclesiastics in Europe. Likewise, we have the testimony of a biographer (1121) that when Hugh of Semur was abbot of Cluny, distinguished men were drawn to the monastic life.[2] And this movement was by no means confined to Cluny. The superior level of intelligence was bound to show in both the internal and the external relationships of these brotherhoods.

The assembling and administration of monastic estates called for managerial skills which are generally unsung. Yet they were

---

[1] [This article appears here for the first time. Ed.]
[2] 'Viri celebres converterentur.'

indispensable to keep the illustrious monasteries flourishing and stable in a disturbed period, when new hierarchies of power were developing. Managerial skills were clearly needed in the process of creating new foundations, as often happened, by redeeming desolate or uncultivated lands. Numerous tracts of this sort were given to the monasteries. There are many cases where the monks transformed a Roman or a Frankish villa into an organised monastic complex, such that, in the sequel, a great monastery became the shrine, the refuge, the intellectual and cultural capital of a region, and moreover its agricultural centre and garner, with governmental as well as spiritual attributions.

Where a community colonised, it was often necessary to discover the resources of a new region, and to work out the technical means by which they could be made available. There was increasing need for men who could understand and marshal resources on a more than parochial scale. The Benedictines themselves were typically able to supply the management and accounting skills which were required – they had great reserves of experience along with the formal academic schools which are so much better known.

An excellent case in point is that of Peter Gloc, who did so well with the involved business of Cluny monastery that St Hugh sent him to Rome when Urban II appealed for someone who could put the papal finances in order. Later, under Peter the Venerable, Bishop Henry of Winchester reorganised the economy of Cluny, where he had started his career as a youngster.

The monks had to discover new mechanisms by which the numerous widely separated houses could be joined in spirit to form the pervasive monastic institution of the eleventh and twelfth centuries. This process was unquestionably furthered by Charlemagne, who had been deeply impressed by the spirituality of Monte Cassino on one of his Italian visits, and required all monasteries in the imperial dominions to follow a Rule of Benedictine type.

The resulting interconnections may be illustrated by the example of Santiago de Compostela. Within a few years after Charlemagne's death there had been attached to the tomb a community, believed to have been Benedictine, 'who diligently chanted the divine office and celebrated Mass over the remains of the apostle'.[1] Their festival day, 25 July, became known, through Benedictine connections, at the renowned Choir School of Metz before 860. Thence the knowledge of Santiago spread, and ultimately the famous pilgrimage to this remote Galician site came into being, aided and furthered by Benedictine establishments (among others) along the Way of St James.

The development of the pilgrimage and the expansion of such institutions as Cluny, Hirsau, Cîteaux, and Prémontré involved a very considerable amount of building. It is a popular delusion that these edifices were generated almost spontaneously by the 'faithful'. Modern studies have convincingly shown the contrary – in John Harvey's witty phrase, the buildings have 'descended from the sublime to the aediculous'. We now know of the bands of craftsmen and their foremen, constantly increasing in number as the buildings multiplied and gained in sophistication.

The modern equivalents of these craftsmen, always with a sense of community, are the Italians who cut and set stone and marble everywhere (they have a practical monopoly of this work in the United States), but they, like their medieval and ancient forebears, need direction, and in the middle ages capable monks typically provided this. The men worked in roving bands to some extent: glass painters, bell-founders, and some other metal workers quite often moved from place to place as their services were required.

However, the craft aspect of this work was often dependent on policy decisions at a high level. An obvious case of this is the high quality of the Cluniac work everywhere, which in turn had a salutary general effect on the medieval building art over a wide area. Another example is provided by the Cistercians, who vetoed sculpture and architectural bravura. This deprived their basically Burgundian church architecture of a part of its birthright (rich carvings, handsome towers, bold proportions). But the Cistercians, whose membership included architects (perhaps St Bernard's own brother Gerard was one of them), spread improved masonry and vaulting techniques throughout western Europe in the twelfth century, which is rightly accounted a great achievement.

[1] 'qui super corpus Apostoli divina officia cantassent et missas assidue celebrassent'.

However, such a development could not come out of nothing, and we must therefore postulate that a very considerable body of technical 'know-how' existed in the ambient of the older communities during the eleventh century. It was not merely that buildings had to be raised, but the discovery, the transport, and the essential testing of materials had to be arranged. The craftsmen had to be found and engaged, their quarters and their essential gear provided; moreover, the new work had to be functionally related to the old in many cases, by someone who thoroughly understood the old buildings, the character of the terrain, and so forth. In general, a bishop's or an abbot's delegate intervened significantly in all of this.

The abbot himself, like Gunzo of Baume, might possess the essentials of architectural training. This was the case with Benedict of Aniane, under whose direction a novel and beautiful church was built on his estate near Montpellier. He was also responsible for the model imperial monastery, Cornelimünster near Aix-la-Chapelle, and doubtless participated in drawing up the prototype plan for a monastery which was adopted by the Synod of Aix-la-Chappelle in 817. The famous plan of St Gall is a copy of this, sent before 823 to Abbot Gauzbert of St Gall (who did not attend) with the admonition to exercise his sagacity on examining it thoroughly.[1] For this, Gauzbert must have possessed some architectural knowledge.

At Aix-la-Chapelle there was a policy decision on the highest level. Of course, within the adopted formula, many modest structures, particularly those in wood, could be left to the responsibility of the craftsmen.

But in the general revival of the building industry after the dark ages we are in debt to the monks – Benedictines especially – without realising it. There are other cases of the same sort.

Few people are aware, for instance, of our debt to early Benedictines and their ambient in the matter of writing and bookmaking. Actually these men found the secret of clarifying the difficult earlier writing, and created the characters which have come down to us, with slight modifications, as the printing types of the present day. The scribes developed the book hands into cursive by inventing clever ligatures and standardising

---

[1] 'sollertiam exerceas tuam, perscrutinanda'.

them for easier, speedier writing and reading. The ligatures, which represent both logic and experience, are an important contribution to the technology of writing, paralleled by Greek developments of the age of Photios.

The hideous débacle of penmanship in our times resulted from supposedly enlightened 'educators' who taught their followers a book hand without ligatures of the sort which the great medieval scriptoria worked out. The pupils develop undisciplined ligatures of their own which degenerate with time, and make the handwriting indecipherable or nearly so. One penman cannot decipher the letters and ligatures of another, which differ from his own.

The medieval calligraphers not only created practical cursive and book hands, but they also developed the book itself (the codex) as we know it, with its hierarchies of lettering for titles, chapter headings, subsections, and – by no means least – lively decorations and opportune illustrations.

These features often have great artistic merit. In their turn they stirred the imagination of sculptors. At first the sculptures, especially in stone, were crude, and the attempts at the human figure were often laughable. With time they acquired a calligraphic grace, partly because the designs were painted in line on the blocks prepared for carving, obviously by men who found their subjects and exercised their art in the scriptoria. Bronzework and stucco never fell so low as stone sculpture had done, but all of the arts benefited by Benedictine skill and patronage. The number of Benedictine practitioners who are known by name is considerable.

But this is not the whole story. When, as in the early period, the choice of subject was left to a craftsman, the carvings were episodic and heterogeneous. As the style advanced, and the monastic intellect entered in (as it began to do late in the eleventh century), the sculptures were better arranged, and had a lesson to teach. The patterns of great symbolic and iconographical compositions were created. Some of these, especially in the twelfth century, are extraordinarily impressive, though still somewhat hieratic and abstract. Their power and appeal were long misunderstood, but there can be no doubt that these monastic achievements were the basis for the development of the more facile Gothic sculpture.

Another case of unacknowledged debt is offered by music. The monks created and performed beautiful plainsong, but it was traditional, and it depended for a long time on simple mnemonic systems and a complex, inadequate notation. Beginning perhaps with Abbot Odo of Cluny and certainly among the Benedictine musicians, key progress was made in methods of instruction, and then towards a more practical notational system. In this, William of Volpiano, or of Dijon (likewise a musician), was a participant, for he devised a new notation. Elsewhere in the Cluniac ambient – at St Martial, Limoges, and at Hirsau in the Black Forest – advances were made, also, in the understanding and performance of liturgical music.

The importance of exact notation, taken up and developed by other churchmen, was that it encouraged original compositions, for such music could be accurately recorded and published. Later it became possible to create directly, and to record, elaborate works with several voices – works which went far beyond the organum and the heterophony of the earlier time. Here we see applied to music the same practical Benedictine talents which, at the same time, were creating the economic basis of medieval Europe, and covering it from end to end with substantial buildings in a novel style.

William of Volpiano was a reform leader, as well as a musician, and he was unquestionably an architect as well. He was sent in 999 from Cluny with a group of monks for the reform of St Bénigne, Dijon. The new church which they built (1001–18) was one of the notable achievements of the time – they made it 'the most wonderful church in the whole of Gaul' – a quite exceptional entirely vaulted building.[1] It was 301 feet in length, and it contained the germ of many later romanesque designs, including the great churches of the Way of St James. The contemporary text says that the abbot gathered experts and told them what he wanted, so that they strove to erect a church worthy of the divine office.[2] Elsewhere the text reports that the design had symbolic features. This is taken to mean that the dimensions contained certain of the symbolic numbers

[1] 'mirabiliorum basilicis totius Galliae'.
[2] 'Reverendus abbas magistros conducendo et ipsum dictando, insudantes dignum divino cultui templum construxerunt.'

which had fascinated early Christian and medieval writers. The destruction of the building makes it impossible to corroborate this at present, but we are more fortunate with regard to Cluny.

St Mayeul, abbot of Cluny, who received William of Volpiano into the community, presided over the construction of the abbey church there, Cluny II (948–81). In this case excavated remains and old texts make it clear that the design incorporated, as a module, the symbolic number 7. There were dimensions of 7, 14, 21, 28, 35, 42, 49, 84, 91 and 140 feet; moreover the nave and aisles had 7 bays and consequently 28 windows altogether, and there were 35 more distributed in the eastern part of the building. 7 sanctuaries – the principal apse and 6 chapels – opened on the transept. Since the high altar was the Lord's (*dominicum*), it is likely that the sevens so persistently used in the design were intended to symbolise the gifts of the Holy Spirit.

Surely a design of this sort would not have been produced by an ordinary 'master'. However, in the conventual structures raised by Odilo, Mayeul's successor, there seems to have been modular building of a more usual kind – edifices, 3, 5 and 9 times the length of a key dimension. The guest-house, 30 by 135 feet, was probably laid out on a quadrille of 15-foot squares.

The great church Cluny III, begun in 1088, was the epitome of the Benedictine accomplishment in architecture and sculpture. It was always, until demolition for building material (1798–1824), the largest and one of the most impressive churches in France. The designer architect, Gunzo, and the job architect, Hazelo, were both Cluniac monks. No ordinary 'master' could have conceived the remarkable scheme, involving advanced architectural skills which would be respected in any age.

There was clearly a desire to have the design embody philosophical and symbolic as well as aesthetic values. The apse was built up on a 7-foot module, presumably in symbolic reference (as at Cluny II) to the gifts of the Holy Spirit, for the dedication of the high altar was first of all to the resurrection of our Lord. Careful measurements by the Mediaeval Academy's mission show that symbolic dimensions like 100 (for plenitude or perfection), the 'perfect numbers', mean and extreme ratio, and special Vitruvian geometrical constructions were used. For instance, four adjacent 50-foot squares, with their various diagonals, yield the whole series of basic transverse dimensions of the church (with a minimum tolerance, always less than four inches).

Pointed arches, nearly two hundred in number, were here decisively introduced into church architecture for the first time, and the resulting aesthetic problems were satisfactorily solved. These pointed arches were not just a fancy on the part of the architects: they marked a functional improvement in the vaulting. Later, when the solution proved to be insufficient in one section, the vault was strengthened by flying buttresses (1130) which were among the earliest in western architecture.

The elegance of the general solution at Cluny III, though arrived at by processes differing from our own, betokens a fine architectural intelligence able to imprint on the energy of this wonderful design the seal of a fastidious spirit. The foundations of this great work were laid broad and deep in the terrain at Cluny, but they were laid equally in the wide field of accomplishments – some novel, some practical, some work-a-day – of the preceding Benedictine centuries.

6 Aldebald the Scribe of Cluny and the Bible of Abbot William of Dijon.[1]

BERNARD DE VREGILLE

These few pages, offered as a filial tribute to Father Henri de Lubac, are an attempt to extend the charters and documents of St Bénigne at Dijon by the addition of a short metrical text, which shows how devoted to Holy Scripture the monks of Cluny were around the year 1000.[2] They may also serve to draw attention to the remarkable Bible in which these nine couplets are inscribed.

It was amongst Father Pierre-François Chifflet's notes that I first came across these verses beginning 'Hic utriusque gerit legis praecepta libellus. . . .' ('Commands from either law this little book doth hold. . . .'), and I found them again amongst the papers which Dom Lanthenas passed on to Mabillon.[3] But it was Hans Walther's invaluable *Initia Carminum* which put me on the track of the manuscript from which these seventeenth-

[1] The article translated here contains considerable modifications of the original article published under the same title, 'Le copiste Audebaud de Cluny et la Bible l'Abbé Guillaume de Dijon', in *L'Homme devant Dieu, Mélanges offerts au Père Henri de Lubac*, ii ('Théologie', 57, Paris, 1964) pp. 7–15. The writer had not actually seen MS. Hamilton 82 and was misled, as were others, as to the character and date of this manuscript. Thanks to the excellent description given in the new catalogue of the Hamilton Collection, published in 1966 (see below, p. 87, n. 2), it has been possible to rectify a serious error. What was originally said about Aldebald, author of the colophon, a later addition to MS. Hamilton 82, remained valid, however, and that was the main point of the article. It is not possible to indicate all the corrections of the original article, but the most important insertions are in italic type.

[2] G. Chevrier and M. Chaume, *Chartes et Documents de Saint-Bénigne de Dijon*, ii (Dijon, 1943).

[3] MS. 220, Collectanea Burgundica, in the Bollandist Library, Brussels, contains Père Chifflet's notes. The papers of Dom Lanthenas are in the Bibliothèque Nationale, Paris, Collection de Bourgogne, MS. 12, fol. 207.

century scholars got them – a manuscript of note, being none other than the splendid Carolingian Bible from the Abbey of St Bénigne at Dijon, long believed to have been written for the most famous of its abbots, blessed William (990–1031).[1]

A vague tradition of some such Bible survived amongst historians of Dijon, but none of them in the nineteenth or twentieth centuries seems to have found a trace of it.[2] The term 'St Bénigne Bible' normally denotes another very beautiful one, dating from the twelfth century, which has always been kept at Dijon.[3]

Hans Walther's *Initia* refers under 'Hic utriusque gerit . . .' to an article by W. Wattenbach on the manuscripts in the Hamilton Collection.[4] The couplets copied out by Father Chifflet and Dom Lanthenas, together with several other verses, were published for the first time in this article.[5] Wattenbach found them on the end page of the 'very large and exceptionally beautiful biblical manuscript written for Abbot William of Dijon', which had recently passed from the Hamilton Collection to the royal collection in Berlin. In that same year a brief account of this MS. Hamilton 82 was given in the *Catalogue of the Hamilton Collection of Manuscripts*, printed in London and limited to a few copies only.[6]

---

[1] Hans Walther, *Carmina medii aevi posterioris latina*, I (Göttingen, 1959).

[2] See, for example, Mgr Bougaud's preface in his edition of the *Chronique de Saint-Bénigne* ('Analecta Divionensia', Dijon, 1875) p. vi. Sackur followed him: *Die Cluniacenser*, II (Halle, 1894) p. 352. Similarly Bernard Prost, *Le trésor de l'Abbaye Sainte-Bénigne de Dijon* (Dijon, 1894), p. 301, based on Dom Lanthenas' reference. The oldest reference known to me concerning this Bible occurs at the beginning of Père Chifflet's list of MSS Codices Benigniani, MS. Phillip, 1866, Staatsbibliothek, Berlin, fol. 37v: 'Biblia descripta tempore Guillelmi Abbatis, adeoque ab annis fere septingentis'.

[3] Bibl. de Dijon, MS. 2. This occurs second on Père Chifflet's list mentioned in the preceding note: 'Biblia descripta ab annis circiter quingentis'. The municipal officers of Dijon, visiting St Bénigne in April 1790, noted that among the 283 manuscripts 'one which appears to us to be very valuable, is a Bible written on vellum, not dated, but well preserved save for one page which has been cut'. (Prost, *op. cit.* p. 149.)

[4] 'Die Handschriften des Hamiltonschen Sammlung', in *Neues Archiv*, VIII (1882) 327–46.

[5] Ibid. pp. 330–1.

[6] *Catalogue of the Hamilton Collection of Manuscripts* (privately printed, London, 1882) pp. 13–14: '82. *Biblia latina* cum Prologis Sancti Hieronimi.

Shortly after the publication of Wattenbach's article, the Hamilton manuscripts acquired by Berlin were divided between the royal library and royal museum, but only those sent to the museum were catalogued.[1] The ones which went to the royal library (now the German national library in Berlin), including this particular MS. 82, were never described in the fine series of catalogues of this library.

It was only in 1966 that there appeared at Wiesbaden, under the name of Dr Helmut Boese, a very careful catalogue of the 'Latin Manuscripts of the Hamilton Collection in Berlin', giving a full description and analysis of MS. Hamilton 82.[2] This publication was most welcome as previously the only description of the manuscript was the short entry in the few existing copies of the English catalogue

Venerable Manuscript on Vellum (19½ by 14 inches), oak boards covered in russia. Royal folio. saec. x. – This important Manuscript appears to have been written by Aldibaldus the Monk, by command of Guilielmus the Abbot. To the New Testament is prefixed the Canon of Eusebius, written between 5 painted columns, and filling 8 pages. After the Gospels and Acts of the Apostles follow the seven Canonical Epistles, then the Apocalypse, and lastly the Epistles of St Paul. The reading of this venerable codex merits attention, as the conclusion of the Epistle to the Romans differs from the Vulgate.' This conclusion, of little significance, is as follows: 'solo sapienti Deo per Dominum nostrum cui . . .'. A cursory examination shows that the manuscript belongs to the Alcuin group classified by Dom H. Quentin. MS. Hamilton 82 is mentioned by E. Lesne, *Histoire de la propriété ecclésiastique*, IV 121, n. 4, following Wattenbach. It was also from Wattenbach that the Benedictines of Bouveret reproduced the colophon from Hamilton 82 in *Colophons de manuscrits occidentaux des origines au XVIe siècle*, I (Freiburg, Sw. 1965) no. 36.

[1] *Catalogue of Ninety-One Manuscripts on Vellum . . . chiefly from the famous Hamilton Collection and till lately in the possession of the Royal Museum of Berlin* (London, 1889).

[2] *Die lateinischen Handschriften der Sammlung Hamilton zu Berlin*, beschrieben von Helmut Boese (Wiesbaden, 1966) pp. 40–2. On p. xi the author indicates that MS. Hamilton 82, still at Dijon in the eighteenth century, appeared before 1819 in the Alexander Douglas collection (no. 10 in the catalogue of this collection by W. Clarke, *Repertorium bibliographicum* (London, 1819)). Here I must acknowledge a debt of gratitude to Professor Dr Hans Lülfing, director of the manuscript section in the Deutsche Staatsbibliothek, Berlin, for information he gave me in 1963. I would also like to acknowledge the assistance of Dr Ingeborg Stolzenberg, keeper of manuscripts at the Marburg/Lahn Staatsbibliothek: it was at Marburg (in the Stiftung Preussischer Kulturbesitz, Staatsbibliothek, formerly the Westdeutsche Bibliothek) that MS. Hamilton 82 was found in 1963.

H.C.M.

with the addition of a few words in Wattenbach's article. This explains why such a remarkable manuscript is so little known.

In this present article we do not propose either to describe 'Abbot William's' splendid Bible or to examine the peculiarities of its text. *The 1966 catalogue furnishes ample details of this masterpiece from the scriptorium of Tours, written about the middle of the ninth century.*[1] *The compiler of the catalogue goes into the question of whether the manuscript belonged to St Bénigne as early as that: in any case it was certainly there from the time of Abbot William's rule.*

We intend to concentrate on the colophon on folio 435r – that is, the nine couplets reproduced with some variations by Father Chifflet, Dom Lanthenas and Wattenbach. Finding the name of Abbot William mentioned in them, these scholars supposed that the Bible had been copied for him. *Actually it is a case of a text from about the year 1000 being added to a manuscript dating from the middle of the ninth century.*

The verses run as follows:

> Commands from either law this little book doth hold,
> And mystic actions too within its text unfold;
> Designed with zeal to serve forever one whose name
> Is rightly 'St Benign', a martyr of great fame.
> An energetic man, named Abbot William, bade
> From two books counterset these extracts to be made.
> So Aldebald obeyed with readiness of heart,
> But how his fingers ached from labour at his art!
> The faithful reader now he begs in humble tone
> To pray for him to God on high upon his throne.
> Whoever reads within to seek for gifts of light,
> Should thank our holy Lord with every grateful rite.
> All powerful maker he, of heaven and of earth,
> Gives to his servants all the world contains of worth.
> His children exiled now in this far distant land
> Must celebrate his praise with every power to hand.

[1] Boese, loc. cit. p. 40, dealing with no. 97 in E. K. Rand, *Studies in the Script of Tours*, I (1929) p. 147; II (1934) pp. 112–13 and pl. LV. The microfilm of MS. Hamilton 82 made at my request by the library at Marburg has been deposited in the Bibliothèque Municipale, Dijon.

Do you, who read this book, bear Aldebald in mind,
Who scribed with his own hand the contents that you find.[1]

We do not think that there is any reason for supposing that Aldebald's colophon was necessarily composed to go at the end of a Bible. On the contrary, the expressions 'little book' and 'extracts' seem to point to some biblical compilation, the work of Aldebald himself.

But before directing our attention to the contribution, however modest, that these lines may make to an understanding of medieval exegesis, we should first assess their historical value, which will be a more fruitful study, itself by no means unconnected with devotion to Scripture.

First of all, what connection is there, if any, between the ninth-century Bible and this colophon dating from the end of the tenth century? The author of the catalogue of the Hamilton collection suggests the following ingenious explanation: Aldebald, the scribe who claims to have done the work at Abbot William's request, no doubt made a copy of the Dijon Bible (perhaps William wanted to take it with him to Fécamp, which was entrusted to him in 1001); on completing his task he may well have added a colophon of his own composition, and then it may have occurred

[1]
    Hic utriusque gerit legis praecepta libellus,
      Mystica gesta suis astruit indiciis.
    Marthiris egregii, uocitati iure Benigni,
      Deditus assiduis nam manet obsequiis.
5 Strenuus hunc abbas Uuillelmus nomine dictus
      Excerpi grammis iussit ab oppositis.
    Aldebaldus et hoc compleuit mente benignus,
      Fessis articulis nempe labore suis.
    Lectoremque humili rogitat sub uoce fidelem
10   Fundat vota Deo propter eum supero.

    Perlegis haec quisquis capiens pia commoda lucis,
      Grates solue sacro multimodas Domino.
    Omnipotens cum sit caeli telluris et auctor,
      Destinat haec famulis quod super arua suis.
15 Hunc cunctos ideo peregrini ruris alumnos
      Concelebrare suis condecet ingeniis.
    Quis legis haec, Aldebaldi studeas reminisci
      Dicta refert scriptis talia qui propriis.

In line 14 *haec* refers to *arua*, not very happily. This is not the only obscurity in this laboured verse.

[The main text of this article, including the verses, has been translated by Dame Frideswide Sandeman, O.S.B., of Stanbrook Abbey. Ed.]

to him to transcribe it on to the Carolingian Bible, which he had used as a model.

It was only natural that the work, done to Abbot William's order, should be dedicated to the famous martyr himself. There are other instances of similar dedications at Dijon.[1] No better adjective could be found than 'energetic' to describe the remarkable zeal which characterised this famous abbot, disciple of St Mayeul of Cluny and great restorer of St Bénigne. One has only to think of his exceptional breadth of view and the wealth of his achievements: the vast basilica – a marvel in itself – erected by him and consecrated on 30 October 1016, or the thoroughgoing reform which he carried out in forty houses. It was William who had first attracted St Odilo of Cluny to St Mayeul's school, and shortly after his death Odilo wrote of him (with forty years of his own prodigious abbacy behind him): 'He laboured more than any of us.'[2]

Who was this scribe Aldebald, who obeyed William 'with readiness of heart', and twice demanded, as price of his labours, prayers from all readers drawing 'gifts of light' from his work? This unmistakable name is not to be found in any chronicle or in any of the innumerable charters of Dijon, which go back to the time of Abbot William. There is no reference to an Aldebald corresponding to the note about Girbert in the St Bénigne chronicle: 'One of the first to be trained by Abbot William, surnamed the scribe on account of his office'.[3] Then too, although this same Girbert is to be found more than once working on charters instead of books, not a single one of the St Bénigne deeds was drawn up by Aldebald. And what is more,

[1] E.g. Bibl. Nat. MS. lat. 9518, fol. 252v.: a dedication in verse, which appears as no. 303 in *Chartes et Documents de Sainte-Bénigne*. Ibid. no. 280 is another dedication in verse, but see p. 10, n. 12 of the article on which the present translation is based for a fuller treatment of no. 280.

[2] 'Plus omnibus laboravit'. Odilo, *Vita beati Maioli* (*BHL* 5180): *PL* 142, 954. On the activity of William, see especially the *Regeste* of the *Chartes et Documents de Saint-Bénigne*, II 243–8. On the relations between Cluny and Dijon at the time of William, see *Annales de Bourgogne*, XXXI (1959) 6–9.

[3] *Chronique de Saint-Bénigne*, ed. Bougaud, p. 162; *Chartes et Documents de Saint-Bénigne*, II 246, 279 and nos 272, 274, 276, 297. The necrology of St Bénigne, quoted below, does not fail to mention the qualification *scriptor* if merited by the deceased: e.g. for Hugo (4 Feb), Oddo (8 March), Girardus (14 June), Girbertus (16 Dec).

there is evidence that there was no monk of that name at St
Bénigne during its golden age under Abbot William: the foundation charter of Fruttuaria was signed by all the monks resident
at Dijon between 1020 and 1021, and the name Aldebald is not
amongst them.[1]

Though not to be found in the chronicle or charters, the name
Aldebald does occur in an early Dijon document, the St Bénigne
necrology, where it is noted on January 24.[2] This fact did not
escape the Benedictines in the seventeenth century: they identified the Aldebald of the necrology with the one of the Bible,
and assumed that he was a monk of Dijon.[3] There is everything
to be said for such an identification, but it does not follow that
he was a Dijon monk; quite the contrary. The St Bénigne
necrology is arranged in a special way, described by Father
Chifflet as follows: 'The old obit book of St Bénigne consists of
two lists, "opposite" each other as the term goes, i.e. parallel.
One is of actual members of the community, together with outstanding benefactors and special friends; the other is of members
of the confederation elsewhere and of people who had asked the
community for prayers.'[4] This second list, on the right-hand
page, generally indicates to which abbey the deceased belonged:
Cluny, Fécamp, Tournus, St Germain at Paris, Luxeuil, Baume,
etc., but in the case of the earliest entries it does not do so. Now
it is precisely amongst these names of deceased outside the community that the name Aldebald occurs: no further qualification
is added; it heads the list on 24 January. Everything leads one
to suppose that this is none other than the scribe who worked
for Abbot William. If this is so, then that monk was certainly

---

[1] *Chartes et Documents de Saint-Bénigne*, no. 274.

[2] A twelfth-century necrology transcribed from an older one: Bibl. de
Dijon, MS. 634, fol. 129 (a seventeenth century copy in the Bibl. Nat.,
Coll. de Bourgogne, MS. 12, fol. 242).

[3] Bibl. Nat. MS. lat. 12662, fol. 273v; Coll. de Bourgogne, MS. 12, fol.
207. See Prost, op. cit. p. 301; Sackur, op. cit. II 491.

[4] Pierre-François Chifflet, *Histoire de l'Abbaye Royale et de la Ville de Tournus*
(1664) p. cxliv (see Bibl. Nat. Coll. de Bourgogne, MS. 12, fol. 204):
'. . . l'ancien livre des Obits de Saint-Bénigne . . . est composé de deux rangs
qui sont, comme on parle, *e regione*, c'est-à-dire, à costé l'un de l'autre. L'un
est des domestiques, ausquels ils joignent leurs insignes bienfaicteurs, & amys
particuliers: l'autre est du reste de leurs confederez, ou qui s'estoient
recommandez à leurs prières.'

not a member of the community of Dijon, and any record of him must be sought in one or other of the abbeys associated with St Bénigne in the time of Abbot William.

Obviously Cluny ranks foremost amongst these, and the records there are perfectly clear. Amongst the charters of Cluny there are about fifty which enable one to trace out the monastic career of an unmistakable Aldebald between 975 and 1004.[1] At first he appears merely as a witness in November 974 or 975; then from 976–7 onwards he draws up a whole series of deeds: 'Aldebald wrote this', 'by the hand of Aldebald', 'Aldebald, acting chancellor, wrote this'.[2] From 978 a further qualification is found: 'Aldebald the deacon wrote this', and so again in 990–1.[3] Towards the end of St Mayeul's abbacy the situation changes: having witnessed his abbot's signature once in 991–2, Aldebald draws up two more documents in 992–3, adding on one of them: 'Aldebald the priest wrote this'.[4] At the end of 993 he appears at the abbatial election of St Odilo, as 32nd out of 78 electors.[5] After that he is no longer official notary, but often witnesses important transactions for the abbey. In such cases his name always comes next to that of St Odilo, except on one occasion when he himself represents Cluny.[6] The last of these deeds with a definite date is that of 22 August 1004.[7]

These then are the facts: Aldebald, disciple of St Mayeul and deacon by at least 978, was one of the busiest scribes in the chancellery at Cluny up to about 991. Ordained priest shortly before the election of St Odilo (end of 993), which was followed by the death of St Mayeul (11 May 994), he was closely associated with the new abbot for at least ten years.

There is evidence of a different kind of the activity of a member of the community at Cluny named Aldebald, a con-

---

[1] BB II 1218, 1406–1725; III 1743–2594. Only those charters in which the actual name Aldebaldus occurs have been taken into account here. Approximate forms – Albaldus, Adalbaldus – have been discounted.

[2] BB II 1406, 1433: 'Aldebaldus scripsit'; 'per manum Aldebaldi'; 'Aldebaldus ad vicem cancellarii scripsit'.

[3] BB II 1457: 'Aldebaldus LEVITA scripsit'; ibid. 1845.

[4] BB III 1900; ibid. 1933, 1934: 'Aldebaldus SACERDOS scripsit'.

[5] BB III 1957 (78 names, not 177 as in *PL* 137, 780, following d'Achery, *Spicilegium*, III 379).

[6] BB III 2313.   [7] BB III 2594.

temporary and assistant of Abbots Mayeul and Odilo. We know that the first biography of St Mayeul was begun shortly after his death, and that it was to the monk Syrus that Prior Garnier had entrusted the task. Syrus himself describes in a letter to St Odilo the circumstances in which the work was carried out.[1] His biography is well documented and carefully written. He has a taste for garnishing the narrative with quotations, which are on the whole well chosen: St Augustine alternates with Vergil and Juvenal; there are even a dozen or so more obscure poetic citations, taken for the most part from the life of St Germanus, put into verse a hundred years previously by Héric of Auxerre.[2]

Not even all these literary embellishments could satisfy contemporary taste, and on the death of Syrus Aldebald undertook the completion of the work, setting about it in the most astonishing way.[3] He left the life as it was, except for the beginning of the first book, where he inserted a whole legendary story about the seizure of Lérins by the Saracens.[4] But the excerpts from the life of St Germanus he saw fit to extend, and himself added many others, plastering them anyhow onto the narrative, content merely to substitute 'Maiolus' for 'Germanus'. Using the same method he was able to enhance the work by the addition of a number of prologues. The ones introducing the

---

[1] *Vita sancti Maioli*, preceded by the *Epistola domni Syri ad domnum Odilonem*: *PL* 137, 745–78. On the successive stages of this biography, see *BHL* 5177–8 and the different conclusions of Sackur, op. cit. II 338–40. Sackur's conclusions are followed by the present writer as the main source. Manitius, *geschichte der lateinischen Literatur des Mittelalters*, II (Munich, 1923) pp. 137–8, has studied the question well and supports Sackur. He recognises the poetic interpolations of the prologues but does not refer to the dedicatory epistle.

[2] *BHL* 3458; the text is in *PL* 124, 1131–1208 and *AA SS* July VII, 221–55 (3rd ed., 232–66). A better edition is in *MGH, Poetae latini aevi carolini*, III, 421–517.

[3] *Vita sancti Maioli*, amplified by Aldebald (*BHL* 5179) is in *AA SS* May II 668–84. See also the notes published in the appendix of *AA SS* May VII. It may be noted that the Bollandists used, among other manuscripts, one from St Bénigne transcribed by Père Chifflet. Formerly quoted as A3 (Bouhier C41), it is in fact MS. 68 of the Montpellier Faculty of Medicine.

[4] This detail led Sackur to suppose Aldebald was a monk of Lérins. The reference by Syrus to the ravages of the Saracens explains such a conclusion. Dom J. Hourlier, *Saint Odilon de Cluny* (Louvain, 1964) pp. 156–7, refers simply to 'Aldebald of Lérins'.

various sections consist of somewhat mauled extracts from the lyrical prologues of Héric of Auxerre, while the main prologue to the whole book is in prose and contains, along with other blatantly pirated passages, an extract from Héric's dedicatory letter to Charles the Bald! 'Syrus's work', Dom Rivet remarks, 'could well have dispensed with the service which this revising editor presumed to render it.'[1] If only Aldebald had been less pretentious, he would certainly have had it in him to produce a tribute to the memory of St Mayeul which would have been more informative for us and more edifying as well.[2]

It is difficult to give the exact date of this strange composition. Probably it was compiled soon after the biography, which was completed not long after 995. The date would then coincide with Aldebald's active period of collaboration with St Odilo.

Finally we must mention the rather vague evidence afforded by a necrology which gives the names of many of the early monks of Cluny, including that of Aldebald. According to the researches of J. Wollasch, the manuscript commonly known as the 'Necrology of Villars-les-Moines' was only brought to this Swiss priory (in the diocese of Lausanne) in the

---

[1] *Histoire littéraire de la France*, VII (1746) p. 410: 'L'écrit de Syrus se serait fort bien passé du service que ce réviseur a prétendu lui rendre.' Dom Rivet believed, like his predecessors, that the verses cited by Syrus and Aldebald were of their own composition. Sackur continued to believe it of Aldebald's prologues.

[2] Such literary devices are surprising on the part of a biographer who knew his subject personally. There are, however, other examples. Thus, when the chronicler of St Bénigne wrote an interesting entry on William's successor, Abbot Halinard, who had died only a few years previously and who had himself 'formed' the chronicler by 'gentle and paternal teaching', the writer copied word for word from the *Vita Maioli* of Syrus, revised by Aldebald, all those passages which could be applied to the virtues of Halinard (*Chronique de Saint-Bénigne*, ed. Bougaud, pp. 182–92 and *PL* 142, 1337–46; *PL* 162, 839–48). The fact did not escape the attention of Père de Lubac, who noted the similarity of language used to describe the 'good captive' in both biographies (*Exégèse Médiévale*, 1 i 297 n. 7). A quotation from Héric of Auxerre, speaking of St Germanus, applied to St Mayeul, then to Halinard, is used again by Hugh of Flavigny of Bishop Berengar of Verdun (*PL* 154, 181):

> Factus apostolici consors et compar honoris
> Duxit apostolicam factis et nomine vitam.

(*Vita Germani*, str. 46. See also str. 60, 'Omnibus hospitii . . .'.)

second half of the twelfth century.[1] *It had been compiled at the beginning of that century in the nuns' abbey of Marcigny, its main contents being long lists of the deceased monks of Cluny up to the death of St Hugh.*[2] *The name Aldebald (not counting Albald and Adalbald) occurs as many as four times, on February 5, July 12 and 13, and October 16 respectively. Clearly none of these dates corresponds with that in the Dijon necrology (January 24). This fact however is not in itself conclusive: it is not inconceivable that a commemoration might have been made on another day in a different church; or else a name might have got misplaced in the process of copying and recopying the necrology.*

There seems little reason to doubt that Aldebald of Cluny, notary for many years in the chancellery of the great abbey, and a man capable as well of literary ventures, successful or otherwise, was also the expert scribe and compiler to whom Abbot William entrusted the work he had in mind. William, it will be remembered, had been brought from Italy to Cluny by St Mayeul in 985. In 989 the bishop of Langres, Brun de Roucy, called for a reform of the abbey of St Bénigne of Dijon; this task was entrusted to William and eleven other monks. It would not be surprising if, at the time when he was introducing monks from Cluny and Cluniac usages at Dijon, he should also have had recourse to the parent abbey for restocking the Dijon library. St Bénigne was soon to be independent in this respect, and Girbert would, like Aldebald, be dividing his time between the library and chancellery.

As regards contents, Aldebald's verses simply echo a piety which embraces both the Old Testament and the New with the same reverence, and interprets them in the same way. They are also the song of thanksgiving of a scribe, privileged to devote his pen to the word of God.

We were at first misled by others into supposing that these lines referred to the Bible in which they are to be found inscribed; but since this is now out of the question, it remains for us to consider for what work they were actually intended. We have already mentioned H. Boese's suggested explanation, according to which the lines might have been written for another Bible which was being copied from this one, and the scribe might then have copied them out again in the first Bible. This

---

[1] Bibl. Nat. MS. nouv. acq. lat. 348, 'Fonds de Cluny' no. 98.

[2] [See below, pp. 143 ff. where the history of this manuscript and its use by scholars is examined. Ed.]

hypothesis seems rather far-fetched, and does not take Aldebald's actual terminology sufficiently into account: to refer to a whole Bible as a 'little book' would be strange indeed.

The book compiled for St Bénigne contained 'commands from either law'. It was Abbot William's desire that a single volume should be filled with treasures from the two Testaments which complement each other: '. . . [he] bade from two books counterset these extracts to be made.' This phrase suggests the integral harmony of the Old and the New Law. It would seem to indicate a small volume showing type and antitype in the characters of the two Testaments and parallel passages for comparison.[1]

Strictly speaking there is no reason why the compiler of such a work should not have collected his material from the actual copy of the Bible in which evidence of his work is to be found (but in that case it would almost seem as though he must have come to Dijon to work).

In the original lines the unusual word *grammae* is employed to designate the Scriptures. It is rather pretentious, half Greek and half Latin, and in the middle ages was sometimes used in a general sense for 'letter' or 'writing'. Here it corresponds to the Greek plural form *grammata*. 'Mystic actions' is a happier turn of phrase, and succeeds in expressing sacred history in which the Spirit is revealed.[2]

One of the community of St Bénigne decided some years later that these lines were inadequate, so he added onto them some old, traditional verses composed by St Isidore of Seville for use in his library, either on furniture or wall-paintings.[3]

The first is a couplet destined for the biblical shelf. While Aldebald has 'either law', for Isidore it is a 'twofold law', resplendent with a single light. Here too we find the New Law coupled together with the Old:

---

[1] This hypothesis was advanced in the first edition of the present article.

[2] This brief and rich formula approximates to those studied by Père de Lubac in *Exégèse Médiévale*, I ii 493–6: *gesta allegorumena, mystica historia, typica historia, res prophetice gestas, mystice gesta, historia prophetica, facta figurativa.* Similarly of the New Testament: *facta mystica* (p. 511).

[3] The collection *Versus sancti Isidori* appears in *PL* 83, 1107–10. A better edition is C. Beeson, *Isidor-Studien*, pp. 133–6. References are also given in *Clavis Patrum*, no. 1212, and J. Fontaine, *Isidore de Séville et la culture classique dans l'Espagne wisigothique*, II 738–40.

The sacred tomes of twofold Law here shine,
Which treasured things both old and new enshrine.[1]

After that come three lines addressed to St Jerome and
originally intended to be attached to his portrait.[2] Isidore composed a number of verses in honour of the doctors and other
writers: Father de Lubac has quoted the first of the series,
addressed to Origen.[3] Here none of them have been retained
save the lines to St Jerome, but then after all, the translator of
the Vulgate did devote himself to the service of the actual word
of God:

Most learned translator from divers tongues, Jerome by name,
Whom Bethlehem city reveres, the whole world tells your fame;
Our library too through your books does your praises
    proclaim.[4]

By adding St Isidore's verses onto Aldebald's, another scribe
at St Bénigne fittingly extended the liturgical *Deo gratias* which
his predecessor began on the last page of his work on the
Scriptures.

The same cannot be said of his successors who transcribed
onto the same page a very different sort of document – a writ
served on Archbishop Hugh III of Besançon by the legate
Hugh of Lyons, bidding him restore the church of Notre-Dame
at Salins to St Bénigne.[5] This time the Holy Scriptures are called
upon to hallow by their proximity the legitimacy of a claim!

[1]   Hic geminae radiant ueneranda uolumina Legis,
     Condita sunt nempe hic noua cum ueteri.
This first couplet has *pariter* instead of *nempe* in the edited versions.

 [2] H. Walther, *Initia carminum*, no. 8160, indicates three manuscripts which
contain the verses on St Jerome.

 [3] *Exégèse Médiévale*, 1 i 268, n. 6; 280, 281.

 [4]   Hieronime interpres uariis doctissime linguis,
     Te Bethleem celebrat, totus te personat orbis,
     Te quoqe nostra tuis promit bibliotheca libris.
The scribe has plainly indicated that the *e* in *bibliotheca* is unstressed. A text
of 3½ lines has been omitted between this quotation and the preceding one.

 [5] This letter, written between 1088 and 1093, is edited in *Chartes et Docu-
ments de Saint-Bénigne*, II 147–8, no. 370, after the editions of Baluze and
Mabillon. Three copies made by Père Chifflet survive (Staatsbibliothek,
Berlin, MS. Phillip, 1757, vol. v, fol. 15v; Bibl. des Bollandistes, MS. 220:
2 copies) and one made by Dom Lanthenas (Bibl. Nat., Coll. de Bourgogne,
MS. 12, fol. 238). All derive from the ancient copy in MS. Hamilton 82.

7 Monastic Movements in the East Pyrenees[1]

ANSCARI M. MUNDÓ

It was in the second half of the tenth century that signs began to appear in Catalonia and in the ancient ecclesiastical province of Narbonne of movements tending towards the formation of groups of monasteries. This period has been chosen as our starting point the more easily to make clear the true part – in this district a modest one – played by Cluny, and to assess precisely the relative importance of Moissac as it drew some of our monasteries into its orbit.

There can be no doubt that the impetus of the congregational movement came from Cluny, but from the outset this impetus made itself felt through the mediation of certain great abbeys which, while imitating Cluny's monastic reform, were in no juridical dependence on her. The leaders of the movement were men who had assimilated the Cluniac spirit and introduced it into their own monasteries. Later, other abbots rose up in succession to the great monks who had led the movement, abbots who followed them in doctrine or were fascinated by their personal qualities. But juridical bonds between monasteries were forged too late, and for this reason premature attempts to form congregations promptly collapsed on the death of their promoters.

This state of affairs continued until the middle of the eleventh

[1] [Translated from 'Moissac, Cluny et les mouvements monastiques de l'Est des Pyrénées du Xe au XIIe siècles', in *Annales du Midi*, vol. 75, n.s. no. 64 (Toulouse Oct 1963) 551–70. Ed.]

century, when the first thrusts of the Gregorian reform began to be felt in these regions. Here was a new type of movement, tending towards centralisation by keeping reformed abbeys closely tied to their mother house like simple dependent foundations. Such a system clashed with a desire for autonomy in monasteries which thus found themselves subject to a foreign house, and which, having their own history and enjoying political and cultural importance, could not but regard a merely dependent role as an unmerited humiliation. Reaction was not slow in coming, and the system fell to pieces. Even before the end of the eleventh century similar movements had reappeared, but these were now local in character, grouping monasteries in a given area under the authority of a mother abbey which made some attempt to centralise or at least to guide the group's activities.

Our study will deal with some of those monastic movements that saw the light of day in the eastern Pyrenees. The earliest was that which linked Lézat and Cuixà to Abbot Garí in the second half of the tenth century. Then came the movement directed by Oliba, abbot of Ripoll and Cuixà and bishop of Vic, which lasted throughout the first half of the eleventh century. At the end of the same century a kind of congregation formed round Sant Cugat del Vallès, near Barcelona. The last congregational movement was that of Lagrasse, in the county of Carcassonne, in the early twelfth century. By way of preface to this study, however, some brief consideration of the political and religious situation in Catalonia at this period is necessary to throw into relief the evolution of its monastic institutions.[1]

The house of the counts of Barcelona was then in the most vigorous period of its existence. Its activity began in 987 with a gesture of refusal made to King Hugh Capet, who had offered to Count Borrell, on condition of feudal allegiance, military aid against the Moorish attack under Al-Mansur. The refusal was

[1] For the general history of Catalonia in this period, see the following recent syntheses: F. Soldevila, *Història de Catalunya*, I (Barcelona, 1962) pp. 73–146; R. d'Abadal, *Els primers comtes catalans* ('Biografies catalanes', I, Barcelona, 1958); S. Sobrequés, *Els grans comtes de Barcelona* ('Biografies catalanes', II, Barcelona, 1961); J. Vincke opened the theme of this study in his article 'Klöster und Grenzpolitik in Katalonien-Aragon während des Mittelalters', in *Spanische Forschungen*, I 3 (1931) 141–64.

of some consequence for the history of the reconquest of the country. A new political development, natural enough in itself, must be recognised: nearly all the Catalan counts, not only the counts of Barcelona but also those of Urgel and especially those of Cerdanya, Besalú, Empúries and Rosselló, were to marry into the families of the counts of Languedoc and Provence during the period that concerns us. It is hardly necessary to point out how far-reaching were the political consequences of the bonds created by these family alliances. A tight network of counties was formed across the eastern Pyrenees to produce a new political entity, equidistant from the peninsular kingdoms, the Capetian monarchs, and the imperial domains in Italy. Monastic history in Catalonia clearly reflects this varied political pattern.

GARÍ'S CONGREGATION, CENTRED IN LÉZAT AND CUIXÀ

Ramon d'Abadal, the much-respected historian of the counts of Catalonia, has recently thrown light on the process whereby the Cluniac spirit of renewal penetrated into the eastern Pyrenees. We need only follow him and summarise his conclusions.[1]

A request was made to Abbot Odo in person to take under his jurisdiction the new abbey of Lézat, founded in 940 in the neighbourhood of Toulouse by the viscounts. To this was immediately added the viscounts' other foundation, Mas-Garnier. On Odo's death in 942 his disciple Adasius, who had been Odo's administrator for the Cluniac houses in the Midi, was left in charge, with Daniel as coadjutor abbot at Lézat. In 949 Cluny received from Pope Agapitus II her fundamental privilege regarding the whole future organisation of the order. This bull of exemption caused a stir, and the monks of Cuixà, in the heart of the Pyrenees, were promptly aware of it. In the following year, 950, they were the first to obtain from the same

---

[1] R. d'Abadal, 'L'esperit de Cluny i les relacions de Catalunya amb Roma i la Itàlia en el segle X', in *Studi medievali*, 3rd ser. II (Spoleto, 1961) 2–41, and *Com Catalunya s'obrí al món mil anys enrera* (Barcelona, 1960).

4.6639

pope a similar bull placing Cuixà under the direct protection of the holy see.[1]

Exemption, however, was only the first step. If monastic reform on Cluniac lines was to be introduced, an experienced man who knew its spirit was needed. It is impossible to say whether the initial impulse came from the monks of Cuixà themselves or from Count Sunifred of Cerdanya, but it was certainly the latter, a devout layman, who in about 965 requested Abbot Garí of Lézat to take Cuixà under his care. Garí needed no persuading: the abbey of Cuixà, fortified with its papal privilege, was a good deal more important than Lézat. Accordingly Garí established himself in his new house and made it the virtual centre of that monastic congregation of which he was dreaming. In 969 Cuixà gained possession of Tramesaigues in the province of Toulouse for the purpose of building a monastery there. On the occasion of the discovery of the relics of St Hilary in 978 Garí was also established as reforming abbot of the monastery of that name in Carcassonne.

Garí was a great traveller. He had taken the initiative in a movement to aid pilgrims to the Holy Land, and this venture had led him to Rome, Venice and the Near East. In 993 Pope John XV juridically confirmed the congregation in his favour: 'We deliver and confirm to your Reverence jurisdiction over five abbeys', that is, Lézat, Mas-Garnier, St Hilaire, Alet and Cuixà, over all of which Garí ruled as abbot general.[2] The bull proves that this congregation was entirely detached from Cluny; it retained however the Cluniac spirit and methods.

Apart from these abbeys which were closely linked with Garí other new foundations are known to us which, while receiving their initial impetus from him, remained juridically independent. In 978, for example, a caravan of Venetians with St Romuald among their number arrived as escort to the Doge Peter Orseolo, who, inspired by Garí, was to become a monk at Cuixà.[3] Only four years later Orseolo's intimate friend, John

[1] JL 3651; *Marca Hispanica*, ed. Baluze, app. 87, cols 864–5.

[2] JL 3850; *GC* XIII, instr. 149; *Marca Hisp.* app. 157, cols 966–8 (attributed to Pope John XIX, 1008!).

[3] R. d'Abadal, 'Com neix i com creix un gran monestir pirinenc abans de l'any mil: Eixalada-Cuixà', in *Analecta Montserratensia*, 8 (1954–5) 218–32.

Morosino, returned to his native land to found the abbey of
San Giorgio on an island in Venice in 982.[1] There can be little
doubt that he breathed into San Giorgio the new monastic
spirit that he had himself received from his spiritual father,
Abbot Garí of Cuixà.

Yet another recruit joined the congregation, the Piedmontese
abbey of San Michele della Chiusa, in the Susa valley near
Turin. Its founder was a nobleman from Auvergne, Hugh
de Montboissier, and he entrusted its government to Abbot
Advert, who had been Garí's coadjutor at Lézat. Advert
arrived at San Michele some time between 983 and 987,
accompanied by a few monks.[2]

Garí was undoubtedly the moving spirit of the congregation,
its true centre and heart. For lack of a written constitution to
ensure that it should continue to function, however, it was
destined to disappear after his death in about 998. From this
time onwards the most powerful abbeys in the group went their
own way independently, leaving Cuixà alone with only a few
daughter houses, and perhaps St Hilaire. Around the year 1000
Count Bernard Tallaferro entrusted his foundation of Sant Pau
de Monisaten (or de Fenollet) to Abbot Guifred of Cuixà,
Garí's successor:

> that you may set this foundation on a firm footing and
> introduce there those monastic usages in which your pre-
> decessor Garí of venerable memory nurtured you according
> to the Rule of our beloved father Benedict, for we know that
> you have yourself held, like him, to the straight path, turning
> aside neither to right nor to left, even to this day.[3]

This text is enough to show that Garí's idea of making Cuixà
the nucleus of a congregation was still in the air in spite of
everything. The document is signed by Count Oliba de Berga,
Tallaferro's brother, who became a monk at Ripoll in 1002 and

[1] G. Damerini, *L'Isola e il cenobio di San Giorgio Maggiore* (Venice, 1956)
pp. 9, 11 and 239–40; see the review of this book in *Studia Monastica*, 2 (1960)
296.

[2] G. Schwartz and E. Abegg, 'Das Kloster San Michele della Chiusa und
seine Geschichtsschreibung', in *Neues Archiv*, 45 (1923–4) 235–55.

[3] d'Abadal, 'Com neix', app. doc. 119, pp. 336 f.; *Marca Hisp.* app. 147,
cols 954 f.

abbot of Ripoll and Cuixà in 1008; as such he was to gather up and make his own Garí's spiritual legacy.

OLIBA'S CONGREGATION, CENTRED IN RIPOLL AND CUIXÀ

Count Oliba, after six years of life in seclusion as a monk, was elected abbot of Ripoll in 1008, and in the same year abbot of Cuixà also. The votes of both communities were unanimous and they were fortunate in their choice: Oliba was to be the providential figure in the religious affairs of Catalonia in this first half of the eleventh century.[1] Some concrete details may perhaps be of use to us in understanding the part Oliba played as a spiritual leader, exercising certain powers discernible by the historian.

If the counts of Barcelona and other Catalan counts had retained anything from their direct contacts with the three emperors Otto on visits to Rome it was a pronounced taste for interfering in ecclesiastical affairs. In certain solemn documents Count Raymond Borrell had from the beginning of the century asserted that his rights of supervision and intervention in the bishoprics of his territory had been committed to him by God:

Raymond, by the grace of God count and marquis, and by God's gift supervisor of the episcopal sees belonging to our dominion . . .

and he demands that the bishops should be present at the county judicial assizes, even to the point of requiring them to sign the documents:

I have readily given my consent to this contract, and order that it shall be confirmed and signed by the aforesaid bishops.

The bishops, particularly those of Barcelona and Girona, felt at home in the count's household: Peter Roger was the brother of Countess Ermessenda, and had not given up his co-regency over the counties of Carcassonne and Foix. They were quite

---

[1] The two fundamental works on Oliba remain those of A. Albareda, *L'abat Oliva, fundador de Montserrat* (Montserrat, 1931) and R. d'Abadal, *L'abat Oliba, bisbe de Vic, i la seva època* (Barcelona, 1962).

willing to accept the count's authority. Deusdedit of Barcelona on this same occasion in 1014 spoke in these terms:

> I, Bishop Deusdedit, together with the canons my brethren ... with the consent of our lord Count Raymond who is a worshipper of God and has care of the bishops of the universal Church who belong to his dominion, and after consultation also with the bishops of neighbouring provinces. . . .[1]

Although Oliba of Elna, a former canon of Barcelona, may often have been among these bishops,[2] that other Oliba who had now been bishop of Vic since 1017 always refused to attend. Only one journey made by him to Barcelona is known for certain, and that was towards the end of his life, in 1044.

Bernard Talleferro, count of Besalú, had no intention of being left behind, and since the dioceses of Vic, Girona and Urgel lay within his county he dreamed of having a bishopric at his disposal. He secured it from Pope Benedict VIII in 1017. Countess Ermessenda, with her grandson Raymond-Berengar I, concluded a treaty in 1056 which guaranteed the cession of all the abbeys in the county and diocese of Girona. The grave consequences that these lay usurpations in the ruling of ecclesiastical institutions were bound to have are plain to see.

Such were the main factors in the situation, but others may be added as having considerable relevance to a clear understanding of subsequent events. The custom had been introduced in Catalonia, more markedly there perhaps than elsewhere, of appointing as bishops men who continued in their former office as abbots of their monasteries. Thus Odo, bishop of Girona, was abbot of Sant Cugat (d. 1010); Arnulph of Vic was abbot of Sant Feliu of Girona (d. 1010); Berengar III of Elna was abbot of Arles-sur-Tech (d. after 1036); Guifred of Carcassonne retained the abbey of Camprodon (d. after 1050). In continuing to hold office as abbot of both Ripoll and Cuixà until his death, therefore, Oliba of Vic was merely following the custom of his country and more especially the example of his friend Gauzlin

---

[1] *Marca Hisp.* app. 172, col. 996; J. Mas, *Rúbrica dels Libri Antiquitatum de la catedral de Barcelona*, 1, no. 322, pp. 142 f.

[2] A. Mundó, 'Entorn de les famílies dels bisbes Oliba de Vic i Oliba d'Elna', in *Boletin de la Real Academia de Buenas Letras de Barcelona*, 28 (1959–1960) 172.

of Bourges, abbot of Fleury. One must admit that the system sometimes bore unquestionably healthy fruit. Oliba did not disappoint his subjects.

It is time now to examine the way in which he became Garí's heir as head of a monastic congregation. Through an erroneous interpretation of a passage in the history of the counts of Barcelona, Mabillon said of him that he ruled thirty-eight monasteries.[1] The phrase did not in fact mean that he ruled thirty-eight monasteries, but that he was abbot of Ripoll and Cuixà for thirty-eight years. It is not to be assumed, however, that Oliba's authority was restricted to these two monasteries; Cardinal Albareda has shown that Oliba enjoyed a direct influence over a good many other communities.[2] It has even been suggested that they formed a group analogous to a monastic congregation of the early Cluniac type. If I presume to refer to it as such I do so on the strength of evidence provided by the best modern authority on Oliba. Here is a brief summary of the facts.

Let us begin by listing the monasteries linked to Cuixà at the time of Oliba's election in 1008. Over and above Cuixà and Ripoll – which were to be twin brothers from now on, with the latter sometimes slightly in the lead – Oliba became abbot general over Sant Pau de Fenollet and over Ste Marie d'Arles-sur-Tech, although the rights of their residing abbots were kept intact. It was in fact Oliba who obtained bulls in their favour from the chancellery of Sergius IV in 1011, on the same date as those destined for Ripoll and Cuixà.[3] As for St Hilaire at Carcassonne, there can be little doubt about the direct influence that Oliba must have continued to exercise there as abbot of Cuixà, in view of his close ties with the co-regent Count Peter, bishop of Girona, and with the latter's sister, the Countess Ermessenda of Barcelona.

A year after Oliba's abbatial election the first foundations in which he was concerned took place. In 1009 his brother, Count Guifred of Cerdanya had his new monastery of Canigó

---

[1] *AA SS OSB* vii 850, n. 9: 'rexit cenobia XXXVIII': the misinterpretation is of a passage in the *Gesta comitum Barchinonensium*.

[2] Albareda, op. cit. pp. 83–7.

[3] JL 3975 (for Fenollet); JL 3977 (Arles); JL 3974 (Ripoll); JL 3973 (Cuixà).

consecrated, and Oliba was the only abbot to sign the deeds. In 1011 moreover he obtained a papal privilege for this house also, and no abbot is mentioned.[1] It was not until 1014 that the monk Sclua was elected, probably as a secondary abbot under the direction of Oliba.[2] However this may be, Oliba remained the community's spiritual father, so much so that after his death the monks of Canigó referred to him as their 'dearest father',[3] while the community of Cuixà, writing to Canigó, expressed themselves thus:

> Seeing that we were formerly governed by the authority of those two most noble brothers, princes of our country, our lord Oliba, bishop and abbot of blessed memory and *father in God to all of us in common*, and his brother the lord Guifred, of one mind with him and pre-eminent in worldly honour, you are right to entreat us to do reverence to their memory together with you. . . .[4]

Leaving Canigó aside for the moment, let us glance at the new monastic foundations promoted by Oliba. The first was Sant Pere de la Portella, founded by the tenants of the castle of that name who had been Oliba's vassals in the days of his regency of the county of Berga. In 1018 the abbot of Ripoll, newly appointed as bishop of Vic, despatched the first two monks there, himself continuing as superior for a time.[5]

The next foundation was that of Santa Maria de Montserrat in 1022 (or 1023). The story of this would make for lengthy telling, but we may pick out the main points.[6] In 1011 a monk John, who had been Oliba's companion and had done his studies at Ripoll, was sent, presumably by Oliba, to Santa

---

[1] JL 3976. On the authenticity of the original on papyrus, preserved at Perpignan, see A. Mundó, 'Notes entorn de les butlles papals catalanes més antigues', in *Homenaje a Johannes Vincke*, i (Madrid, 1962–3) pp. 115f., n. 10.

[2] J. Puiggarí, *Catalogue biographiques des évêques d'Elne* (Perpignan, 1842) p. 18, and *Notice sur l'ancienne abbaye de S. Martin de Canigou* (Perpignan, 1848) 'Inventaire d'archives de 1586'.

[3] Reply to the obituary letter of Guifred of Cerdanya (d. 1049), ed. L. Delisle, *Les rouleaux des morts* (Paris, 1866) n. 19, p. 52.

[4] Ibid. n. 104, p. 93.

[5] J. L. Moncada, *Episcopologio de Vich*, ed. J. Collell (Vic, 1891) pp. 235–6.

[6] The story has been told with admirable erudition by Albareda, op. cit. pp. 175–200, and *Festes jubilars. Fonament històric* (Montserrat, 1931).

Cecília de Montserrat, an already ancient monastery on the same mountain. But in 1018 John became aware of the attractions of St Benoît at Fleury, and departed thither to end his days in 1022, after resigning his abbacy into the hands of his spiritual father, Oliba of Ripoll (this last point is a personal deduction). The latter, all in good faith, lost no time in seeking juridical backing for this act of cession, and presented a request in due legal form before the tribunal of Berengar-Raymond I, count of Barcelona.[1] The annexation did not succeed, however. In 1026 Santa Cecília regained its independence through the efforts of its energetic abbot Bonfill Halim, a man probably of Arab or Jewish extraction. Oliba consented and signed to that effect.[2] Thereafter the destiny of Santa Cecília de Montserrat diverged from that of its neighbour Santa Maria, which Oliba turned into a monastery in about 1023. This little priory of Montserrat, which Oliba retained for his lifetime, was to become in the centuries that followed the sole heir to all the monasteries of Catalonia.

Finally in 1045, in his capacity as abbot of Cuixà, Oliba founded on this monastery's estates the abbey of Sant Miquel de Fluvià, in the Empordà.[3]

The cases where abbots were chosen from among the disciples of Oliba are significant, for they wove round him a network of enduring spiritual bonds. Thus for example the abbot of Tabèrnoles in the county of Urgel, who acted as intermediary between the bishop of Vic and King Sancho of Navarre, was called by Oliba 'the lord abbot Pontius, our brother and son' because he was a former monk of Ripoll.[4] There can be little doubt that he often went to seek advice from Oliba for the welfare of his community.

Another example, that of Sant Feliu de Guíxols, speaks eloquently of the bonds that united nearly all the Catalan monks to Oliba at this time. The monks of Sant Feliu, on the seaboard of Girona, approached Countess Ermessenda in 1043 to request a pastor for their community. Ermessenda got in

[1] *Marca Hisp.* app. 195, cols 1035–7.
[2] Barcelona, A.C.A., perg., Santa Cecília de Montserrat, original and interpolated copy.
[3] *Marca Hisp.* app. 228, cols 1087–8.
[4] *Ep.* 1, to Sancho of Navarre, 1023: *PL* 142, 600.

touch with Oliba, who was passing through Girona and who 'with devoted pastoral care regulated the observances of monks', begging him to send the monk Arnau, his inseparable companion and secretary. Arnau very humbly refused the offer, and Oliba would not force him. Disappointed, Ermessenda reproached the bishop, reminding him that 'I have given you a thousand men for the service of God; do not stand in the way of one being granted to me.' Oliba yielded, but Arnau, the abbot elect, was willing to accept only on condition that he should not be obliged to take the title of abbot; he in fact assumed it only after Oliba's death.[1] The episode indicates that Guíxols had joined Oliba's congregation, since there too the system prevailed whereby the local abbot was the delegate of his superior.

Since I have embarked on a hunt for monasteries which can be said to have belonged in some way to Oliba's congregation, perhaps I may be allowed to turn to good account the letters of condolence sent to Cuixà on the occasion of Oliba's death in 1046. I think that the monasteries which refer to him as 'father' do not merely out of sympathetic courtesy towards the orphaned monks to whom they are writing, but because they recognise him as the spiritual father who united them all in the same upsurge of renewed monasticism. Thus the monks of Sant Pere de Rodes wrote, 'We and you regarded him as our common father'; those of Sant Pere de Besalú spoke of 'our father Oliba, bishop and abbot'; at Serrateix they eulogised 'our devoted superior'; while others again called him 'gentlest father' (Banyoles) or 'holy father' (Casserres and Camprodon).[2]

There is moreover one proof which in my judgement is decisive for the existence of such a Catalan monastic confederation under Oliba's direction. This is a hitherto unpublished document in solemn form emanating from Count Guifred of Cerdanya, given on 12 November 1025 in favour of the monastery of Canigó which he had founded earlier. The document was drawn up by his brother Oliba, bishop and abbot. In God's name Guifred there lays it down that all his descendants

---

[1] J. Villaneuva, *Viage literario*, xv, app. 1, pp. 209–13.

[2] Details are given in the edition by E. Junyent, 'Le rouleau funéraire d'Oliba, abbé de N. D. de Ripoll et de S. Michel de Cuixà, évêque de Vich', in *Annales du Midi*, 63 (1951) 249–62.

shall favour the aforesaid monastery of blessed Martin with every privilege and the most generous freedom. They shall not permit it to be liable to the jurisdiction of any see or any other monastery or church, nor shall they themselves so subject it, except in so far as the custom of honourable communities in the neighbourhood shall demand.

The sole restriction placed on the total exemption granted was the established custom of neighbouring monasteries, and hence, we may infer, that of the nearest of them all, Cuixà. It was presumably Oliba who inserted this restriction in view of the superior right of inspection willingly accorded to him.[1]

If we keep in mind Oliba's exceptional stature, both human and spiritual; if we take into account what had been happening in Burgundy since the tenth century round Cluny and its great abbots, whom Oliba had no reason to envy; if we remember that he was the friend of all the counts in Catalonia and of several in the French Midi, as also of the king of Navarre; if we give due weight to the fact that this abbot of Ripoll and Cuixà had despatched monks and abbots to Canigó, La Portella, Tabèrnoles, Santa Cecília de Montserrat and Guíxols, and that he had founded Santa Maria de Montserrat and Fluvià, I think we are justified from the historical point of view in attributing to him the organisation and direction of a congregational movement that united our monasteries on both sides of the Pyrenees during the first half of the eleventh century.

This moreover is the assertion of an anonymous monk of Cuixà a century after his death, the author of the Life of Sir Peter Orseolo:

[Oliba] was the distinguished father of many abbeys, but especially of Santa Maria and Sant Miquel.[2]

The statement pinpoints exactly the character of this type of primitive congregation in which a distinction was drawn between those abbeys subject to the direct control of their superior – those which were materially his property, one might say – and

[1] The text ends with 'Signum Olibe pontificis ac notarii'; it will be published in the *Diplomatari d'Oliba* prepared by E. Junyent; one copy exists in Paris, Bibl. Nat., Baluze, 109, fols 48–48v.

[2] *AA SS OSB* vii 860, n. 21.

those which were bound to him by relationships of spiritual dependence only, having received from him their abbot or some of their monks, or having been influenced by counsels or friendly visits which could not but leave them with a feeling of reverence for this wonderful father of monks.

In Oliba's official documents there is never a word to remind us of Cluny, and yet his eyes were fixed on that beacon of western monasticism. At the end of his life he was inspired by the God-fearing ordinances of his contemporary, Odilo of Cluny (d. 1048). In a letter addressed to his successors at Ripoll, Oliba enjoined them to make an annual commemoration of all departed brethren on the day when the gospel of the raising of Lazarus was sung; the abbot was to sing the Mass that day and to wash the feet of thirteen poor folk while serving them at table.[1] A similar decree by Odilo on this matter had preceded Oliba's by only a few years.[2]

The fact that this congregational movement never received a papal bull on the model of that which Garí obtained from John XV for Cuixà proved its undoing. On the three or four occasions when he visited Rome, Oliba does not seem to have given any thought to ensuring the permanence of his work, or at any rate there is no evidence to suggest that he did. We know that at most his monasteries shared certain usages; they cannot be spoken of as united by an actual codified observance. It should be emphasised once again that the juridical bond needed to maintain their cohesion was missing. Hence the role played by Ripoll as head of the congregation did not last after Oliba's death in 1046; only a few small priories founded during the eleventh century remained united to Ripoll, and thirty years later we find it reduced to the status of a daughter house of St Victor of Marseilles.

What had happened? At this period, unfortunately, simony was more or less widespread, and the same greed for bishoprics and abbeys had seized the civil and ecclesiastical powers in Catalonia. Count Guifred of Cerdanya bought for his three sons the archbishopric of Narbonne and the bishoprics of Girona and Urgel. Raymond Bernard Trencavel, viscount of Albi and

---

[1] Villaneuva, op. cit. VI, app. XXXII, p. 310.
[2] *PL* 142, 879: *c.* 1037–8: probably after 1030: the prescriptions are completely different from those of Oliba.

Nîmes, sold the city of Carcassonne, together with the abbeys of Lagrasse and St Hilaire, to the count of Barcelona in 1067, receiving in exchange rights over various abbeys in Languedoc. No shame was felt about openly recording this traffic in sacred goods in the relevant documents. It is not difficult to imagine what disastrous effects on monastic discipline must have followed these simoniacal contracts between all-powerful lay lords.

Throughout his reign as abbot and bishop Oliba must have had to struggle against such abuses, ever on the increase. If he had only had as his heir someone of wide-ranging intelligence and comparable spiritual calibre the failure might have been delayed, or even minimised by the new wave of reform set in motion by Gregory VII and his legates. But alas, no such providential churchman was forthcoming.

ATTEMPTS BY CLUNY AND MOISSAC, AND THE SUCCESS OF ST VICTOR OF MARSEILLES

The first attempts to remedy this state of affairs came from certain lay lords animated by the best intentions. In the course of their travels in Italy they would have stopped at the great hospitable abbeys in Piedmont, Liguria and the French Midi; they would have been struck by the number of monks there and by the severe discipline imposed by a reforming abbot. Once home again they dreamed of placing their own new family foundations in the hands of those observant monks.

The earliest donations of Catalan monasteries to abbeys abroad seem to have followed no preconceived plan; that abbey was chosen which had made the most vivid impression on the traveller or pilgrim. Already in 1026 Sant Pere de Riudebitlles had been offered by Guifred and Guisla, the rulers of Mediona, to San Martino dell'Isola Gallinaria.[1] In 1042 Gombau de Besora, the friend of Abbot Oliba, ceded his little monastery of Sant Miquel del Fai to the abbey of St Victor of Marseilles;[2]

---

[1] G. de Argaiz, *La perla de Cataluña* (Madrid, 1677) p. 56.
[2] E. Martène, *Veterum scriptorum . . . amplissima collectio* (Paris, 1724) vol. 1, cols 406 and 447–8 (of 1059).

his action was to be the first of a series. Ten years later, in 1052, Gombau's daughter Guisla and her husband the powerful Mir Geribert, prince of Olérdola, introduced monks from Marseilles to man their monastery of Sant Sebastià dels Gorcs, in Penetès; the monks were under the direction of an Abbot Miró, a somewhat mysterious figure.[1] Then again, the widowed Countess Ermessenda granted to Marseilles in 1048 the abbey of Sant Pol de Mar,[2] although in the event her grandson, Raymond-Berengar I, count of Barcelona, was to hand it over to Lérins in 1068.[3] Lastly a childless couple, Silvi Llobet and Adalets, ceded their foundation of Santa Maria de Cervià to La Chiusa in 1054.[4]

Unlike the other foreign abbeys which in this way accepted the gift of monasteries, Cluny preferred to decline an initial offer made to her by the famous Arnau Mir de Tost, leader of the Christian reconquest in the valleys of the Segre. The latter had founded and amply endowed the monastery of Sant Pere d'Ager, for which privileges of exemption had been secured from Popes Nicholas II and Alexander II. Arnau wrote to Abbot Hugh of Cluny in 1066 informing him that he was handing over the monastery, its goods, and the right to appoint its priors, and that he would deliver all the deeds and documents belonging to Ager on the occasion of an impending visit to Cluny.[5]

Why should Cluny have shown herself so unwilling, or at least so unenthusiastic, at the chance of getting a foothold in the counties of Catalonia? I can see no way of explaining it satisfactorily except by some fear on Cluny's part at the prospect of a new crusade.[6]

---

[1] Ibid. cols 431 and 447–8 (of 1059).   [2] Ibid. col. 414.

[3] H. Moris and E. Blanc, *Cartulaire de l'abbaye de Lérins* (Paris, 1883) nos 274–5, pp. 280–2.

[4] *Marca Hisp.* app. 238, col. 1099. Before the end of the century Sant Miquel de Cruïlles had also passed to La Chiusa: see F. P. Kehr, *Papsturkunden in Spanien*, I 1, p. 356; C. Baraut, article on 'Cruilles' in DHGE xiii, cols 1075 f. La Chiusa also attracted St Hilaire (Carcassonne) and Mas-Garnier: see P. Schmitz, *DHGE* xiii, col. 177.

[5] BB iv 3409; J. J. Bauer, 'Sankt Peter zu Ager . . .', in *Spanische Forschungen*, 19 (1962) 1095–8; F. P. Kehr, 'El papat i el principat de Catalunya', trans. d'Abadal, in *Estudis Universitaris Catalans*, 13 (1928) 6.

[6] [See below, pp. 191 ff. for Cluny's attitude to the Crusades. Ed.]

Some light is however thrown on the question by other factors, political and economic, which may explain the refusal. The popes were at this juncture using Cluniacs to preach in favour of a crusade in Spain, and it was thus Cluniacs who had directed to Spain many soldiers from among their own compatriots. In the reconquest of Catalonia things were different: there were no French or Aquitanian knights enrolling in the armies of the count of Barcelona, but at best his own vassals from Languedoc or Provence, and it was these together with the Normans (referred to as the English) who fought at his side to regain Tarragona.

Count Raymond-Berengar I the Old, who had married Almodis, daughter of the count of the Limousin, was considered to be one of the richest in gold among all the princes of the Christian west. His main source for this gold was the tributes paid to him by Arab kinglets in the peninsula, who were very appreciative of his favour and relied on it to maintain their precarious sovereignties. It is scarcely to be supposed that Count Raymond-Berengar I or his two sons would have considered renouncing this political *entente* with its economic advantages to respond with alacrity to the admonitions of a Gregory VII or an Urban II, who were exhorting them to undertake a crusade against the Moors. Such a course would have led far more surely to material losses for themselves than to immediate gains for the cause of religion. It is true that they were not unmindful of the obligation imposed on them both by the head of the church and by their Christian conscience, as the reconquest of Tarragona in 1089 testifies, but their first care was for their own political interests. With gold obtained from the tributes Raymond-Berengar I and Almodis bought rights of succession in several counties in the Midi, and their policy was carried to a triumphant conclusion by their grandson Raymond-Berengar III, who in 1112 received as the dowry of his wife Dolça, heiress to Provence, all sovereign rights over those vast territories. These facts are important if we are not to judge the religious evolution of Catalonia (particularly as regards its monasticism, with which we are here concerned) in the same way as that of the rest of the Iberian peninsula. The special conditions obtaining in Catalonia explain to some extent why Cluny's role was so much more modest here than it was in

Castile and León or even in the ancient kingdoms of Aragon and Navarre. One more instance of this is that the popes had no need to employ Cluniacs to introduce the Roman rite into the Catalan liturgy, since it had been in use there since the ninth century.

So Cluny had let slip her first opportunity, but another was offered in 1074. That restless knight Mir Geribert, who had already presented two monasteries to Marseilles, conceived the idea before his death in 1073 of founding a fortress-monastery on the furthest frontier of his domains on land reconquered from the Arabs. Its centre was to be the castle of Roda de Berà, on the Roman road through Tarragona. The abbot of Cluny was to send four monks there 'to take their stand in this country', instructing them to support the knights 'who will defend the country against the Saracens'.[1] The temptation for Cluny to embark on a crusading adventure was powerful, but Hugh of Cluny certainly refused the offer, for no mention of the fortress-monastery occurs in Cluniac documents. Had she adopted Mir Geribert's idea, at once inspired and original, Cluny might have stolen a march of several decades on Cîteaux in organising the military orders. However that may be, Cluny let slip another opportunity, and when in 1079 the viscounts of Cardona and Ausona offered her Sant Pere de Casserres it was too late to establish a solid Cluniac nucleus in the counties of Catalonia.[2] Casserres was an undistinguished monastery, and badly situated. The direct Cluniac possessions in Catalonia were to amount to no more than a couple of other priories – Clarà and Corbera – and a house in the city of Barcelona.[3]

It should be noted however that Cluny did maintain a more stable bond with Catalonia through the mediation of Moissac.

---

[1] BB IV 3465: it concerns the executing of the will, made on 25 January 1074, during the six months following the death of the testator.

[2] BB IV 3541.

[3] Clarà was given by Adalets Guadald in 1080 (BB IV 3554); the original documentation for Corbera has been lost but it is mentioned among the priories of Cluny in 1277: see U. Robert, in *Boletin de la Real Academia de Historia*, 20 (1892) 342. For Barcelona, see the document quoted in n. 40 above and also Montserrat archives, perg. Bages, no. 1590 of 11 August 1088.

The first of the Catalan counts to be won over to the Gregorian reform was the devout Bernard II of Besalú. When in 1077 the papal legate Amat d'Oloron was expelled by the simoniacal Archbishop Guifred from Girona, where he had convoked a council, Count Bernard hastened to welcome him, together with the bishops, into his own palace at Besalú. The pope rewarded him with a personal privilege, in consequence of which Bernard styled himself 'St Peter's special soldier'.[1] His action further earned him, however, the hostility of certain bishops, abbots and nobles of the region.

Bernard had already given his consent to the gift of the small monastery of Santa Maria de Cubières to Moissac in 1073, but in this case the initiative had been taken by the lord of Peyrepertuse in Narbonne.[2] Only in 1078, the year following that reforming council to which he had given hospitality in Besalú, did Bernard decide to affiliate to the Cluniac congregation three monasteries belonging to his jurisdiction as count, not directly but again by using Moissac as intermediary. He emphasised the fact that the donation was made 'into the hands of our most dear cousin, the lord abbot Hunald of Moissac'.[3] So it was that the destinies of Sant Pere de Camprodon, Sant Pau de Vallosa or de Fenollet, and Ste Marie d'Arles were to remain linked with Moissac for centuries. Bernard II of Besalú was in fact only distantly related to Hunald – they had merely a common great-grandfather in Duke Sancho of Gascony – but this motive may nonetheless have been sufficient to determine Bernard's choice of Moissac and his gift to Hunald.

It would be wrong, however, to assess Moissac's spiritual influence in Catalonia solely on the basis of its connection with these three monasteries. If it is to be appreciated justly, other factors must be remembered. We know, for example, that musical compositions and rhythmic poetry originating at Moissac found their way into Catalan liturgical manuscripts in considerable quantity, and the studies of Anglès and Moragas

---

[1] *Liber Feudorum Maior*, ed. F. X. Miquel Rosell, II (Barcelona, 1947) no. 501.

[2] Monsalvatje, *Noticias históricas*, VIII (Olot, 1896) app. 26, pp. 171–3.

[3] *Marca Hisp.* app. 289, col. 1168; J. Miret i Sans, *Relaciones entre los monasterios de Camprodon y Moissac* (Barcelona, 1898) pp. 14–18.

have shown their importance.[1] Consideration should also be given to the artistic influences on which my friend Ainaud has informed us.[2]

Whatever may have been the extent of Cluny's and especially of Moissac's penetration into Catalonia, we cannot estimate its precise importance unless we see it in the context of the congregational movements that were jostling one another in the country. The two leading monasteries of the Cluniac congregation were too far away to make themselves felt. These facts are undeniable.

For all his deeply religious sentiments and devotion to the cause of reform, Bernard II of Besalú did not lose his political sagacity. He had no mind to let all the monasteries in his domains fall into the hands of a single great abbey abroad. He had begun by giving to Marseilles in 1070 the most important of all the Catalan monasteries, Ripoll, together with its dependent priories including Montserrat.[3] In the same year he had handed over Sant Martí de Lez to St Pons de Thomières.[4] In the following year, 1071, he affiliated Sant Pere de Besalú to St Victor,[5] and it was again to Marseilles that he made over the very ancient abbey of Sant Esteve de Banyoles,[6] certainly before 1081, and in 1083 that of Sant Joan de les Abadesses. This last had been originally a house of nuns, but in 1099 it was taken

---

[1] H. Anglès, La música a Catalunya fins al segle XIII (Barcelona, 1935): see the index, p. 289; B. Moragas, 'Contenido y procedencia del himnario de Huesca', in Liturgica, 1: Cardinali I. A. Schuster in memoriam ('Scripta et documenta', 7, Montserrat, 1956) pp. 277–93. Other literary contacts are mentioned in J. Ainaud, 'Supervivencias del Pasionario hispánico en Cataluña', in Analecta Sacra Tarraconensia, 28 (1955–6) pp. 15f., n. 8.

[2] J. Ainaud de Lasarte, 'Moissac et les monastères catalans de la fin du Xe au début du XIIe siècles', in Annales du Midi, 75 (1963) 545 ff.

[3] Guérard, Cartulaire de l'Abbaye de Saint-Victor de Marseille (Paris, 1857) II, nos. 817 and 819.

[4] Monsalvatje, op. cit. VIII, app. 25, pp. 168–70.

[5] Guérard, op. cit. II, no. 820.

[6] According to G. Constans it could have been given from 1077 onwards: see 'Monacologi de Banyoles', in Anal. Mont. 8 (1954–5) 422; reformed by the legate Amat d'Oloron and his counsellor Frotard de Thomières in 1078 (Marca Hisp. app. 281, cols 1168–70); the donation is dated 1080 (Guérard, op. cit. II, no. 821); Banyoles is mentioned in the bull of Gregory VII of 1081 in favour of Marseilles (ibid. no. 841).

over by canons.[1] As regards the canons, he subjected the collegial church of Santa Maria de Besalú to St Ruf d'Avignon in 1084.[2]

But in his desire to reform the monasteries Bernard of Besalú had overstepped the bounds of all reasonable expectation. The dispersal of powers on the one hand and the mutual jealousy of the various new proprietors on the other could not but impede the progress of the reform sooner or later.

The preponderance that the congregation of St Victor of Marseilles was to enjoy in Catalonia is already clear, and it was to grow continually until the end of the century. A complete list of Catalan monasteries owned by Marseilles at this period would total more than fifteen, and among them were the abbeys of Canigó, Cuixà and Gerri besides those already mentioned.[3] The reasons for the pre-eminence of Marseilles among those monasteries on the French side of the Pyrenees which owned daughter houses in Catalonia are varied and strangely paradoxical. The earliest in date and the most obvious was undoubtedly the favour accorded by Popes Gregory VII and Urban II to Bernard de Rodez, abbot of Marseilles (d. 1079), and to his brother and successor Richard, who became cardinal legate and then archbishop of Narbonne. But effective as desire for reform on the part of the popes may have been in stimulating lay authorities to make such donations, the holders of ecclesiastical power in the country did not look kindly on this habit of withdrawing the great monastic estates from their jurisdiction. Moreover the subjection of local abbeys to foreign rule entailed for many families of the aristocracy the loss of the highly productive benefices that these abbeys represented. Hence a new tension was set up involving the lay authorities also, which sometimes got the better of the reform.

We have seen that the counts of Barcelona had extended their sovereignty over most of the counties in Languedoc and Provence. Lagrasse, Thomières and St Victor of Marseilles had made their way, one by one, into the political field in Barcelona. In order to handle the lesser and greater lords of these terri-

[1] Villaneuva, op. cit. VIII 77–83 and apps XIV–XVII, pp. 241–7.
[2] *Marca Hisp.* app. 296, col. 1175.
[3] For Cuixà see Guérard, op. cit. II, no. 826, of 1091; donation of Gerri in 1096: ibid. no. 824.

tories who attempted from time to time to withdraw from his control, the count of Barcelona was often obliged to rely on the loyalty of the bishops and abbots, and had to grant them wealth and properties to keep them on his side. Yet at the same time such liberality simply increased the desire of these abbots to gain possession of new monasteries and unite them to their own congregation on pretext of reforming them. Confidential friend of Gregory VII though he had been, Cardinal Richard, abbot of St Victor, was a greedy man whose rapacity knew almost no limit. Pope Victor III, Gregory's successor, was forced to excommunicate him and deprive him of his legatine dignity in 1087. Nevertheless Urban II restored him to his place of trust and confirmed him in possession of all monasteries acquired since the reign of his brother, Abbot Bernard.[1]

It is my belief that the full import of the policy of the counts of Barcelona in religious matters during the second half of the eleventh and the first half of the twelfth century has not yet been grasped. It must have been extremely difficult for them to hold the balance in this confrontation of opposing forces which so often clashed with their personal interests, the political interests of their country, and religious sentiment.

THE EFFORTS OF THOMIÈRES AND OF SANT CUGAT DEL VALLÉS

The employment of very subtle family policies, adapted to the needs of each concrete case, seems to me indisputable. The various attempts to implant monastic reform in Catalan soil by means of regrouping monasteries reveal how the great counts of Barcelona made the best of the situation.

First, Raymond-Berengar I. He had a brother named Sancho Berengar who had renounced the world and become a monk at St Pons de Thomières, but who still held extensive landed property very near to Sant Benet de Bages. Suddenly in 1075 there appeared in this rich monastery near Manresa both Abbot Frotard of St Pons, claiming the title of abbot of Bages

---

[1] For the excommunication of Victor III, see JL 5346; for Urban II's rehabilitation in 1089, see JL 5392.

also, and Sancho Berengar as its prior.[1] By this manoeuvre it was possible to further the reform preached by the pope and at the same time prevent the revenues of the abbey being drained away from the country.

On the death of old Count Raymond his two sons, Raymond-Berengar II and Berengar-Raymond II, ruled together until the latter killed the former in 1082. The murderer, not being convicted at once, was still able to swear an oath of allegiance to the holy see in 1090. Shortly beforehand he had offered to Abbot Frotard of Thomières the great abbey of Sant Cugat del Vallès, close to Barcelona. According to the opinion of Dalmace, archbishop of Narbonne and former abbot of Lagrasse, it was Prior Sancho Berengar, 'the cause of all the discord and dissension', who induced the pope to authorise the incorporation of Sant Cugat and of Sant Pere de Rodes, another great Catalan monastery, into Thomières.[2]

There was a sharp reaction. The bishop of Barcelona and the new Count Raymond-Berengar III allied themselves with the archbishop of Narbonne to defend the liberty of Sant Cugat and of its monks, expelled by Frotard. Raymond in public session declared the acts of his predecessor, the fratricidal count, to be null and void. Pope Urban II, approving the decree, severely admonished the abbot of Thomières, rebuking him for having taken advantage of his situation to transgress the canons and the express commands of the reforming popes.[3] Paschal II further obliged him to restore the documents and title deeds removed from the archives of Sant Cugat.[4] Welcoming Urban II in his abbey in 1096 had profited Frotard nothing. Sant Cugat's subjection to Thomières did not last beyond 1098.

Pending Rome's settlement of the juridical question the count of Barcelona obtained for a near relative of his, perhaps a

[1] Villaneuva, op. cit. vii, p. 217; there are also many documents in the archives of Montserrat for Bages during these years.

[2] Kehr, op. cit. i₂, nos 15–16, pp. 274–7.

[3] Ibid. no. 17, p. 278. Pope Urban II reprimanded Frotard in 1098: 'cum eiusdem cenobii investituram de manu laici et fratricide contra canonum decreta et contra sanctissimi predecessoris nostri Gregorii prohibitiones antea recepisses'. See ibid. nos 18–21 and 24–8, between 1089 and 1093, for the documents referring to the whole affair.

[4] Letter of 1099? Ibid. no. 32, pp. 298 f.; Cartulario de Sant Cugat, ed. J. Rius i Serra, ii (Barcelona, 1946) no. 779.

E

cousin, the monk Berengar, the position of abbot of Sant Cugat, and in 1099 endowed him with the bishopric of Barcelona, which Berengar subsequently ruled without renouncing his abbacy.[1] Having now secured this key post for his kinsman, Raymond-Berengar III believed the time to be ripe for an attempt to form a monastic congregation round Sant Cugat. Accordingly the monasteries of Santa Cecília of Montserrat[2] and Sant Llorenç del Munt with La Llacuna and Sant Salvador de Breda were handed back or confirmed to Sant Cugat in 1097, 1098 and 1099, as also were other churches subsequently transformed into priories dependent on del Vallès; these included Sant Pau del Camp near the walls of Barcelona, Santa Maria del Coll or Fontrúbia and Sant Pere de Clarà.[3] The count added to their number all the churches that were to be reconquered in the diocese of Tortosa. In spite of its rather modest size and the losses it was to suffer at the beginning of the following century, the little congregation of Sant Cugat was able to survive throughout the twelfth century, whereas Thomières by the end of the same period had lost all her daughter houses in Catalonia.

A BLUNDERING ATTEMPT BY LAGRASSE

Bitter conflicts were however to result from the domination by Marseilles and from the obstinacy of Richard and his successors in maintaining abbots who were foreigners to the country in

[1] J. de Peray, San Cugat del Vallés (Barcelona, 1931) pp. 115–16. The previous bishop, Folc, of the viscountal dynasty of Cardona had given to Ste Foy de Conques in 1099 the priory of Tagamanent in Montseny; see the document in G. Desjardins, Cartulaire de l'abbaye de Conques (Paris, 1879) pp. cxvii and 337 f., no. 467. Since 1065 Conques had owned estates in the county of Manresa: 'in comitatu Minorise, in campo Bagies, in loco vocitato ad ipso collo de Excollatis', and not on the island of Minorca as Desjardins says, ibid. pp. cxix and 288, n. 389.

[2] Given from before 1058, it seems: see Cartulario de Sant Cugat, II, no. 615; confirmed in 1097: ibid. no. 767. It is also mentioned in the bull of Urban II in 1098: JL 5715; Cartulario, II, no. 774; Marca Hisp. app. 317, cols 1203–5; see also Cartulari, II, no. 797.

[3] All these monasteries are mentioned in the bull of 1098: in addition, for Fontrúbia, see Cart. II, nos 771–3, and for Sant Llorenç, Cart. II, nos 169 and 777.

monasteries attached to the congregation. Though Ripoll did not succeed in detaching itself from St Victor for good until after a whole century of dependence, Lagrasse obtained its coveted liberty more quickly. This latter abbey, closely linked from its origins with the house of the counts of Carcassonne-Barcelona, had been incorporated, possibly about 1070,[1] into the possessions of St Victor by Ramond Berengar I, and the donation had been confirmed by Gregory VII in 1081.[2] The struggle for freedom soon began and the counts of Barcelona found themselves in a delicate situation, not knowing which of the two monasteries it would be more advisable to help in the dispute. Once more it was the policy of the family that induced them to favour a solution more advantageous to the private interests of their house. A new congregation to be centred in Lagrasse was set up in opposition to faraway Marseilles. From 1107 onwards other monasteries were subjected to Lagrasse: Sant Sepulcre de Palera, Sant Andreu de Sureda (1109)[3] and Canigó (1114).[4] In this same year, 1114, Lagrasse finally broke away from St Victor.[5] There can be no doubt that the count of Barcelona had a hand in this, since in the following year, 1115, he placed his brother Berengar, hitherto a monk of Thomières, over the monastery in Carcassonne. During the three ensuing years Raymond-Berengar III gave to Lagrasse the abbeys of Sant Pere de Galligans at Girona (1117) and of Sant Feliu de Guíxols (1118).[6] Unfortunately the methods employed to reduce these abbeys to subjection often relied on armed force,

[1] One can deduce the date from what Count Bernard de Besalú said in the donation of Ripoll: Guérard, op. cit. II, no. 817, p. 167; *GC* VI, col. 941 suggests perhaps around 1080 under Gregory VII.

[2] JL 5211, of 18 April: see Guérard, op. cit. II, no. 842, though it was retracted the same year, 1081: see JL 5223 and *Bibl. de l'École des Chartes*, 35 (1874) 433.

[3] Monsalvatje, *op. cit.* VIII, app. IV, pp. 120–1; *Marca Hisp.* app. 341, col. 1234. For Palera, see the act of dedication of 1085, Monsalvatje, op. cit. IV, app. VI, pp. 185–7. Santa Maria de Ridaura also belonged to the domaine of Lagrasse: ibid. pp. 28–9 and app. IV, pp. 180 f.

[4] For Canigó, see ibid. IX, p. 74, but the reference to Martène, *Thesaurus novus anecdotorum*, IV, col. 131 is not correct: see the following note.

[5] *GC* VI, col. 942; *GC* I, 'Instrumenta', pp. 115–16.

[6] *Marca Hisp.* app. 359, cols 1248–9: 'de congregatione Scae. Mariae Crassae'.

and this fact destroyed all hope of a genuine congregational movement. Guíxols, which had suffered a violent invasion by reforming monks from Lagrasse under the leadership of Abbot Berengar, a man 'equipped with worldly power and enticed by abominable greed', had to be abandoned in the course of the same year 1118 after a decision by the bishop of Girona in favour of the monastery.[1]

Thus ended the last of these attempts in Catalonia to form a monastic congregation on the model of the old centralising types. Not until the early thirteenth century would there appear a modern congregation of a federalist type more suitable to the Catalan temperament. At the time of the Fourth Lateran Council under Pope Innocent III in about 1215 the monastic congregation of Tarragona came into being. For more than six hundred years it was to unite all the Catalan monasteries that had managed to recover their liberty during the twelfth century.[2]

When we consider those poor monasteries subjected to the domination of men who often cared little for reform and were more concerned to increase the revenues of the abbey that formed the nucleus of the congregation, we may well wonder whether Villanueva was not right when he said that these affiliations were the result of 'the ambition of some and the weakness of others'. Under pretext of necessary reforms humiliating and often unreasonable subjugations were demanded. The lamentable consequences of the system were out of all proportion to its undeniable benefits. But do we not belong to a world in which the best things often come to the most wretched end?

[1] Ibid. app. 362, cols 1251–2.
[2] See the important study by A. Tobella, 'Cronologia dels Capítols de la congregació Claustral Tarraconense i Cesaraugustana', part 1, in *Anal. Mont.* 10 (1964).

8 The Monastery of St Benedict, Polirone, and its Cluniac Associations[1]

HANSMARTIN SCHWARZMAIER

In a survey which he produced more than ten years ago concerning recent works on research into Cluny and Cluniac monks, Professor G. Tellenbach came to the conclusion that we were still a long way from any positive knowledge of Cluny and its influence. At the same time he suggested methods of research into areas which still remained to be explored.[2] Several of these have, in the meantime, been followed up, not least by Tellenbach himself.[3] As a result, it has been realised that a clearer understanding of the nature of Cluny is made possible by research into the history of individuals as shown in the contents of Books of Life, calendars and necrologies.[4] Fundamental to this were W. Jorden's views on the extreme importance which Cluny attached to the commemoration of the dead.[5] Necrologies

[1] [Translated from 'Das Kloster S. Benedetto di Polirone in seiner cluniacensischen Umwelt', in *Adel und Kirche*, Festschrift for Professor G. Tellenbach (to whom this article is dedicated), edited by J. Fleckenstein and K. Schmid (Herder: Freiburg/Basel/Vienna, 1968) pp. 280–93. Ed.]

[2] G. Tellenbach, 'Zum Wesen der Cluniacenser', in *Saeculum*, 9 (1958) 370, and 'Zur Erforschung Clunys und der Cluniacenser', introduction to *NF* pp. 3 ff.

[3] From a number of works the following may be quoted: H. Hoffmann, 'Von Cluny zum Investiturstreit', in *Arch. f. Kulturgesch.* 45 (1963) 165 ff.; A. Becker, *Papst Urban II*, part 1 (1964); G. Tellenbach, 'Der Sturz des Abtes Pontius von Cluny', in *QFIAB* 42–3 (1963) 13 ff.; J. Fechter, 'Cluny, Adel und Volk' (diss. Tübingen, 1966); and especially the article by J. Wollasch [translated below, pp. 143 ff.]; also his 'Die Überlieferung cluniacensischen Totengedächtnisses', in *Frühmittelalterliche Studien*, ed. K. Hauck, 1 (1967) pp. 389 ff.

[4] G. Tellenbach, 'Zur Bedeutung der Personenforschung für die Erkenntnis des früheren Mittelalters', in *Freib. Universitätsreden*, n.s. 25 (1957); and K. Schmid, 'Über das Verhältnis von Person und Gemeinschaft im früheren Mittelalter', in *Frühmittelalter. Studien*, 1 227 ff.

[5] W. Jorden, *Das cluniacensische Totengedächtniswesen* (1930).

could thus be classified as characteristic liturgical books for
Cluniac monasteries. This will necessarily lead to a certain
amount of investigation modifying the results already obtained.

The possibilities for research are naturally not as favourable
elsewhere as in the vicinity of the mother house. If we turn to
Italy, to its Cluniac priories and more especially to the
Benedictine monastery in Polirone, this research suffers from
the almost total lack of precisely that kind of information which
has become proverbial for Cluny itself. Yet it seems not
irrelevant to call to mind the traces left behind by Cluny in the
intellectual landscape, or even in the very scenery, of Italy.
A delightful example is that of the subsequently Cluniac
monastery of SS Mary and Nicolas of Piona, at the northern tip
of Lake Como.[1] Records do not prove the church's existence
until between 1236 and 1244, yet it was built nevertheless in the
first half of the twelfth century and bears such an undeniable
Franco-Burgundian stamp that we tend to place its Cluniac
history one hundred years earlier than the oldest records, on the
simple basis of this proof. Other examples of this nature could
be quoted.

The extent to which the great Cluniac Abbots Odo, Mayeul,
Odilo and Hugh tried to influence and mould monastic life in
Italy has not passed unnoticed, and the reforming effect of
Cluny, which had such decisive results in the very land where
Benedictine monasticism originated, is also known. The gift of
St Peter's, Pavia (967) to the Burgundian abbey – shortly
afterwards it took the name of Abbot Mayeul[2] – the taking over
of S. Salvatore in Pavia, the reform of the famous abbey of
S. Pietro in Ciel d'Oro by Mayeul and his reforming work in
S. Apollinare in Classe, Ravenna, created for the Cluniac
abbots positions of strength in northern Italy which were of
benefit to them and their brothers on their extensive journey-

[1] A kind suggestion from Prof. W. Goez of Würzburg; for Piona, see
Cottineau, *Répertoire topo-bibliographique*, II 2286, though no further references
are given. See also D. Sant'Ambrogio, 'Recenti contestazioni intorno a
S. Nicolò di Piona', in *Riv. Arch. lomb.* 2 (1906) 150 ff.; BB 4704 (1236–44).
E. Gufanti (see below, n. 5) p. 163 quotes an unpublished document of
4 May 1154 (Milan, Arch. St. fondo rel. Cart. 126) in which the estates
sancti Nicolai de Piona are named.

[2] C. Manaresi, 'La fondazione del monastero di S. Maiolo di Pavia', in
Spiritualità, pp. 274 ff.

ings.[1] With the acquisition, in Rome itself, of St Paul's without the Walls, St Mary's on the Aventine and S. Andreas ad Clivum Scauri, already achieved by Odo, he and his successors were assured a foothold in the city of the popes.[2] Reform in Subiaco and Farfa led to the introduction of Cluniac customaries into the most staunchly traditional Benedictine monasteries of Italy. This list need not be continued further: if it were transposed to a map, it would result in an impressive picture of the journeyings of the great abbots of Cluny, such as has been drawn for Abbot Hugh.[3] Not until his abbacy did the wave of substantial gifts from the nobility begin, which led to the founding of countless priories and thus to an organised concentration of Cluniac control. These foundations can be described as the poor relations of research, for in Italy itself they passed unnoticed for a very long time. Disregarded until then, their learned discoverer drew them, one by one, from the Cluny records and made them known in countless studies.[4] A French scholar published a first survey, but it is no longer valid.[5] On the contrary, Polirone, as the richest Cluniac monastery in Italy from the point of view of possessions and influence – it was never reduced to the status of a priory – has

---

[1] E. Sackur, *Die Cluniacenser* (1892) I 226 ff.

[2] Ibid. pp. 101 ff.; G. Antonelli, 'L'opera di Odone di Cluny in Italia', in *Benedictina*, 4 (1950) 19 ff.

[3] H. Diener, 'Das Itinerar des Abtes Hugo von Cluny', in *NF* pp. 355 ff.

[4] Numerous articles by D. Sant'Ambrogio written between 1900 and 1910 are listed in L'Huillier's article mentioned in the following note.

[5] A. L'Huillier, 'I priorati cluniacensi in Italia', in *Brixia Sacra*, 3 (1912) 14–29, 61–9, 97–104, trans. from the French by P. Guerrini. See also G. de Valous, *Le monachisme Clunisien des origines au XVe siècle*, II (1935) pp. 266 ff. The best, though not systematic, list of Cluniac priories is in P. Bognetti, *L'Abbazia benedettina di Civate* (1957) pp. 76 ff. All the researchers tend to work from the list of Cluny's houses in the bull of Urban II, 1095: JL 5551; *PL* 151, 410 ff.; *Bibl. Cl.* col. 516 and (for a list of priories) cols 1744 ff. Professor Violante of Pisa kindly made available a work quoted by P. Zerbi, 'I monasteri cittadini di Lombardia', in *Monasteri in alta Italia, Relazioni e comun. al 32 congresso stor. Subalpino in Pinerolo 1964* (Turin, 1966) p. 305: n. 88 there cites an unpublished dissertation by E. Guffanti, 'I monasteri cluniacensi nele.'attuale Lombardia' (Università Cattolica del Sacro Cuore, Milan, Feb 1965). It is particularly useful for the attached maps. See also Dom G. Charvin, *Statuts chapitres généraux et visites de l'ordre de Cluny*, I (1965) p. 376, no. 92; II p. 243, no. 180, p. 286, no. 190 etc. for a survey of the Lombard Cluniac priories in the thirteenth century.

always claimed the scholar's interest.[1] Its history, particularly
towards the end of the eleventh century, is of singular fascina-
tion when set against the great political events in which, unlike
most other monasteries, it was caught up. The results of this
research will provide the basis, in the following paper, for the
indication of certain factors which come to light when we
consider Hugh of Cluny's 'monastic policy' and start asking
questions aiming at a more intimate knowledge of Cluniac
influence in the life of the Italian monasteries.

On the fringe of the historical events linked with the name
Canossa, one event of particular significance for S. Benedetto
di Polirone is to be noted. Towards the end of January 1077,
when Pope Gregory VII was staying at the castle of Countess
Matilda, he took this monastery, which she owned and con-
trolled, under papal protection.[2] Not much later, or perhaps at
the same time, he endorsed the transfer of the monastery to
Abbot Hugh of Cluny, then at Canossa.[3] Until that moment the
destiny of S. Benedetto had been considerably influenced by
the relationship between its founders and abbots.

About 961 or 962 Count Adelbert of Canossa had acquired
the territory between the Po and the Lirone in an exchange of
land. At that time there was already mention of the Isle of
St Benedict, on which a castle was built.[4] In the following year
the bishop of Mantua relinquished the adjoining territory on
which was situated the chapel of St Benedict which gave its
name to the island.[5] The present course of the Po has altered

---

[1] For general literature on Polirone, see P. Kehr, *It. Pont.* 7, 1 (1923)
323 ff. On the relation of Cluny and Polirone, see G. Schreiber, *Kurie und
Kloster im 12. Jahr.* 2 (1910) pp. 313 ff. P. Hofmeister, 'Cluny und seine
Abteien', in *Stud. Mitt. OSB*, (75 (1964) 203 ff.) is somewhat inexact. Still
indispensable is B. Bacchini, *Dell'istoria del monastero di S. Benedetto di Polirone*
(Mantua, 1696). The documents have been published by P. Torelli, *Regesto
Mantovano*, 1 (1914) ('Reg. Chart. It.' 12); on the manuscripts, see
B. Benedini, 'I manoscritti Polironiani della Bibl. comunale di Mantova'
(1958), in *Atti e mem. d. accad. Virgiliana di Mantova*, n.s. 30; see also G. Fasoli,
'Monasteri padani', in the collection mentioned in n. 5 above: *Monasteri in
alta Italia*, pp. 189–97.

[2] For the date of Gregory's diploma, see *It. Pont.* 7, 1, 329; the main part
in Kehr, *Urk.* 5 and JL 5287 does not give *ad regendum illud idem monasterium
Cluniacensis monasterii . . . fratrem Widonem nobis donasti* as does *PL* 148, 719.

[3] Diener, loc. cit. p. 366.   [4] Torelli, op. cit. 24, p. 18.

[5] Ibid. 27, p. 20 and particularly 32, p. 23.

the insular character of the monastery, set as it was in lonely isolation, though with natural protection, in marshy country away from all main routes.[1] The completion of the monastery's church of St Benedict – certainly planned by Adelbert – was carried out by his son Count Tedald, who in 1007 testified that the basilica of SS Benedict, Mary, Michael and Peter, built by him and endowed by him with lands, was destined for the monastery.[2] In 1016 (on 26 July) there died in the vicinity of Polirone the hermit Simeon, a man of Armenian origin, who was formally canonised by Pope Benedict VII only a few years later.[3] A new basilica, built over his bones, was dedicated by Pope Alexander II. Simeon thus became, together with Benedict, patronal saint of the monastery, which in subsequent years attracted numerous pilgrims. Little more than their names is known of the abbots of the pre-Cluniac period. Until 1076 Peter was abbot; in February of that year he was mentioned for the last time on the occasion of the acceptance of a gift.[4] His successor was Wido of Cluny. In a document dated 7 April 1080 he was named once more and here we also learn something of his origins.[5] He was a nephew of Archbishop Haderich of Orleans (1063–7), removed from office for simony. On his advice, his relatives in the family of the lords of Pithiviers (dep. Loiret) donated extensive allodial lands, belonging to their family seat, to Cluny, who built there the priory of Gué de Pithiviers (which came later under the jurisdiction of St Martin des Champs).[6] In the donations, to which the deposed bishop as well as Wido's brothers Godfrey and Gibald contributed, Wido himself was already mentioned as abbot of Polirone. His origins

---

[1] V. Colorni, *Il territorio mantovano nel sacro Romano impero*, 1 (1959) pp. 45 ff. and maps; also K. Schrod, *Reichsstrassen und Reichsverwaltung im Kgr. Italien* (1931) pp. 56 ff.

[2] Torelli, op. cit. 44, p. 31.

[3] On Simeon, see *BHL* 7952–4 and *Vita et Miracula* in *AA SS* July VI 319 ff.; *It. Pont.* 7, 1, 329.

[4] Torelli, op. cit. 95, p. 66 and U. Nicolini, *L'Archivio del monastero di S. Andrea di Mantova* (1959) no. 10, p. 13.

[5] M. Prou, *Recueil des Chartes de Philippe Ier* (1908) no. 99, p. 255; BB IV 3552.

[6] BB 3398 and 3438 [and n. 22 of the original article]. On the donation, see H. Diener, 'Das Verhältnis Clunys zu den Bischöfen', in *NF* pp. 158 ff. On the significance of Pithiviers, see also Sackur, op. cit. 1 271.

and his family's gifts throw some light on the problems which Cluny had in store for him in Polirone.

The transfer of the abbey of Polirone to Cluny was marked by a change in the domestic policy of the counts of Canossa. In February or April 1076 Countess Matilda's husband and mother, Duke Godfrey and Countess Beatrix, both died; from then on she alone disposed of the immense wealth of her house. A glance at the map shows that Polirone can be considered one of the key positions of Matilda's estates.[1] Yet it was not the only monastery to benefit from the favours of the noble family. Their burial vault was at S. Apollonius in Canossa – which also reverted to the holy see in 1077 – whilst Boniface was buried in Mantua and Beatrix in the cathedral at Pisa. Among the numerous gifts made by the Canossa family to monasteries and churches, those made in Matilda's early days to the royal monastery of Nonantola are particularly noteworthy. Polirone was then coming more and more to the fore. In the last years of her life Matilda made it her sole allodial heir in the diocese and county of Mantua. The privileges and gifts of the years 1113–5 gave Polirone exclusive control of the Po islands and of countless priories.[2] Its abbot became liege lord of the countess herself and her knights.[3] Abbot Pons of Cluny seems to have spent Christmas here in 1114 and then to have visited the countess, living in Bondeno (near Gonzaga).[4] A short time later the countess died, and, breaking with family tradition, was buried in St Benedict's, whose greatness owed all to her. Formerly it had also had to surmount all the struggles and difficulties to which Matilda herself had been prey.

Wido's successor, Abbot William, who apparently came to office in 1083, was, without doubt, sent from Cluny itself to the Italian abbey in the same way as his predecessor and his successor. Whilst a gift made to Polirone in 1090 was accepted by two monks, Ubald and Peter, we hear two years later that Abbot William was staying with the countess in the mountains,

---

[1] A. Overmann, *Gräfin Mathilde von Tuscien* (1895) *passim*; also maps.

[2] Torelli, op. cit. 153–66, pp. 111–20; Fasoli, loc. cit. (see above, p. 123 n. 1) p. 193.

[3] Overmann, *Reg.* 114.

[4] Donizo, *Vita Mathildis*, ed. Simeoni, *Rer. ital. Script.* v 2, 103 and Torelli, op. cit. 167, p. 121.

having been driven out of his monastery by the Emperor Henry IV.[1] It is not necessary to follow in detail the latter's position during the campaigns of these years. In 1090 Matilda, together with Duke Welf, was imprisoned in Mantua. In the summer of that year she retired to her castles in the mountains and abandoned to its fate the town which opened its gates to the king the very next year. The records for 1092 refer to the distressed condition of the abbey, whose estates had been used and impoverished by the troops of both sides. The gift of 1090 was made expressly for the support of the brethren in the absence of the abbot, who had fled. Very soon, however, there could no longer be any question of distress in Polirone. Abbot William probably died in 1099. Under his successor Alberic a cultural and spiritual renaissance started in the abbey. Let us examine this more closely.

Under Abbot Alberic a remarkable manuscript was begun. It is known to scholars as the Gospels of Matilda, although it is doubtful whether the codex is right in bearing this name.[2] G. Waitz presumed that the countess had the Gospels prepared in order to present them to Polirone. This theory was supported by the magnificence of the volume, the high quality of the miniatures and initials – even if not completely finished – and the elegance of the writing. Scholars have not hesitated to compare this manuscript with the best examples of the medieval miniaturist's art, and they have sought, and believed to find, a particular connection with the famous Donizo manuscript of the Life of Matilda,[3] which appeared only a little later, some

[1] Torelli, op. cit. 118, pp. 84 f.; for the text, see my article 'Der *Liber Vitae* von Subiaco', in *QFIAB* 48 (1968) 127 and n. 139.

[2] On the manuscript, which is in the Pierpont Morgan Library, New York, see G. F. Warner, *Gospels of Mathilda, countess of Tuscany* (The Roxburghe Club, New York, 1917: facsimile ed.) and also the incomplete edition by A. Mercati, 'L'Evangeliario donato dalla contessa Matilda al Polirone', in *Atti e Mem. Dep. Mod.* ser. 7, vol. 4 (1927), reprinted in *Saggi di storia e letteratura* (Rome, 1951) pp. 213–27. See comments on the manuscript by G. Waitz, *Neues Archiv*, 4 (1879) 591 and Tiraboschi, *Memorie storiche Modenensi*, 2 (Modena, 1793) 64, no. 270 (part edition).

[3] Warner, op. cit. p. 18, where similar material is compared; the attribution to Farfa is now hardly tenable: see Schwarzmaier, loc. cit. pp. 91 f. On Vat. lat. 4922, see pp. vi ff. of H. Simeonis's edition of Donizo; the miniatures are reproduced in *MGH SS* 12.

fifteen years after the Gospels.[1] A closer comparison, especially
of the two types of writing, but also of the miniatures, does not
however support the view that one school produced the two
most representative codices from the sphere of Matilda's court.

At the same time G. Warner, the editor of the Gospels,
undertook the remarkable task of discovering the identity of the
scribe. A record from Abbot Alberic's time which contains
details of an anniversary gift made by the countess bears as its
conclusion on the final pages the signatures of the monks of
Polirone, all written in their own hands. Waitz thought that he
recognized among them the writing of John the Deacon, who
had written the whole codex. This rather questionable theory –
with similar reasoning one could perhaps select the priests
Bonizo or Genesius – shows nevertheless that Waitz believed
the codex to have been written in Polirone, and indeed it does
bear the unmistakable stamp of the Benedictine monastery.
A book which was either originally intended for, or commissioned by, the countess would however be expected to
contain a dedication similar to that of the Donizo manuscript,
and the final records for 1109, without a doubt written by a
contemporary hand and signed by the monks living at that
time, could hardly be of interest anywhere else but in the
house of Abbot Alberic who had them drawn up.

It is of particular importance that the Gospels should contain,
at the end, a *Liber Vitae* whose introduction alone claims our
interest. The writer, perhaps the signatory abbot himself,
quotes a biblical basis for this Book of Life (Luke 10:20; Ex.
32:31–2; Ps. 68:29). Probably, too, the relevant chapter in
St Gregory's *Moralia* to which he refers determined the form.[2]
It would seem, then, that Abbot William followed this example
and had the volume produced (*fecit scribi*) so that it could lie on
the altar and the names of the *familiares* written in it could be
quoted in the monks' prayers. The name of Pope Urban II was

[1] See Donizo, ed. Simeoni, IV 1110–15, for the origin and character of the
manuscript.

[2] Introduction to Warner, op. cit. p. 39; besides this, in the text of Gregory
the Great, *Moralia in Iob*, lib. 24: *PL* 76, 167: 'Liber vitae est ipsa visio
advenientis iudicis etc.' On memorials in general, see K. Schmid and
J. Wollasch, 'Die Gemeinschaft der Lebenden und Verstorbenen in
Zeugnissen des Mts', in *Frühmittelalter. Studien*, 1 366 ff.

to be placed at the beginning 'as he is the head of all the faithful',[1] followed by that of Abbot Hugh of Cluny and finally by that of Countess Matilda, her relatives, friends, *familiares*, and the benefactors of the monastery. The other entries then follow.

The *Liber Vitae* must on no account be considered as an appendix to the Gospels, as a filling in of blank pages with more or less indifferent names. Rather it belongs to it by its very nature, just as the hand which wrote it is identical with that of the Gospels. The reference to the commissioning of the book does not refer solely to the *Liber Vitae* but to the whole codex.[2] Abbot William appears to have commissioned it, most probably between 1092 (the year of his return to Polirone) and 1099 (the year of his death). It must have been finished soon afterwards, for pope Urban II, mentioned in the *Liber Vitae* as still alive, died in 1099. We can directly conclude that the Gospels appeared in 1099, the year of the change of abbot at Polirone.[3] After what has been said, the countess must naturally be discounted as the donor of the codex. The book appeared in Polirone and remained in use there for centuries.[4] The manuscript had a few further names added which take us on to the middle of the twelfth century. Certain restrictions which formerly prevailed in a monastery whose monks, only a short time before, had scarcely known how to keep body and soul together, had by then been lifted, for it is known that the library of the Benedictine abbey was relatively complete.[5]

---

[1] 'sicut est caput fidelium omnium'.   [2] 'fecit fieri hunc librum'.

[3] From the introduction to the *Liber Vitae* it is clear that Abbot William was dead at the time of its composition and that Pope Urban II was still alive. But Abbot William witnessed a transfer of the monastery of St Bartholomew in Lucca to Polirone on 17 June 1099 (see Guidi-Parenti, *Regesto del Capitolo di Lucca*, I (1910) ['Reg. Chart. Ital.' 6] no. 573, p. 245; *Mem. Doc. Stor. Lucca*, IV 2 app. p. 120), and Urban II died on 29 July in the same year. This narrows the time for the death of Abbot William, the choice of his successor Alberic and the composition of the preface to the *Liber Vitae* to a few days in July 1099, a surprising precision but hardly questionable. See also my article mentioned p. 129 n. 1 above.

[4] On the history of and observations on the manuscript, see Mercati, loc. cit. p. 129 above) pp. 214 ff.

[5] Benedini, see p. 126 n. 1 above, and M. Venturini, *Vita ed attività dello 'Scriptorium' Veronese nel secolo XI* (Verona, 1930). Dr. U. Muroni, director of the Bibliotheca Comunale in Mantua, kindly allowed me to see his catalogue of Polirone manuscripts which is about to be printed and which contains an

In Mantua alone we can still find today approximately one hundred manuscripts of the twelfth century; these are almost exclusively of patristic, hagiographical or liturgical content. Among them is an especially well-known codex with Remigius' commentary on St Matthew.[1] This codex is adorned with an interesting initial. To the left of the initial 'A' sits the evangelist Matthew, to the right stands the Abbot Peter. The latter is more likely to be Abbot Peter of Polirone, who died in 1076 or 1077, than Peter the Venerable of Cluny, the manuscript having been hitherto attributed to the beginning of the twelfth century. Only a little later than this appears a psalter, endowed with numerous delicately worked miniatures, some rather obliterated in places, and bearing on the first page a miniature of King David playing on his harp, and other figures.[2] In common with the Gospels, this psalter reveals the trend towards ornamental decoration of details. Finally we must mention a missal whose initials can only belong to an extraordinarily highly developed school of writing: it appeared at the beginning of the thirteenth century.[3] Reference to these manuscripts may suffice to place the Gospels in a series of artistically illuminated volumes from Polirone; the Gospels themselves reveal the finest execution of the series.

The *Liber Vitae* reflects the relations of the monastery with the pope, Cluny, and the Tuscan countess. The thoughts expressed in the introduction contain a high ideal and help us to understand how the monks conceived the communion between the living and the dead in their house. The Gospels, representative in themselves, are thus joined, in the Book of Life, by a most illustrious company of men following a religious way of life, whom the monks recognised as their brothers. And so we should logically expect to find in the *Liber Vitae* the same groups of Cluniac abbots, counts of Canossa, and reformers surrounding Pope Gregory VII and Anselm of Lucca. In fact, the persons introduction showing what eventually happened to all the books of the monastic library.

[1] Mantua, Bibl. Comun. 342 (C IV 1); Benedini, loc. cit. p. 37.

[2] Mantua, Bibl. Comun. 340 (C III 20); and 448 (D IV 2) fols 140 and 203. Attention should be drawn to the likeness between MS. 340 and MS. Vat. lat. 4922 (see p. 129 n. 3 above) as regards script and illumination technique.

[3] Ibid. 441 (D III 15) with calendar, pls 173 ff. Reproduced in Paccagnini-Gnudi, *Mantova, Le arti*, 1 (1960) pls 316–22; see further MS. 447 (D IV 1).

and groups of persons whose names are actually inscribed appear most modest. They are distinguished by the note 'who freely became *fideles* of this house',[1] whilst two groups to whom attention is especially drawn by the fact that their names are encircled – and these are surprisingly enough the greatest nobles among the persons mentioned – bear the comment 'these do not belong to those who swore allegiance'.[2] A high proportion of the names, as far as it is possible to identify them, can be attributed to the time around 1110.[3] As the final records of 1109 form a kind of conclusion to the *Liber Vitae*, one can place the main entries of *fideles* in the decade between 1099 and 1109–10. As to the meaning of this *fidelitas*, G. Fasoli has recently expressed an opinion, without however reaching a convincing conclusion.[4] She starts from the observation that the second half of the list contains the names of several artisans from Milan, Mantua, Gonzaga and Cremona, whose relationship with the monastery is not at all clear.[5] And so she thinks that she can detect in the *fideles* the early form of a brotherhood, directly comparable with a third order or group of lay oblates, and attributes great importance to the *Liber Vitae* as an indication of religious movements of the later middle ages. Yet starting from the actual content of the manuscript, we deduce that the real group of *fideles* can be identified with those of Mantua.[6] We must then ask exactly why two groups, one of Venetians, the other of particularly high nobility, should be thus carefully distinguished, for they had sworn no oath. This being so, they would not normally have been entered in a confraternity record. So why should they, as 'non-oath-takers', and considering the conditions for commemoration and the funda-

---

[1] 'qui fidelitatem in hac domo sponte gratisque fecerunt'.

[2] 'isti non sunt de illis qui iuraverunt fidelitatem'.

[3] See the identifications made by Warner, which according to Torelli need to be more precise. The following may be added: Tebaldus *abbas* (*Liber Vitae*, p. 40), abbot of S. Andrea in Mantua: see *DH* IV 449, 1097–1106; Raginerius (*L.V.* p. 41) *de Burbasio, habitator in Mantua*, in 1098 renounced some possessions in Formigosa in favour of Abbot William of Polirone: see Nicolini (as on p. 127 n. 4 above,) no. 18, p. 23; Hugo *massarius* (*L.V.* p. 40): see Overmann, *Reg.* 96f., 1106. On p. 40 of the *Liber Vitae*, and the persons *Gandulfus fil. Ugonis*, see Overmann, *Reg.* 63, 1100.

[4] Fasoli, loc. cit. p. 192.

[5] Following Mercati, see above p. 129.   [6] Fol. 103.

mental customs of such confraternities, be included at all?

Another possible solution is very obvious. On 18 March 1109, that is, only a few weeks before the above-mentioned anniversary gift, Countess Matilda gave both the castle and fortified town of Governolo on Benedict's Island to Abbot Alberic and then took them back in feudal tenure.[1] In the records it is specifically stated that Matilda's knights at the manor of Villola and on the island itself should hold their fee, from then onwards, from the countess, who was bound in vassalage, on their behalf, to the monastery. At her death, however, the fees in question and those of her knights were to revert to the monastery. A serious rift within Matilda's militia is revealed in this agreement. The ageing princess, who had turned not inconsiderable sections of her allodial estates into church lands, seems to have acted quite against the advice of her knights, who had suffered great military losses during the hard struggles of previous years. Apparently Polirone put its actual and future vassals and knights under oath in 1109 and bound them to the monastery. This explains why the countess's most powerful knights and, in particular, her commander-in-chief Arduin de Palude and his sons refused to agree to the abbot's bond of vassalage and swear fealty to him.[2] Among the *fideles* on the list, on the other hand, are numerous servants of the countess, indicated by name; several are distinguished by the addition of *de Castello Ariano* (Castellarano), which had been transferred to the abbot of Polirone in 1092. Lotharingians like Constantinus and Ulrich Lotherengus remind us of the countess's first husband, several *teutonici* of her second; her chamberlain Arduin (evidently not the same as Arduin de Palude) and Roland are among those who took the oath. The latter appears, together with Arduin de Palude (whose two sons are mentioned, by way of corroboration, in the same year) and Rudolf Piloso, in the records of 1109 among the witnesses; this is also an indication that the list of *fideles* must have been drawn up in this connection.[3] The fact

---

[1] Torelli, op. cit. 144, p. 105. On the allegiance of Countess Matilda, see *Vita Anselmi Lucensis*: *MGH SS* 12, 34.

[2] F. Fabbi, 'Le famiglie reggiane e parmensi che hanno in comune l'origine con la contessa Matilda', in *Atti e mem. prov. Mod.* ser. 9, vol. 3 (1963) 184 and family tree. See also n. 3 above.

[3] Torelli, op. cit. 143–4, pp. 104f.

that Arduin de Palude enjoyed the monks' esteem although he never entered into any sworn service with the monastery is gathered from the anniversary records, in which he is described as 'most faithful to us in all things for the love of Christ our Lord', almost as if he were the countess's executor. His was a *fidelitas* beyond that of an oath of allegiance.

What does this mean for the form of the *Liber Vitae*? We have already stated how its introduction and arrangement bear the stamp of Cluny. The Book of Life itself, however, reveals another facet. It was probably discontinued for ten years and then begun again, in a completely new style. In an almost register-like sequence were inscribed the names of those men (female names are completely lacking!) who, as we believe, depended upon the monastery as vassals or tenants and who had changed their direct bond with the countess for one with the abbey. Among the artisans of the second page we find, perhaps, tenants of monastic leaseholds and houses in the nearby towns, especially in Mantua and Gonzaga. At that time the knights, at least, took the oath of allegiance to the abbot, which is shown by the form in question. The *Liber Vitae*, drawn up in 1099, has thus acquired a secular nature. Not only are the abbots of Cluny and Polirone omitted, as well as those of neighbouring priories, but there is no mention either of brothers from other monasteries or of those laymen, together with their families, who had close spiritual ties with Polirone. Above all, no mention is made of Polirone itself. And so this *Liber Vitae*, in its origins an expression of Cluniac spirit, comes to have, as it is carried on, just as little to do with the commemoration of the dead as the Gospels themselves have to do with Countess Matilda. Pragmatism has supplanted idealism.

We obtain a completely different impression from a calendar from Polirone taken from a lectionary of the late twelfth century.[1] In the litany, immediately after the saintly Bene- dictines, come the Abbots Odo, Mayeul, Odilo and Hugh, who also appear as saints in the calendar. Here are inscribed, as

[1] G. A. Gradenigo, *Calendario Polironiano del XII secolo* (Venice, 1795) pp. 7–18, following Mantua, Bibl. Com. 133 (A v 3) pls 347–8. On the liturgy and the *Consuetudines* of Polirone, see S. J. P. Van Dijk, 'The customary of St Benedict of Padolirone', in *Miscell. liturgica in honorem L. Cuniberti Mohlberg* (Rome, 1949) II 451 ff.

solemn commemorations, Count Boniface, Count Teodald, Countess Willa and Countess Matilda, Abbots Rotho (18 May), Venerandus (5 April), Rainfred (11 May), Alberic (7 April) and Herman (28 November), all of Polirone; St Simeon (26 July and octave) and finally, also as a solemn commemoration, Hubert, prior (31 December).[1]

The calendar in question answers the queries raised in the introduction of the *Liber Vitae*. All Souls' Day on 2 November and the 'Commemoration of all our dead relatives' on 12 November point once again to Cluny.[2] But the question of when the calendar was drawn up and when it was written down is harder to answer. As we have said, the manuscript would indicate that it was written between 1180 and 1200. The deaths of Matilda and Abbot Herman of Polirone are the last to be recorded in it! The latter must have died on 28 November 1124.[3] It is surprising to find that the names of the three Abbots Peter, Wido and William are missing, that is, those of the very first two Cluniac abbots of Polirone. On the other hand, the anniversaries of the first three abbots of the beginning of the eleventh century were apparently well known. The lost calendar which served as a model for our manuscript must therefore have been begun under Alberic, at the earliest, and completed according to a later text. That does not, of course, provide any explanation for the omission of perhaps the most important abbots of the Benedictine monastery.

There is another liturgical source in Polirone which we can mention. It has only come down to us, however, in fragmentary form.[4] 'In an ancient manuscript, scarcely legible because of its age' Arnold Wion, a monk at Polirone, found a list of its abbots with the names of Rozo, Venerandus, Rainfridus, Landulfus, Petrus, Wido, Willelmus, Albericus, Ermanus, Heinricus,

---

[1] Gradenigo has a misreading: 'Ubertus Parmensis'; the person referred to is a prior of Polirone, mentioned in Abbot Alberic's document of 1109 (see p. 133).

[2] 'commemoratio omnium parentum nostrorum defunctorum'.

[3] He is mentioned as still alive in July 1124; on 30 November 1125 his successor is referred to: Torelli, op. cit. 191–3, p. 136.

[4] Arnold Wion, *Lignum Vitae, ornamentum et decus ecclesiae*, pars 2, lib. II (1595) 233–4; mentioned by Bacchini, op. cit. p. 50, who no longer knew which copy Wion had used.

Willelmus, Ubertus, Gervasius, Rainerius; in short, a list which covered the period from the beginning until about 1180 and which appears to be complete and fits in with the facts. This list is followed by the names of 1309 monks. Wion counted them through and found that 844 were written in the first handwriting, then there were additions in a different hand. Unfortunately Wion only edited the names of persons designated abbot or bishop, together with the appropriate numbers. What did the text he used look like? 'Evidently a necrology', wrote G. Fasoli, who referred to the list.[1] But the list of abbots contradicts this. A comparison with a similar list from St Martin-des-Champs leads us further. We have already come across this important Cluniac priory; we said that Abbot Wido of Polirone's family foundation in Pithiviers had later been put under St Martin. Besides the great necrology, a whole series of lists were kept there (the editor speaks of diptychs); these were written down in the second half of the twelfth century.[2] Chapter One contains the prayer for the dead; Chapter Two the twenty-six names (numbered by the editor) of priors and highly placed personages, kings and bishops; Chapter Three nine further names of benefactors. Then there begins a list of names extending from no. 36 to no. 713, among whom we find more bishops and abbots. The list is incomplete, being cut short at the ninth page. It is the list of monks at St Martin and their brothers; its arrangement follows the order of their death, as the editor is able to show. Contrary to the necrology, reference to the actual day of death is omitted here, the day which was to be celebrated with an office and which was firmly fixed in the necrology. Here, on the other hand, the community finds all the dead brothers who were remembered at the monastery. It is obvious that we can interpret in the same way the lists from Polirone: one list is for abbots, another for monks. Of the twenty-five names which Wion reproduces, too few can be positively identified to provide clear enough proof. It is only of the last names that we can say with any certainty that they date from about 1180, whilst the earliest names must belong to the middle of the eleventh

[1] Fasoli, loc. cit. p. 192.

[2] J. Depoin, *Recueil des Chartes et Documents de Saint-Martin des Champs*, III ('Arch. de la France monastique', 18, 1917) pp. 1 ff.

century.[1] We can only be absolutely clear about this when the text used by Wion comes to light. We suppose it to be a list of obits of the monks in Polirone and of the brothers connected with them, compiled at the time of Abbot Alberic or Abbot Herman, on the basis of an earlier text, and taken up to about 1180.

Thanks to this we become acquainted, through a *Liber Vitae* which is Cluniac in its drafting, and a calendar as well as the obits which remind us yet again of a Cluniac model, with the rest of those notes which were drawn up for the commemoration of the dead in Polirone. It was worth the trouble to search for similar relics of tradition reflecting the spiritual links with Cluny. Of course the situation in Polirone is much more favourable than elsewhere since the tradition found here in books has been preserved near its place of origin.

The fact that the names of the Cluniac abbots appear in both the calendar and the litany at St Benedict's becomes a foregone conclusion. Whether the names of the abbots of Polirone are also to be found in the necrology at Cluny cannot be ascertained, for we only know the date of death of Abbot Alberic, which perhaps, put back by two days, is in the necrology at St Martin-des-Champs.[2] It is well known that Anselm of Lucca, possibly like the Empress Agnes, was included in the prayers of the monks at Cluny. Others, like Matilda or, for example, Prior Albert of Pontida, later honoured as a saint, whose dates of death are known, do not appear. And yet there must have been a firm relationship between the Burgundian abbey and its Italian dependencies, which, after all, continually received new impetus from their mother house.

A document which has been ignored until now points to such a relationship between Cluny and Lombardy. At the time of Abbot Hugh seven men, Paganus, Mainfred, Lanfranc, Totdilus, Alberic, Lanfranc and Petrus, requested permission to have the names of relatives mentioned in the martyrology as

[1] No. 39, Rainfredus *abb.* and 301, Wido *abb.* are perhaps the abbots of the same name in Polirone. No. 54, Stephan *eps.* is perhaps the bishop of Ancona, *c.* 1030. No. 1040, Mainfredus *abbas*, died at Fruttuaria after 25 April 1142; no. 1044, Ribald *eps.* is certainly of Modena, *c.* 1136–48. Nos 1295 and 1296 list Bishops Theodinus of Porto and Petrus of Tusculum: both were consecrated on the same day, in May 1179: Petrus only is recorded in 1179, Theodinus in 1181.

[2] Ed. Molinier, *Obituaires Sens*, I 412.

they had presented a church to Cluny.[1] The document is without doubt of Italian origin and concerns a gift made jointly by a large circle of kinsmen. In our attempt to define this more closely we find ourselves right in the middle of the great priory foundations of the time of Hugh of Cluny.

In the Book of Life of the royal monastery of S. Giulia and S. Salvatore in Brescia there was entered, seemingly towards the end of the eleventh century, a family group which can be identified.[2] The very first four names, Giselbertus, Enricus, Lanfrancus and Albericus, point to the Martinenga family, definitely the most widespread and influential family in Lombardy, counts of Bergamo (whose bishopric was, as it were, passed on in the family), holders of high office and landed proprietors in the region of Como, Bergamo and Brescia.[3] Count Giselbert of Bergamo, son of Count Maginfred, was the founder of the priory of S. Paolo, Argano, on the southern tip of Lake Iseo, which priory was transferred in 1079 to neighbouring Sarnico.[4] We conclude from the name of his consort Matilda that Giselbert was related to the house of Canossa; Giselbert himself was a feudal tenant of Matilda's monastery at Nonantola. His brother Henry was made count of Verona by Henry III in 1048.[5]

To this family belonged Berta, Lanfranc of Martinenga's daughter, who, together with her second husband Wifred, founded the priory of S. Maria di Laveno on the eastern shore of Lake Maggiore. Her sons by her first marriage, Counts Winizo and Albert (sons of Count Arduin of Bergamo, a brother of the above-mentioned Count Maginfred), gave their consent to the foundation, which was certainly made on property belonging to their side of the family.[6] In the same year, 1081,

---

[1] BB 3312.

[2] *Codice necrol.-liturg. del monastero di S. Salvatore o S. Giulia in Brescia*, ed. A. Valentini (1887) p. 87 on fol. 47r in an eleventh-century script.

[3] P. Guerrini, *I conti de Martinengo* (Brescia, 1930) and E. Odazio, 'I conti del comitato Bergomense', in *Bergomum*, n.s. 8 (1934) 271 ff. with numerous supplements.

[4] BB 3536. For the monastery, see *It. Pont.* 6, 2, 389; Cottineau, op. cit. 1 148; Guerrini, op. cit. pp. 101 f. For the entire group of Cluniac priories in Lombardy. See the map on p. 294 of the original article cited on p. 123, n.1.

[5] Guerrini, op. cit. p. 103.

[6] BB 3583; on the genealogy of the benefactor, see Guerrini, op. cit. p. 106.

Countess Berta (Lanfranc of Martinenga's daughter and Wifred's wife) also presented estates to the newly founded priory of Pontida (near Lecco).[1] The founders of the church of St Paul on Lake Iseo, which was later united with St Paul, Argano can, thanks once again to our Book of Life reference, be placed in this very same family, for the names of the donors Ferlinda, Oprandus, Albertus and Johannes, appear in that order in the Brescia group.[2] We know them as a branch of the Martinenga family, named Mozzo.[3] Johannes de Muzo, with his sons Aubrand and Albert, was also the donor of the chapel at Clizano, dedicated to SS Gervasius and Protasius (1093), out of which was formed the Cluniac priory of Clusa.[4] It would finally appear that the benefactors Ambrosius and Opprand (son of Albertus de Tocingo) belong to the same family; theirs was the foundation of the priory of Provaglio, not far from Lake Iseo.[5]

As a result of this we have at least marked out the compass of the family in which can be placed the church donors who wished to see the names of their kinsmen included in the Cluny martyrology. The ladies Oliza, Adelasia and Odda, entered among the names of the dead, appear in the Brescia group after the Martinengas, and one name which is typical of this family is that of an entry for 18 February in the necrology: Rolinda. It may finally be noted that there are names which sound very similar to those of the approximately fifty noblemen of Como and Milan who, as joint benefactors, transformed the fortress of Vertemate into a Cluniac priory.[6]

This brief survey contains two points worth noting. The first refers to the increasingly close ties binding the nobility of northern Italy with Cluny. We could have referred to the

---

[1] The document is in M. Lupus, *Cod. Dipl. Bergom.* II 723–4; a valuable literature on Pontida may be found in Kehr, *It. Pont.* 6, 1, 392.

[2] BB 3658–9.   [3] Guerrini, op. cit. pp. 117 f.

[4] BB 3668.   [5] BB 3603; Cottineau, op. cit. II 2368.

[6] BB 3606; see F. Forte, 'Como e i Cluniacensi', in *Periodico della Soc. Comense*, 28 (1931) 13 ff. Whether the benefactors in BB 3312 refer directly to Vertemate is questionable, though worth considering. It would be difficult to find another group of benefactors so numerous and with such similar names existing apart from those connected with Vertemate. It remains to be seen whether the names of the dead recorded in BB 3312 are to be found in any Cluniac necrology.

importance, in the province of Valsesia, of the counts of
Biandrate, in whose domains five Cluniac priories were founded.
They themselves founded and endowed the one in Locarno.[1]
We have already realised the importance of the Martinengas
for Cluny in the region of the north Italian lakes. In the vicinity
of Polirone, Count Ubald of Parma and Countess Matilda
represented the nobility which was motivated by the desire to
guarantee for itself the intercession of the monks at Cluny; this
held the greatest certainty of salvation. This movement towards
the Burgundian abbey is certainly not surprising, nor do we
wonder at the moment in time at which it became effective in
Italy. It is certainly worth investigating who was affected by it.

The other aspect turns our attention to Cluny itself, whose
active 'monastic policy' can certainly not be denied. A glance
at the map reveals one undisputable fact: chance alone did not
cause the massing of priories and churches among the north
Italian lakes in the foothills of the Alps and on the approach
roads to the passes leading to Swabia and Burgundy.[2] The fact
that, at this time, Cluny also founded, near Aosta, the priory
of S. Helena in Sarre which depended on St Victor in Geneva,
is gleaned from the map of the Burgundian priories which were
to be found as far away as Lake Geneva.[3] The region which
contained the western Italian passes came under the influence
and authority of the counts of Turin and had its own spiritual
centre in Fruttuaria, which did not lag behind Cluny either in
the esteem it enjoyed or in the reforming zeal it possessed.
Bearing this in mind no one would wish to question the political
neutrality of Cluny and the intelligent weighing up of this

---

[1] BB 3600: on the Counts Biandrate, see Kehr, *It. Pont.* 6, 2, 38; also C. G.
Mor, *Frammenti di storia Valsesiana* (Varallo, 1960) p. 47.

[2] P. Bognetti, op. cit. (see above, p. 125 n. 5); P. Guerrini, *Brescia e
Montecassino* (1942) p. xxii; P. Zerbi, 'Monasteri e riforma a Milano dalla
fine del sec. X agli inizi del XII', in *Aevum*, 24 (1950) 44 ff., 166 ff. and esp.
p. 170, with notes; *Storia di Milano*, 3 (1954, G. L. Barni) 218 f. C. Violante,
'Il monachesimo Cluniacense di fronte al mondo politico ed ecclesiastico',
in *Spiritualità*, pp. 194 ff.

[3] L. Kern, 'Notes sur le prieuré clunisien de Sainte Hélène à Sarre', in
Mélanges P. E. Martin, Mem. Soc. d'Hist. et d'Arch. de Genèves, 11 (1961)
329 ff. P. Ladner, 'Das St Albanskloster und die burgundische Tradition in
der Clunizenserprovinz Alemannia', in *Basler Beitr. z. Geschichtswiss.* 80
(1960) 31 ff. and maps.

mediator, its greatest abbot, so conscious of his responsibility. But we should also ascribe to Cluny and its monks an eminently practical attitude in their comprehension of given political interests. In its change from abstract idealism to practical politics the *Liber Vitae* of Polirone seems to us to provide a clue to the disposition of the Cluniac monasteries at the beginning of the twelfth century.

9 A Cluniac Necrology from the Time of Abbot Hugh[1]

JOACHIM WOLLASCH

There is an increasing tendency nowadays among historians to rely on necrologies of the early middle ages for data in research on reformed monasticism.[2] But none of the surviving medieval necrologies come from any of the famous centres of monastic reform, such as Cluny,[3] Gorze,[4] Hirsau or Fruttuaria;[5] and from St Vanne at Verdun there is only one from the late medieval period and a new edition of an old necrology.[6] In the

[1] [Translated from 'Ein cluniacensisches Totenbuch aus der Zeit Abt Hugos von Cluny', in *Frühmittelalterliche Studien*, ed. K. Hauck, 1 Berlin (1967) pp. 406–43. Ed.]

[2] The decisive influence in this direction came from K. Hallinger, *Gorze–Kluny*, and is certainly one of the great merits of that work. On the methods of research see, however, G. Tellenbach in *NF* pp. 4 f.; J. Wollasch, 'Muri und St Blasien, Perspektiven schwäbischen Mönchtums in der Reform', in *DA* 17 (1961) 427 ff.; also his 'Qu'a signifié Cluny pour l'abbaye de Moissac?', in *Annales du Midi*, 75 (1963) 345 ff. See also K. Schmid and J. Wollasch, 'Die Gemeinschaft der Lebenden und Verstorbenen in Zeugnissen des Mittelalters', in *Frühmittelalterl. Studien*, 1,365 ff.

[3] A. Molinier, *Les obituaires français* (1890) no. 392, and *RHF Obituaires*, 1, 1 (1902) 419, 519; K. Hallinger, *Gorze–Kluny*, 1 (1950) p. 26.

[4] A modern compilation called a necrology of Gorze (an excerpt from Baluze) was published by C. Aimond, 'Le nécrologe de l'abbaye de Gorze', in *Bull. mensuel de la Soc. d'archéologie lorraine et du musée historique lorrain*, 63 (1914) 76 ff.

[5] In an indirect way, through the necrologies of monasteries connected with Hirsau (e.g. Michelsberg in Bamberg, Zwiefalten, Peterhausen), it is possible to find fragments that approximate to the lost necrology of Hirsau: see J. Wollasch, 'Mönchtum des Mittelalters zwischen Kirche und Welt', *Habil.-Schrift Freiburg i. Br.* (MS. 1963, to appear soon). The fragment of the St Blaise necrology is relevant to Fruttuaria (see J. Wollasch in *DA* 17 (1961) 427 ff.) and is an important roll, especially when compared with the valuable, as yet unpublished, necrological remains from St Bénigne at Dijon (see Molinier, *Les obituaires français*, nos 374–8).

[6] Molinier, *Les obituaires*, no. 322, places the first draft in the fourteenth century and so does H. Bloch (*Jahrb. d. Ges. f. lothr. Gesch. u. Altertumskunde*, 14 (1902) 133), who published it in summary form. (Hallinger, op. cit. p. 31,

face of such serious losses, one begins to doubt whether the ones
that have been preserved can really serve as worthwhile sources
for historical research on the subject. On the other hand, most
medieval manuscript necrologies from about 1100, when
monastic reform was at its height, are accessible.[1] This certainly
points to some connection between the preservation of
necrologies and the reform itself. So it seems best to start with
the question of their preservation when estimating their value
as historical evidence.

Scholars have obviously accepted the fact that there is no
surviving medieval necrology from Cluny. They have been
able to do so the more readily since at the end of last century
Molinier spoke of the possibility of a partial reconstruction of
'the' lost necrology of Cluny.[2] He found that the twelfth-
century necrologies from the Cluniac monasteries of St Martial
of Limoges, St Martin-des-Champs and Notre-Dame of
Longpont had so many entries in common that it would be
possible to reconstruct part of the lost original at Cluny. Experts
were relieved by this reliable opinion, but Molinier's suggestion
led to no practical results.[3] The necrologies of St Martial of
Limoges, St Martin-des-Champs and Notre-Dame of Longpont

---

believed that this edition represented the complete text.) Sackur, *Neues Archiv*,
15 (1890) p. 126 ff. also printed extracts, but from the eighteenth-century
copy. As yet the complete necrology remains unedited. H. Dauphin, *Le
bienheureux Richard, abbé de Saint-Vanne de Verdun* ('Bibl. de la Rev. eccl.' 24,
1946) places its beginning in the fifteenth century. The entries belonging to
the eleventh and twelfth centuries can, for the most part, be established by
comparing them with other necrologies of the same period, like the still
unpublished one of St Airy of Verdun, begun about the year 1100: on this
see J. Wollasch ('Mönchtum des Mittelalters', as in n. 5 above); I am very
grateful to Dom Huyghebaert of St André, Bruges, who placed at my
disposal photocopies of this necrology (Bibl. Verdun, MS. 10) and of another
copy of the necrology (Bibl. Verdun, MS. 11).

[1] There is a great need, as regards research, for a complete, detailed list
of all the surviving medieval European necrologies, such as has been drawn
up for France by A. Molinier.

[2] A. Molinier (see above, n. 3) even spoke of the 'ancient obit book of the
order of Cluny'. There are no grounds for stating that there was at Cluny
during the two and a half centuries from Abbot Berno to Peter the Venerable
only one necrology.

[3] G. Schnürer, 'Das Necrologium des Cluniacenser-Priorates Münchenwiler (Villars-les-Moines)', in *Collectanea Friburgensia*, n.s. x (1906) xviii f;
Hallinger, op. cit. 1 p. 26.

have never been published in their entirety to this day,[1] so it is still impossible to ascertain from reliable publications to what extent the entries in them actually do coincide. Instead the originals have to be consulted. But even were this not so, we would still have a long way to go to carry out Molinier's suggestion. He thought that it would be possible to track down the missing records of Cluny's deceased with the help of necrologies from other Cluniac monasteries, but this would in fact entail consulting all surviving necrologies from such houses, if any certain conclusion were to be reached.

Necrologies from other abbeys and priories dependent on Cluny do actually exist. When Moissac in Gascony joined Cluny in the middle of the eleventh century and began to draw its abbots from there, a necrology was started which contained about 4000 names by the thirteenth century. So far, not even extracts from it have been published.[2] But the most comprehensive Cluniac necrology known to us contains about 10,000 names, and as far as we can see may be the most outstanding of all medieval necrologies.[3] Although published in full more than fifty years ago,[4] it has apparently been completely ignored

---

[1] See the remarks of A. Molinier (*RHF Obituaires*, 1, 1 (1902) 419); or those of E. Molinier in his summarised version of the necrologies of St Martial de Limoges (*Doc. hist. bas-latins, provençaux et français concernant principalement la Marche et le Limousin*, 1 (1883) 65). Most editions are incomplete, including even the nineteenth-century editions of representative necrologies such as those in J. F. Böhmer, *Fontes rer. Germ.* and P. Jaffé *Bibl. rer. Germ.*, where only titles and details of selected persons such as kings, popes, counts, bishops, abbots, ecclesiastics, etc., are given.

[2] Bibl. Nat. Paris, MS. lat. 5548, and also an extract from a later necrology from Moissac: Bibl. Nat. Paris, MS. lat. 12773 (Molinier, *Les Obituaires*, no. 605). I wish to thank Mlle M.-T. d'Alverny (Paris) for microfilms of these necrologies and M. Delvolvé, conseiller d'état and mayor of Moissac, for giving me the opportunity, on the occasion of the nine-hundredth anniversary of the consecration of Moissac church, of seeing the original document there.

[3] It is worth mentioning, by way of comparison, that one of the largest necrologies we possess for the German monasteries (the necrology of Michelsberg in Bamberg) was for Hallinger the supreme piece of evidence for establishing the range of the so-called young Gorze movement. It contains about 2500 names, including those which can be deciphered only with modern techniques.

[4] Ed. G. Schnürer, see p. 144 n.

by modern research.¹ To estimate its value as a source of
historical data regarding Cluny and the whole movement to
which that abbey gave rise, it is necessary to know where the
necrology originated, which community it was intended for,
and where it was actually used. These are the questions which
this article sets out to answer.

It is the only necrology in the collection of manuscripts from
Cluny in the Bibliothèque Nationale in Paris. L. Delisle tried
to trace its origin to the Cluniac priory of Villers in the archdiocese of Besançon, a priory which had previously never
received historical mention.² The name Vilar occurs more than
once in the manuscript containing the necrology, and the
necrology itself also mentions Villarii *monachorum* under the
patronage of the Blessed Trinity. When A. Molinier added this
necrology to his list of French ones, he followed Delisle and
classified it under the name of Villers with others from the
archdiocese of Besançon.³ Chevalier in his topographical index
of sources identified this monastic settlement as Villers ou le Lac,
in the district of Pontarlier (Doubs).⁴ E. Sackur published an
extract from the necrology entitled 'From the Necrology of the
Cluniac priory of Villers, Diocese of Besançon'; he did not so
much as question its place of origin, but quoted Delisle's notes
on the subject.⁵ It was not until 1907 that B. Egger eventually
succeeded in establishing beyond all doubt the identity of Vilar
or Vilarii *monachorum* with its patronal dedication to the
Trinity.⁶ In the days of Abbot Hugh of Cluny there was in the

---

¹ See J. Wollasch, in *Annales du Midi*, 75 (1963) 345 ff. and H. Keller,
'Kloster Einsiedeln im ottonischen Schwaben', in *Forschung z. oberrhein.
Landesgesch.* 13 (1964) 127 and n. 223.

² L. Delisle, *Inventaire des manuscrits de la Bibl. Nat., Fonds de Cluni* (1884)
no. 126.

³ Molinier, *Les obituaires*, no. 338.

⁴ U. Chevalier, *Répertoire des sources historiques. Topo-Bibliographie* (1900)
col. 3309.

⁵ Sackur, *Die Cluniacenser*, 1 383, and n. 7: 'Aus dem Necrologium des
Cluniacenser-Priorats von Villers (Diöcese Besançon)'. A. Potthast,
Wegweiser durch die Geschichtswerke des europäischen Mittelalters bis 1500, 2, 2
(1896, new ed. 1957) p. 839 has *Necrologium Villariensis* ('Villars') *prioratus
ord. Cluniac. dioec. Vesont.*

⁶ B. Egger, *Geschichte der Cluniacenser-Klöster in der Westschweiz bis zum
Auftreten der Cisterzienser* (1907) pp. 93 and 222, n. 4; also pp. 39 f. and nn.

ecclesiastical district of Besançon in the diocese of Lausanne a church of the Blessed Trinity belonging to Cluny and situated in the town called Vilar.[1] In 1228 it was referred to as Vilar-les-Moinos.[2] The editors of the *Bibliotheca Cluniacencis* knew it from a fourteenth century list of Cluniac monasteries as the priory of *villario Monachorum* in the diocese of Besançon.[3]

So it must have been the small Cluniac priory of München-wiler – Villars-les-Moines – near Murten. It was there that the great necrology was used, as B. Egger concluded from entries in it. Records in the manuscript, a table of movable feasts, a number of marginal notes and also a great many entries in the necrology itself confirm this opinion. G. Schnürer goes into all this in his edition of the necrology.[4]

But he also went one step further in his assumption that it was not only used at Münchenwiler but was originally intended for that priory. Since place of origin and use are generally identical where medieval necrologies are concerned, Schnürer's conclusion may at first sight seem an obvious one. However, quite apart from the fact that there are a number of medieval necrologies which originated in one place and were afterwards used in another,[5] we must bear in mind that the large necrology in question was compiled by a woman, Elsendis.[6] She was responsible for about half the entries in it – some 5000 names – which

3 ff.; p. 251, where it is already said that the manuscript came from Münchenwiler.

[1] BB IV 3550 for 18 Feb 1080: 'ecclesia Sancte Trinitatis, que est in villa que vocitatur Vilar, in episcopatu Lausonense'.

[2] See the list of churches in the diocese of Lausanne edited by Cuno d'Estavayer in *Fontes rerum Bernensium*, 2 (1877) no. 77 (15 Sept 1228) p. 89.

[3] *Bibl. Cl.* 1742; see also Schnürer, 'Das Necrologium' (as in n. 9) p. iii, n. 5, on the misleading reference to the diocese of Besançon.

[4] See above, p. 144.

[5] For example: the Bamberg necrology from Paderborn, edited by E. von Guttenberg, 'Das Bistum Bamberg', in *Germania Sacra*, 2, 1 (1937) 8, necr. 2; the oldest necrology fragment from the Austrian monastery of Lambach (*MGH* necr. 4, p. 405), which in fact originally belonged to Fulda; the necrology owned by the Göttweig foundation in the fifteenth century went to Germany from France in the twelfth century (*MGH* necr. 5, pp. 592–5: a Cistercian fragment). For all three examples, see J. Wollasch, 'Mönchtum des Mittelalters' (as on p. 143).

[6] Schnürer, 'Das Necrologium', p. 97 under 31.12: 'Quorum uel quarum nomina hic scripsi meritis peto in cęlis adscribi ęlsendis'.

shows that she must have copied them from somewhere else. Since Schnürer never succeeded in identifying the place where Elsendis lived, which would have determined the place of origin of the necrology and the whereabouts of its source, we are left uncertain as to whether it had originally been copied out for the priory of Münchenwiler or was merely used there. We must first review the proofs adduced by B. Egger and G. Schnürer for the fact that it was used there at all, and then see whether they justify Schnürer's further conclusion that it also originated there.

Schnürer was able to show that the source used by Elsendis stopped before 1109, for the death of Abbot Hugh of Cluny (d. 24 April 1109) was recorded by a later hand, then erased, presumably by the same hand, and entered in the martyrology when Abbot Hugh was canonised in 1120.[1] So we may provisionally take 1109 as the latest possible date for Elsendis' work on the necrology.[2] Was the book used at Münchenwiler as early as that? Once we have discovered when it was used there, we shall know whether it originally belonged to that priory or was only brought there later.

The earliest clue is a deed concerning Münchenwiler, recorded in the manuscript under the date 1146.[3] But even this gives us nothing certain to go by, as the entry may have been made at some later date. This is indeed suggested by the fact that the table of movable feasts in the manuscript extends from 1157 to 1180.

---

[1] Ibid. pp. xxii f.

[2] To establish precisely and methodically the *terminus ante quem* for the work of Elsendis it is necessary to date all her records so that her last entry can be determined. Schnürer, helped mainly by the work of Molinier and Sackur, has been able to identify 94 of the ecclesiastical dignitaries entered by Elsendis. Most of them are correct. Of these the latest are Bishop Peter of Limoges (d. 16 June 1103-4) and Abbot Otger of St Martial, Limoges (d. 9 Dec 1116), whereas most of the bishops and abbots classified as entered by Elsendis occur not later than 1091 (see Schnürer, 'Das Necrologium', pp. xix f.). After breaking down the inscriptions of the names of several thousand dead monks, it is now possible to claim that Elsendis concluded her entries at the beginning of the twelfth century. Later hands continued to insert names of persons who had died in the eleventh century. The entries of Elsendis and many later ones go back, as regards the persons they refer to, far into the tenth century.

[3] Schnürer, loc. cit. p. v and 103, n. 1.

We have to examine entries in the martyrology and those in the necrology by a later hand. The marginal additions to Elsendis' martyrology concern Abbot Hugh of Cluny (29.4), Pope Gregory the Great (3.9), Junianus (16.10), a confessor venerated in Limoges and Cluny, Bishop Florus (4.11), whose burial place, St Flour, passed into the possession of Cluny at the end of the tenth century,[1] Austremonius of Clermont-Ferrand (8.11), bishop and martyr, the feast of our Lady's conception (8.12), and Thomas Becket of Canterbury (29.12). None of these additions have any special connection with München-wiler.[2]

With regard to the continuation of the necrology after the work of Elsendis, Schnürer wrote: 'Undoubtedly the second part was written at Münchenwiler and intended for use there. The increasing number of German and Burgundian names points to this, though of course French names are in the ascendancy in the main section, owing to the connection with Cluny.'[3] However, Schnürer only manages to list fifteen names out of the 5000 entered after Elsendis. The record in the manu-script of the deed dated 1146 is also cited in support of his assertion.[4]

To turn now to the entries which have notes indicating some sort of connection with Münchenwiler and the neighbouring district round Murten. Our interest is aroused, as was Schnürer's, by a group of 106 names of deceased marked with a *t* distinguishing them from the rest. Among these occur the following: Rudolph, who at the end of the eleventh century donated to Cluny the property on which the monastery of Münchenwiler was built;[5] Gerald, whose name was inscribed by Elsendis and later marked with a *t*, probably to be identified with Girald, whom we shall come across again with his brother

[1] Ibid. p. 102, n. 2.
[2] The 'German' saints who are to be found in Elsendis' martyrology (Walburga of Eichstätt, 1.5, Simeon of Trier, 1.6, Ulrich of Augsburg, 4.7, Magnus of Füssen, 6.9, Emmeram of Regensburg, 22.9, Wenceslaus of Bohemia, 28.9, the 11,000 virgins of Cologne, 21.10, Wolfgang of Regens-burg, 31.10, and Othmar of St Gall, 16.11) were already entered in Elsendis' record.
[3] Schnürer, loc. cit. pp. xxv f.   [4] Ibid. p. xxvi.
[5] Ibid. p. 83 under 8.11, and nn. b and 3: 'o. Rodulfus o.T., pro quo officium fiat, qui dedit casalem in quo monasterium istud constructum est'.

Rudolph presenting Vilar to Cluny;[1] 'John, t. prior, founder of
this church',[2] the prior who is said to have built the new church
at Münchenwiler in the twelfth century;[3] 'John, t. II, prior,
a senior whose spirit dwells with God in heaven', Prior John II
of Münchenwiler;[4] 't. Lambert sacristan, monk of this place';[5]
'Cono t. prior', most probably Cono, prior of Vilar 1173–4
according to the records.[6] It is true that we cannot be absolutely
certain about the identity of all these deceased, but one has
only to look at the place names in the appended notes to
realise that entries marked with t have some sort of connection
with Münchenwiler. The names include men and women who
were benefactors of the monastery or artisans employed there:
and the places Geristein, canton Bern;[7] Gurmels–Cormundes,
canton Fribourg;[8] Grussach–Cressier, canton Fribourg;[9] Cour-
tepin, canton Fribourg;[10] Courtion, canton Fribourg;[11]
Gurwolf–Courgevaux, canton Fribourg,[12] Murten;[13]
Guschuburli–Coussiberlé, canton Fribourg,[14] Schnürer was
certainly right in associating with Münchenwiler the 106 entries
marked with t.

He took the connection to be a very concrete one, and
interpreted the t as tumba, tumbatus ('tomb', 'interred'), assuming
that the names with a t against them were those of the dead who

[1] Ibid. p. 34 under 27.4, with n. b and 3.

[2] Ibid. under 18.7: 'Johannes, t., prior qui fuit istius conditor ęcclesię'.

[3] Ibid. p. xxxii.

[4] Ibid. p. xxxii under 30.1: 'Johannes, t., II, prior senex cuius inest celo
spiritus ante deum'.

[5] Ibid. under 10.3: 'Lannbertus sacrista, monachus huius loci'.

[6] Ibid. p. 63 and n. 2; under 20.8.

[7] Ibid. under 25.2: 'Uldricus (t) de Geristen'. The identification of place
names is taken from Schnürer.

[8] Ibid. under 10.4: 'Cono(t) . . . de Curmunns'.

[9] Ibid. under 15.3: 'Agatha (t) (Cresir amica); under 26.5: 'Cono (t
Criseir'); under 13.6: 'Gisla (t Cresir)'; under 28.7: 'Uldricus (t de Crecei)
amicus (noster)'.

[10] Ibid. under 23.4: 'Boso (t) conversus (molinarius Cortibin)'.

[11] Ibid. under 20.6: 'Warnerius (t) de Curtiun'; under 1.9: 'Sibodus miles
(t cuius terram habemus de Cor[t]iu[n])'.

[12] Ibid. under 2.5: 'Wilelmus (t) de Cor[giuolt?]'; under 31.8: 'Rodulfus
(t) de Corgiuolt'.

[13] Schnürer, loc. cit. under 6.8: 'Adalgodi (t) maioris de Mur[ato]'; under
20.8: 'Emma (t de Murat)'.

[14] Ibid. under 22.11: 'Rodulfus (t de Corcebella)'.

were buried in the priory church at Münchenwiler. But one of the names entered by Elsendis (Gerald, 27.4) had a *t* added to it later, which would mean either that the body was transferred there afterwards, or that the fact that Gerald had originally been buried at Münchenwiler was confirmed at a later date. This would certainly bring the compilation of the necrology a little nearer to Münchenwiler. But can one really imagine 106 graves, supposed to date from the twelfth century, in any priory church, even a big one, let alone this one, which we know was small and where in the seventeenth century the community was reckoned to number only four, prior included?[1] Excavations there would hardly be likely to bear out such a surmise, and one can recall nothing like it elsewhere. Also there is no other necrology in which the words for 'tomb' or 'interred' have been abbreviated to *t*. In this so-called Münchenwiler necrology there occurs in an obit note the rubric 'for whom t. there shall be an office' (Osbert, 29.8).[2] This shows the impossibility even from a merely linguistic point of view of taking *t* to mean 'tomb' or 'interred'. It would not make sense if the note after Osbert's name ran: 'for whom a tomb there shall be an office'.

'For whom there shall be an office' (Ebrard, 29.8) is a rubric which is easily understood, being a normal way of noting a commemoration of the dead. Similarly 'for whom *t*.' can be interpreted as 'for whom a thirty days' commemoration shall be made'. This is one of the commonest rubrics in medieval necrologies everywhere.[3] But even if *t* is understood to signify 'thirty days' (*tricesimus, tricenarius, tricenale*), it still means that the 106 entries all indicate an especially close bond with Münchenwiler, since the deceased are given the extra thirty

---

[1] *Bibl. Cl.* 1742.

[2] 'pro quo t., officium fiat' ('Osbertus', under 29.8).

[3] The thirty days' commemoration at Cluny was so well known that it even occurs in charters: e.g. BB v 4183. See also the letter from Peter the Venerable to Bishop Henry I of Winchester in W. Jorden, 'Das cluniazensische Totengedächtniswesen', *Münsterische Beiträge zur Theologie*, 15 (1930) 116. It is also found in the martyrology/necrology of Usuard of St Germain-des-Près, which spans the whole middle ages (*RHF Obituaires*, I, 1 (1902) 248, under 12.1). It was a familiar practice in the monastic customaries of the German monasteries too: see, for example, Albers, *Consuetudines Monasticae*, v 76.

F

days' suffrage. And this particular privilege was accorded at a later date to one of the dead inscribed by Elsendis (Gerald, 27.4).

Evidently certain entries were singled out and marked with a *t* or the addition of a place name. To find out at what date this happened, one has only to notice where they occur on the list of deceased for the particular day. It will be seen that these entries always come last on the list, if they are on it at all and not, as is frequently the case, fitted in as marginal notes. Gerald, inscribed by Elsendis under the rubric 'monks of our community', and who probably donated the property of Vilar to Cluny, was accorded this claim on Münchenwiler by a *t* written in only late in the twelfth century. His brother Rudolph, the necrology tells us, gave Cluny the land on which the priory was built. As he was a founder a note was added prescribing the thirty days' commemoration and office for the dead (8.11), but his name is third from the end of a list of 27. Would that be likely, if the necrology had been written for Münchenwiler in the first place? Prior John, who rebuilt the priory church in the twelfth century, comes last of all on the list of 18 for 18.7! Prior John II, a senior 'whose spirit dwells with God in heaven', is 22nd on the list of 27 entries for 30.1. 'Lambert sacristan, monk of this place' (10.3) is last on the list of 36 for that day. Prior Cono, presumably the Prior Cono of Münchenwiler recorded 1173–4 (20.8) is entered as third from the end of a list of 32 deceased with an additional note as to the thirty days' commemoration. Going through the whole necrology one finds the same thing: entries of especial interest to Münchenwiler are sometimes at the end of the list for the day, but are often just marginal notes added when the necrology was almost full.

It follows that not all the numerous additions to the Elsendis necrology – Schnürer spoke of the 'second part' – were written for Münchenwiler or actually at that priory; only the latest ones were. As far as these can be identified, they occur in the second half of the twelfth century and continue up to the end of it. This fits in with the fact that the earliest deed referring to Münchenwiler in the manuscript is dated 1146, and the table of movable feasts comprises the years from 1157 to 1180. But Elsendis' entries in the necrology, as we have seen, came to an end at the beginning of the twelfth century. Between them and these later entries at the end of the century about 5000 obit notes occur,[1] in fact most of the names were inscribed after Elsendis had finished. The question inevitably arises as to where this necrology was used before 1150 when it passed to München-wiler already almost completely filled in. Where did Elsendis compile her necrology from a source reaching back into the tenth century?[2] And for what monastery was her large book intended? Certainly not for Münchenwiler, as we have shown.

Schnürer, however, assumed that the necrology was written for Münchenwiler in the first place. He wrote: 'Something like this may well have happened: when the priory was founded, the new community needed a necrology and martyrology for the commemorations at chapter, so they obtained from Cluny a necrology which had been brought up to date, but in which the names needed rearranging. The book was already so full that there was no room left in it for further entries. To remedy this, they got Elsendis to make a copy of it. In doing so, she corrected the order of the names, sometimes putting a person marked out for special honour at the head of the list for the day, and adding a few names afterwards. Her work came to an end in about the year 1116. Meanwhile all the rolls of the dead brought to Münchenwiler were stored up until the names could be copied into the necrology. This would account for the fact that Abbot Ademar of St Martial at Limoges, who died on 22.9.1114, was entered in the second part, whereas his successor, Otger I, who died on 9.12.1116, is in the Elsendis section, and Queen Bertha, who died in 966, is recorded in the margin on 9.3, but not by the hand of Elsendis.'[3]

In theory it is not beyond the bounds of possibility that the monks of the new foundation should have obtained a necrology from Cluny to serve as a model, and that this one might have been spared because it was already full and had been replaced by a new one. But then why should they have had a copy of it made? And how could it have occurred to them to ask a woman to do it? Elsendis entered the names of some 5000 individuals in this book, many of whom lived as far back as the tenth century.

[1] And these entries were made by more scribes than there were monks at Münchenwiler! See *Bibl. Cl.* 1742.

[2] See above, p. 148n..

[3] Schnürer, loc. cit. p. xxv.

Is it likely that the small community of a completely new foundation would have ordered for their own use a necrology noting both liturgical and social dues,[1] and containing the names of some 5000 deceased, some of whom had died 150 years before? Take for instance the case of the famous imperial monastery at Farfa: when at the beginning of the eleventh century they wanted to introduce the Cluniac custom of commemorating the dead, all they did was to copy into a chapter of the customary an extract for one day from the necrology at Cluny to serve as a model.[2] Moreover, all that Schnürer elaborates about the rolls of the dead which were brought to Münchenwiler amounts to no more than a mere hypothesis.

We now know that Elsendis finished her work on the necrology at the beginning of the twelfth century – Schnürer himself realised that – also that the majority of the entries, some 5000, were added after that, and that only the latest of these show any connection with Münchenwiler. But obviously the place of origin can be determined only if we can find out something

---

[1] On the problem of the intermingling of spiritual commemorations with social obligations, Peter the Venerable, looking back over the history of Cluny, made a just observation: it is reflected in his reform statute XXXII. See D. Knowles, 'The Reforming decrees of Peter the Venerable', in *Petrus Venerabilis* ('Studia Anselmiana', XL, 1956) pp. 1 ff.; *PL* 189, 1034–5: 'Statutum est ut defunctis fratribus nostris universis scilicet professis, die anniversarii, quo recitari nomina eorum a lectore, sicuti mos est in capitulo solent, quinquaginta praebendae dentur, tali conditione, ut sive plura sint, sive minus, quam quinquaginta, ultra numerum jam dictum nec augeantur praebendae nec minuantur. Causa instituti hujus fuit mira virtutum discretio, quia difficile visum est, et etiam importabile, ut si multiplicitas defunctorum usque ad octogenarium et centenarium, aut forte infinitum numerum [meaning the entries to be read aloud on one day] assidue decedentibus fratribus se extenderet, quod pari modo praebendarum numerus. Nullius enim monasterii substantia, si a prioribus institutus mos servaretur, diu ad hoc sufficere posset. Raris tamen adhuc diebus defunctorum fratrum nomina usque ad quinquagenarium numerum perveniunt.' At the end (*PL* 189, 1050) comes Peter's *dispositio rei familiaris Cluniacensis*: 'Ne vero aliquis miretur hunc infinitum defunctorum numerum certo hoc est quinquagenario numero determinatum, noverit tali hoc factum esse consilio, ne processu temporis crescentes in immensum defuncti vivos expellerent, dum trecentos ad minus vivos et mille fortassis quandoque defunctos parvi Ecclesiae redditus procurare non possent.'

[2] *CF* II 63, p. 204: on this see J. Wollasch, 'Mönchtum des Mittelalters', n. 5 above.

about Elsendis. It is strange enough that such a large necrology should have been written by a woman. We cannot tell why, unless we know who Elsendis was, where she wrote and for whom. We should also have to know where the thousands of additional entries were made before the necrology came to Münchenwiler in the middle of the twelfth century.

However, the editor of the necrology does not attempt to answer these all-important questions: 'Who was Elsendis?' Unfortunately there seems no prospect of anyone being able to answer that question with certainty. Probably she was a member of some monastic community like the many other nuns whose names she recorded. As for which monastery she belonged to, the only way to discover that would be to investigate the circumstances in which she wrote her necrology.'[1] Schnürer also says: 'This [the entry of Abbot Hugh's name][2] proves that the original copied by Elsendis did not go as far as 1109, the year of Hugh's death. The fact that there are some later entries, like those connected with Limoges, can lead one only to the conclusion that they fell within the range of Elsendis' special interest, which was probably centred on Limoges. [There are only two such entries, both mentioned above.][3] The frequent occurrence of the names of nuns in her section of the necrology seems to suggest that, when commissioned to write the necrology for Münchenwiler, she added some entries on her own initiative. Possibly these referred to nuns of some Cluniac priory to which she also belonged. It seems scarcely probable that as early as the eleventh century so many nuns should have lived at Cluny or near to it, and have counted as members of the community.'[4] Although Schnürer himself got little out of his own supposition that Elsendis was a nun in a Cluniac priory, this possibility should be followed up.

For the necrology was not only written by a woman but, as Schnürer points out, it includes the names of a number of nuns. There are more than 150 in the whole necrology, and although only 60 of these were entered by Elsendis, they are of great significance in the matter of identifying the provenance of the necrology. The front of every page has a broad column on the

[1] Schnürer, loc. cit. p. xvii.
[2] See above, p. 148.
[3] See above, p. 153.
[4] Schnürer, loc. cit. p. xxiii.

right for 'monks of our community', and on the left a narrow one for 'associates' (*familiares*). The back of each page has 'monks of our community' on the left, and on the right 'associates'.[1] Since the nuns' names are not in any special place, either at the beginning or end of the list for the day, but interspersed among those of the 'monks of our community', they must have had equal rights with the monks and have counted as members of the same community. So the Elsendis necrology was written in some monastery where there were both monks and nuns, and it must have been used in some such double monastery before it was brought to Münchenwiler. For even in the section added after Elsendis, the nuns' names are scattered about among those of the monks. The question then arises as to whether the necrology written by Elsendis and half a century afterwards used at Münchenwiler originally came from a Cluniac house at all. All the literature about double monasteries either speaks of Cluny's hostile attitude towards them, or else does not mention Cluny at all.[2]

Schnürer believed in the Cluniac origin of the necrology,

---

[1] Schnürer, ibid. pp. xv f., has misunderstood the rubric *nostrę congregationis monachi*. Because Elsendis wrote it first on line 8 of 1 January and followed it with some of her own entries which were added to by later scribes, Schnürer believed the rubric was used to distinguish monks of Cluny from monks of monasteries belonging to the 'congregation' of Cluny. Apart from the fact that he is using the word congregation in a very modern sense, it can be seen, what Schnürer himself missed, that Elsendis wrote again, on the first page of the necrology at the bottom of the left-hand side, the rubric *nostrę congregationis monachi* so that space would be kept in the main column for such as were 'monks of our community'. On the other hand, Elsendis wrote in the right-hand column for 1 January – again after her own entry *Duranni amici nostri* – the rubric (which Schnürer failed to notice) *et aliorum familiarium nostrorum*, and at the bottom of the right-hand side of the first page of the necrology, to complete this column, *et alii familiares nostri*. The twice-given rubrics *nostre congregationis monachi* and *familiares nostri* after Elsendis' entry for 1 January and at the bottom of the page simply serve, it would seem, to differentiate the two columns of the necrology.

[2] S. Hilpisch, 'Die Doppelklöster', in *Beitr. z. Gesch. d. alten Mönchtums u.d. Benediktinerordens*, 15 (1928) 60. On p. 82 he quotes in support of his thesis the statutes of Peter the Venerable, without going further into what Peter himself said about Marcigny: see below, p. 163 and notes. Marcigny is not mentioned by Hilpisch. But see G. de Valous, *Le Monachisme clunisien*, 1 (1935) esp. pp. 382 and 384 f.

since he assumed that it was compiled for Münchenwiler; moreover he also noted the following:

1. The martyrology, which comes before the necrology and was also written by Elsendis, shows Cluniac influence.

2. All the abbots of Cluny up to the lifetime of Elsendis are mentioned: Odo (18.11), Mayeul (11.5), Odilo (1.1) as saints in the martyrology; Berno (13.1) and Aymard (6.10) in the necrology. Amongst the later entries in the necrology are Hugh (29.4), afterwards erased and transferred to the martyrology, Hugh II (9.7), Pontius (29.12)[1] and Peter the Venerable (25.12), who died in 1156.[2]

3. A great many entries in the necrology correspond with the names and days given in the necrologies from the Cluniac monasteries of St Martial of Limoges, St Martin-des-Champs and Notre-Dame de Longpont.

As to the above points:

1. Schnürer gave a list of entries in the martyrology which did not occur in its source, namely a version of the martyrology of Ado of Vienne.[3] They certainly do reveal numerous and unmistakable links with Cluny, as the editor was able to show.[4] They provide a clue, which one cannot afford to overlook, as to the Cluniac origin of the necrology written by the same Elsendis.

2. The abbots of Cluny are mentioned in the martyrologies and necrologies of monasteries in many places which did not belong to Cluny.[5] This somewhat reduces the force of the argument. But one must admit that it would be unlikely for such a complete list of all the abbots to be found in any place not belonging to Cluny.[6]

---

[1] This entry is not obvious. See G. Tellenbach, 'Der Sturz des Abtes Pontius von Cluny und seine geschichtliche Bedeutung', in *QFIAB* 42–3 (1963) 13 ff., esp. pp. 16 f. and 30.

[2] The record of his death occurs in the manuscript as a marginal note because the main column was already full. The same scribe entered for 26.12 the name of a person who died at the end of the twelfth century.

[3] Schnürer, loc. cit. p. 99.

[4] A comprehensive study of the Cluniac *sanctorale* still remains to be made. Meanwhile, see de Valous, op. cit. 1 397 ff. and the general article by P. Schmitz, 'La Liturgie de Cluny', in *Spiritualità*, especially pp. 91 ff.

[5] See Wollasch, 'Mönchtum des Mittelalters', as on p. 143 n. 5.

[6] Schnürer, loc. cit. pp. xxi f.

3. In certain cases the necrology does correspond with those of the Cluniac monasteries of St Martial of Limoges, St Martin-des-Champs and Notre-Dame de Longpont, as Schnürer, relying for the most part on Molinier and Sackur, showed in the notes of his edition; but these cases only concern ecclesiastical dignitaries.[1] It is true that many of them were associated with Cluny, in some cases very closely indeed, and it should be noted too that their names appear in the necrologies of several Cluniac monasteries. Yet we must balance against that the fact that sovereigns, popes, outstanding bishops and famous abbots, according to the extent of their influence, are to be found mentioned in the necrologies of countless communities, without such entries being any indication of the place of origin of the necrologies themselves. If a number of abbots of Cluny are mentioned in a martyrology or necrology, that does not by any means prove that the book comes from a Cluniac monastery.[2] The fact that there are a great many corresponding entries in necrologies from various Cluniac monasteries certainly proves that there was a close common bond between them, which can only be explained by their stemming from the list of deceased at Cluny itself. But the entries of dignitaries in the Elsendis necrology, which Schnürer found recurring in the necrologies of Limoges, St Martin-des-Champs and Longpont, are only a small proportion of the total number. Among some 10,000 entries in the great necrology to which we have kept referring, about 87 represent deceased archbishops and bishops, and about 206 deceased abbots. But what medieval necrologies, and especially those of Cluniac origin, are mostly filled with are the names of thousands of monks of whom nothing is known, though of course some very famous monks are included as well.[3] More

---

[1] The comparisons used by Schnürer, as he himself points out (ibid. p. xix, n. 1) are only extracts from necrologies as yet unpublished.

[2] See above, n. 6.

[3] Thus, for example, among the hundreds of unknown monks entered in the Tegernsee necrology (Clm. 1006: see A. M. Zimmermann, in *Studien und Mitteilungen zur Gesch. d. Benediktinerordens*, 60 (1946) 190–217) one meets, listed according to their anniversaries, Ekkehard of Aura, Fromund of Tegernsee, Frutolf of Michelsberg, Lampert of Hersfeld, Otloh of St Emmeram, Otto of Freising, Wigo of Feuchtwangen and Williram of Ebersberg.

than 9000 monks are mentioned by name in the Elsendis necrology, and the number of secular clergy and laity is relatively small.[1]

To find out whether Elsendis compiled a Cluniac necrology one must get an adequate picture of the degree of correspondence between her necrology and those of Cluniac monasteries, so the only thing to do is to extend the comparison to the enormous number of deceased monks, and check all the names in the various lists. But, as has been said, the monks' names are missing in the published editions of the necrologies of Limoges, St Martin-des-Champs and Longpont.[2] There exists a combined martyrology and necrology of the famous abbey of Moissac,[3] which passed over to Cluny in the eleventh century, but that has never been printed at all. There is nothing for it then but to have recourse to the manuscripts themselves.

Two lines of research have been followed, thanks to Schnürer's helpful observations, in an attempt to ascertain whether the Elsendis necrology really is a Cluniac one. These attempts have fallen far short of systematic and methodical analysis of Cluniac necrologies in general, but they do at least throw light on the question of the origin of the Elsendis necrology. They prove for certain that it stemmed from Cluny. The entries for each day from January 1 to June 30 in Elsendis were collated with those of the earliest necrology on record from St Martial of Limoges.[4] It was found that there were 1709 entries which corresponded

[1] It ought also to be noted that persons other than monks mentioned in Elsendis' copy could be representative. Compatible with this theory is the fact that the fifteen deceased persons on whose behalf a donation was made to Hugh (BB IV 3312) are not recorded. Elsendis did not merely transcribe but edited her entries for use in the community for whom she was keeping the necrology: this is already obvious from the layout of her entries. It also happened from time to time that proportion of which monks, secular clergy and laity appeared in the necrology was changed.

[2] The same goes for many necrology editions (see above, p. 144 f. and n. 10) and is true, also, of the register of the five volumes of necrologies in *MGH*.

[3] For the necrology see pp. 13 ff. of 'Moissac et l'Occident au XIe siècle', *Annales du Midi*, 75 (1963) 13ff. and 345 ff.

[4] Bibl. Nat. MS. lat. 5257. See Molinier, *Les Obituaires*, no. 496; for excerpts from this necrology, together with a later one from St Martial, Limoges, see above, p. 145, n. 2. For a microfilm of this manuscript also I have to thank Mlle M.-T. d'Alverny.

both as to name and date in the first half of the year.[1] This was highly significant, but instead of going on and finishing the year, the section from July 1 to December 26 in Elsendis was checked against another Cluniac necrology, hitherto unknown, from the abbey of Moissac.[2] Elsendis has about 2370 names in these six months and the Moissac one has about 2000 written in several hands: 1276 entries correspond in the two necrologies both as to name and date. So the combined outcome of the collation of Elsendis with the Limoges and Moissac necrologies is a total of nearly 3000 (2985) cases of similar entries. That is to say, two-thirds of the entries in Elsendis are to be found in necrologies belonging to Cluniac monasteries. These two monasteries were situated far apart from each other, they joined Cluny at different times, and their necrologies were drawn up at different periods in the twelfth century. The close correspond-ence between these and the lists in Elsendis cannot be merely accidental; it can only be explained by Cluny, and proves that Elsendis was originally a Cluniac necrology. Schnürer was on right track as far as that was concerned, and having got so far, it is easy to find confirmatory evidence of the fact that Elsendis drew from a Cluniac source.

In the customary of Farfa, which was modelled on that of Cluny, there is a specimen page of entries in the necrology for one day in the year, chosen at random.[3] The model page is not drawn up formally, but simply gives a series of names which

---

[1] These similarities, established from microfilms of the manuscripts, and innumerable other overlaps will first become evident in an edition of the necrologies of Cluniac monasteries. See below, p. 178, n. 4 and Appendix [and the illustrations which appear in the original German article].

[2] On this necrology see above, p. 145, n. 2. See also the remarks of L. d'Alauzier, 'Un martyrologe et un obituaire de l'abbaye de Moissac', in *Bull. de la Soc. archéol. de Tarn-et-Garonne* (1959).

[3] *CF* II 63, p. 183. [See Hunt, *Cluny under St Hugh*, p. 11 and n. 5 for the Cluniac origin of this customary; see above, pp. 56 ff., for Dom Hourlier's use of the description of St Odilo's monastery taken from CF. For other implications following from the Cluniac origin of *CF*], see Valous, op. cit. I 19 ff. and A. Wilmart, 'Le couvent et la bibliothèque de Cluny vers le milieu du Xie siècle', in *RM* 11 (1921). Thus in *CF* II 63, p. 204, the direc-tions for commemorating the dead are those practised in Cluny: see Wollasch, 'Mönchtum' (p. 143, n. 5 above). Many other implications could be cited. The specimen page is in *CF* II 63, p. 205.

can be placed in their original context.[1] The monks mentioned here recur in Elsendis and elsewhere in Cluniac lists. Evidently this specimen page comes from Cluny as well as the rest of the customary. The deceased monks whose names are on it were contemporaries of Abbot Odilo.[2] The formal order of the entries, however, as given in this chapter of the Farfa customary, begins with dignitaries, introduced by the formula: 'The death of Dom . . .',[3] and this is exactly the same arrangement as is found in Elsendis. It corresponds to the form of entries in the Cluny necrology kept in the time of Abbot Odilo but since lost. Further evidence is to be found in a prayer formula given in the manuscript containing the Elsendis necrology. It is a prayer against enemies 'oppressing the domain of this sanctuary'.[4] Schnürer thought that the text might well refer to the skirmishes that harassed the district round Münchenwiler at the time of the contention between King Rudolph of Hapsburg and the duke of Savoy.[5] But the same prayer is to be found in the Farfa customary, which reflects monastic observance at Cluny in the time of Odilo, and was drawn up before 1048, the year of his death.[6] Only the patron named in the prayer for the oppressed church is different in the manuscript with the Elsendis necrology from that in the Farfa customary. The latter gives our Lady as patron,[7] whereas the former refers to 'the church . . . in honour of the holy and undivided Trinity'.[8] So here we

[1] One has to find the anniversary of a King Conrad which coincides with the anniversaries of the four monks whose names are quoted along with his. It was found that the anniversary of King Conrad II of Burgundy (d. 19.10.993), the well-known benefactor of Cluny, and the four names mentioned in *CF* II 63 occurred together and overlapped in the necrologies of Elsendis, St Martial (Limoges) and Moissac (see Wollasch, 'Mönchtum', p. 143 above). Therefore the example of a necrological entry given in *CF* II 63 is taken from 19 October, the king is Conrad II of Burgundy and the four monks were monks of Cluny.

[2] They occur in Elsendis under the rubric *nostrę congregationis monachi* (see below, p. 168) and, since *CF* was written before Odilo of Cluny's death, they were monks of Cluny under Odilo if not under Mayeul as well.

[3] 'depositio domni . . .'.　　　　[4] Schnürer, loc. cit. p. 109.

[5] Ibid.　　　　[6] *CF* II 37, p. 172.

[7] *CF* I: 'Incipit perfectus usus sive ordo'.

[8] Schnürer, loc. cit. p. 109: 'Ecclesia . . . in honore sancte et individue trinitatis'. The dedication to the Trinity mentioned here is important, see below, p. 173.

have a formula dating from as far back as the eleventh century, known to be derived from Cluny and adapted in the twelfth century for use in a particular church by the insertion of a reference to the titular patronage of the Blessed Trinity. We now have evidence from both content and form that the Elsendis necrology was indeed of Cluniac origin.

But where did Elsendis do this work? Which Cluniac monastery can it have been, and how near Cluny was it? Here we come up against a difficulty: this necrology, as we have seen, must have been drawn up in some Cluniac community which included both monks and nuns, and yet literature on the subject represents Cluny as opposing double monasteries. Schnürer too thought it very unlikely that in the eleventh century so many nuns should have lived at Cluny or somewhere near it. Moreover no Cluniac monastery is recognised as having formed one and the same community with a settlement of Cluniac nuns. However, the charters of Cluny point to a monastery of high-born nuns who actually did form one community with Cluny from the spiritual, legal and practical points of view.[1] As there is so far no index to the collection of charters of the abbey of Cluny edited by A. Bernard and A. Bruel, and as no scholarly work on that particular monastery of nuns was available,[2] one can well understand why the editor of the necrology failed to identify it.

This monastery of nuns which formed a single community with Cluny was Marcigny-sur-Loire, a few miles away from Semur-en-Brionnais, the castle from which Abbot Hugh of Cluny came. Right at the beginning of his long abbacy he founded the monastery of Marcigny-sur-Loire with the help of his brother Godfrey II of Semur on the estates of the lords of Semur.[3] There is only one surviving original charter from

[1] BB v 3734, 3804, 3825, 3862. Also the documents of Paray-le-Monial, for example, point in the same direction: U. Chevalier, *Cartulaire du prieuré de Paray-le-Monial* (1891) nos 216, 217, 219.

[2] The painstaking and valuable edition of the cartulary of Marcigny-sur-Loire by J. Richard only appeared in 1957: J. Richard, *Le cartulaire de Marcigny-sur-Loire, 1045–1144* (Dijon, 1957). Nevertheless the old book by F. Cucherat, *Cluny au onzieme siècle* (Autun,⁴ 1885) could have helped Schnürer get onto the right track.

[3] See Richard, *Cart. de Marcigny*, no. 2, p. 2; no. 288, pp. 165 ff.; BB IV 3346, 3347; BB v 3742; letters from Hugh of Cluny for Marcigny: *Bibl. Cl.*

Marcigny; it dates from the year 1102 and affords the following information:[1] 'I, Brother Hugh a sinner, Abbot of Cluny, with God's approval and assistance and the advice and help of our brother, Lord Godfrey of Semur, later himself a monk of Cluny, laid the foundations of this house of Marcigny, humble enough in its beginnings, and a sort of refuge. For it seemed good to us that, just as our holy fathers made provision with their foundation for sinful men to find a haven of salvation at Cluny, if they wished to renounce the world with all its ostentation, so too divine mercy should not deny entrance into the kingdom of heaven to sinful women fleeing here from the snares of the world with heartfelt contrition for their sins. Later we had the main church consecrated by God-fearing men and dedicated to the name of the holy and undivided Trinity, and another built near by, consecrated in honour of the glorious ever-virgin Mary, Mother of God.'[2]

The historical significance of this foundation at Marcigny-sur-Loire has not yet been recognised.[3] Abbot Hugh's mother, sisters, and nieces were nuns of Cluny, and his male relatives held office at the beginning of their ecclesiastical careers as priors of Marcigny.[4] The mother of Peter the Venerable was also a nun there and held the office of cellarer.[5] Marcigny became the abode of the female relatives of abbots, priors and monks of Cluny and Cluniac monasteries.[6] Kings' daughters

322, 491, 493, 497; *Vita Hugonis* (on the founding of Marcigny): *Bibl. Cl.* 420 and 455 ff. See also Valous, op. cit. II 168.

[1] Richard, op. cit. no. 288.   [2] Ibid.

[3] A study of the church is in preparation.

[4] Richard, op. cit. between pp. 240 and 241.

[5] Jorden, 'Das cluniazensische Totengedächtniswesen', see above p. 116; 'Catalogue des noms des dames religieuses du prieuré de Marcigny', in Cucherat, op. cit. p. 237: for the year 1114: 'Raingarde de Semur, veuve de Maurice de Montboissier, morte en 1134!'. She was the mother of Peter the Venerable, abbot of Cluny. See P. Lamma, 'La madre di Pietro il Venerabile', in *Riv. mensile di vita e di cultura*, 54 (Rome, 1958).

[6] Examples are Gisla of Béarn, related to Abbot Hunald of Moissac from Cluny; Aia, mother of Prior Hugh of Paray-le-Monial; Girardus Viridis, monk of Cluny and prior of Marcigny, held in esteem by Peter the Venerable: he had been married to Laurentia Ruffina, and his sister Anna was also a nun at Marcigny. Besides his mother, Peter the Venerable also had two nieces at Marcigny: Margerita and Pontia. Many more examples will appear when the history of Marcigny is properly written. [See p. 422, n. 90

entered as members of the community.[1] When Anselm of
Canterbury had to spend his first year in exile, he met Hugh of
Cluny at Marcigny.[2] His sister was to enter there as a nun.[3]
Héloïse, famous on account of Abélard, was invited by Abbot
Peter the Venerable to end her days at Marcigny, after Abélard
himself had retired into a Cluniac monastery.[4] For on the whole
Hugh had founded this nuns' monastery, attached to Cluny,
not for unmarried women but for mature women of noble

of the original article for supporting evidence and references for all the
details quoted here. Ed.]

[1] Thus Tarasia of Castile: Schnürer, loc. cit. under 9.6: 'Tarasia sanctimonialis'; necrology of St Martin-des-Champs under 9.6: *RHF Obituaires*,
1, 1 (1902) 442: 'Tarasia comitissa'; ibid. (note by Molinier): 'Peutêtre
l'enfante Thérèse de Castille'; Cucherat, op. cit. p. 238 under 1137: 'Sainte
Véraise, fille d'Alphonse, roi d'Aragon'; or Adelaide of Blois (Peter the
Venerable, *Miracula*, 1 26: *PL* 189, 899); Matilda, Hermengard and Emeline
of Boulogne-Blois (Cucherat, op. cit. p. 238 under 1144); for these ladies of
the English royal house, see Richard, *Cart. de Marcigny*, p. 102, n. 2; for others
of royal blood in Marcigny, see Peter the Venerable, *Miracula*, 1 22: *PL*
189, 889.

[2] *Vita Hugonis*: *Bibl. Cl.* 441; see H. Diener, 'Das Verhältnis Clunys zu den
Bischöfen', in *NF* pp. 316 ff.

[3] Diener, loc. cit. p. 316 and note; P. Cousin, 'Les relations de Saint
Anselme avec Cluny', in *Spicilegium Beccense* (Bec-Paris, 1959) p. 446.
R. W. Southern, *St Anselm and his Biographer* (Cambridge, 1963) pp. 9 f.,
contests the theory that the person concerned was sister to the abbot of
Chiusa.

[4] Peter the Venerable, *Epistolae*, lib. vi 21: *PL* 189, 346–53: 'Utinam te
Cluniacus nostra habuisset: utinam te jucundus Marciniaci carcer, cum
caeteris Christi ancillis libertatem inde coelestem exspectantibus inclusisset.
Praetulissem opes religionis ac scientiae maximis quorumlibet regum
thesauris et illarum sororum illud praeclarum collegium, cohabitatione tua
clarius rutilare gauderem . . . concessum tamen est de illo tuo, de illo,
inquam, saepe ac semper cum honore nominando, servo ac vere Christi
philosopho magistro Petro, quem in ultimis vitae suae annis, eadem divina
dispositio Cluniacum transmisit, et eam in ipso et de ipso super omne
aurum et topazion munere cariore ditavit.' After Abélard had died, Peter
wrote to Héloïse telling her about Abélard's monastic life and his last days
in the Cluniac monastery of St Marcel de Chalon-sur-Saône. In Elsendis'
necrology a later hand wrote on Abélard's anniversary, 21 April 1142, under
the rubric *nostrę congregationis monachi*: 'Petrus Magister'. That this is Abélard
is confirmed by entries of the same date in the necrology of Longpont (*RHF
Obituaires*, 1, 1, 523): 'Petrus Abailardus mon. B.D.'; St Victor, Paris (ibid
554): 'It. ob. magister Petrus Abaelardus. Eodem die commemoratio
sollempnis sororum de Paraclito'; see also *PL* 189, 352 and n. 144.

rank.[1] It was to be a refuge for women whose husbands had been killed on the crusades, for some who had been rejected by their husbands and for others whose husbands decided to enter the religious life.[2]

Marcigny was as closely linked to Cluny as it could be. Hugh himself, abbot of Cluny, was its abbot also.[3] Our Lady was regarded as abbess, and for that reason the abbatial throne in church was never occupied.[4] A prior from Cluny administered the property of the sister house at Marcigny, and another was there to attend to the nuns' spiritual needs.[5] As well as this they had a prioress.[6] There were always some old and infirm monks living near the nuns at Marcigny, and this explains why the monastery possessed two churches.[7] In papal documents relating to Cluny, Marcigny appears as its property.[8] Gifts to Marcigny were made over to Cluny and Marcigny.[9] In 1095 Count William of Burgundy donated land to become the property of 'St Peter of Cluny intended for Marcigny'. His mother had entered there as a nun, and he wanted now to become a 'coheir with all the brothers and sisters of Cluny'.[10] So we have evidence that Marcigny-sur-Loire was the place

[1] Hildebert, *Vita Hugonis*: *Bibl. Cl.* 420; Richard, *Cart. de Marcigny*, p. 166, no. 288; Peter the Venerable, *Epist.* lib. VI 39: *PL* 189, 457.

[2] Richard, *Cart. de Marcigny*, nos 109 and 115; e.g. the family of Gerard of Semur: p. 242, 'Girard de Semur', where details of the documentary evidence are given, and nos 201, 202, 291; e.g. Gisla of Béarn (see above, p. 163, n. 6); in general, see Peter the Venerable, *Mirac.* I 22: *PL* 189, 889.

[3] Richard, *Cart. de Marcigny*, nos 7, 15, 269 (document of Pope Urban II, 7 Dec 1095, St Flour: see JL 5603), no. 285; *Index Priorum Marciniaci*, in Cucherat, op. cit. p. 262.

[4] See de Valous, op. cit. I 382.

[5] *Index Priorum Marciniaci*, in Cucherat, op. cit. p. 262.

[6] Ibid. and p. 229.

[7] *Bibl. Cl.* 420 and 455; de Valous, op. cit. I 384. For the two churches, see Richard, *Cart. de Marcigny*, no. 288 and the discussion by J. Hubert in *Annales du Midi*, 75 (1963) 24.

[8] E.g. Victor II, 11 June 1055 (JL 3436; *PL* 143, 803 ff., esp. 805); Gregory VII, 9 Dec 1075, Lateran (JL 4974, L. Santifaller, 'Quellen u. Forschungen z. Urkunden u. Kanzleiwesen P. Gregors VII', 1, in *Studi e Testi*, 190 (1957) no. 107); Urban II, 7 Dec 1095, St Flour (JL 5603, Richard, *Cart. de Marcigny*, no. 269); Calixtus II, 15 Feb 1120, Rome (JL 6816, Richard, *Cart. de Marcigny*, no. 270).

[9] Richard, *Cart. de Marcigny*, nos 102, 170, 176 and pp. xix ff.

[10] Ibid. no. 102.

where reference could be made to both 'brothers *and* sisters of Cluny'.[1]

At the time when Elsendis wrote her necrology Marcigny was the only place where Cluniac monks and nuns formed a single community. This point, once established, is definitive in identifying it as the place of origin of the necrology, which is arranged according to the Cluniac system and includes monks and nuns in one community. This conclusion is therefore practically self-evident.

In the light of all that is known about this sister foundation at Cluny, set up by Abbot Hugh and his relatives, many difficulties about the Elsendis necrology disappear: the fact that it was written by a woman; the names of monks and nuns mixed up together under the heading 'monks of our community'; the astonishing compass of the necrology, whose 10,000 names actually refer to Cluny itself, while out of the 5000 entries by Elsendis almost 3000 recur in the necrologies of the two Cluniac abbeys St Martial of Limoges and SS. Peter and Paul of Moissac; the formal arrangement of the necrology, which is a reproduction of the lost necrology of Cluny from the time of Abbot Odilo; the great number of deceased from as early as the tenth and eleventh centuries who had some connection with Cluny; the martyrology in the same manuscript also written by Elsendis for a Cluniac house, and the prayer formula which can be recognised as Cluniac from its recurrence in the Farfa customary.

Since Marcigny was the first Cluniac house for nuns, and numbered amongst its members mothers, sisters and nieces of abbots of Cluny itself, and of priors and monks both of Cluny and of other Cluniac houses, there is no doubt that it was intimately dependent on the abbey of Cluny. One can quite well see how Elsendis came to compile a combined martyrology and necrology for use in chapter, and how she was offered the one at Cluny as a model. Commemoration of the dead at Marcigny was identical with that at Cluny both as to suffrages

---

[1] Marcigny remained for a long time the sole Cluniac monastery of nuns: see J. Richard, *Cart. de Marcigny*, p. xix and n. 1. Research on the Cluniac monasteries of nuns, as indeed on all nuns connected with the monastic reform movement of the central middle ages, is badly needed. [See Hunt, *Cluny under St Hugh*, pp. 188 for a chapter on Cluniac nuns. Ed.]

and alms-giving. But of course one must bear in mind that Elsendis did not simply copy the book from Cluny,[1] a martyr-ology and necrology dating from the time of Abbot Hugh at the end of the eleventh century and since lost: from some sort of record at Marcigny she added the names of deceased priors, prioresses and nuns of that house to her necrology. Assuming according to the evidence at present available that Marcigny was founded in the 1050s, Elsendis would have had to add the deceased members of this community over about half a century to those given in the book she copied from. If it is true that Marcigny was originally intended for ninety-nine nuns,[2] the number of the deceased recorded by Elsendis – sixty – fits in perfectly with that date.

Finally there are a number of additional proofs that the necrology was written at Marcigny for use in that house. One need only consider the nuns whose names are recorded by Elsendis and by later scribes. To localise them one can compare these entries with those in other Cluniac necrologies, with the reconstructed cartulary of Marcigny or with the catalogue of nuns of that monastery compiled from the archives in the eighteenth century.[3]

There is such a close degree of correspondence between the names of the nuns recorded by Elsendis and later hands in the one necrology, and the necrology entries of other Cluniac monasteries that we can be sure that we are dealing with Cluniac nuns. Collating Elsendis with the necrologies of Limoges and Moissac, we find that of the 150 nuns' names recorded by Elsendis and later hands, 78 – a good half – recur in those of Limoges and Moissac on the same days.[4] So not only the nuns' names recorded by Elsendis were those of Cluniacs but the

---

[1] The very order of Elsendis' entries is sufficient to show this: she places first the names of deceased dignitaries, then noticeably cuts down the number of entries relating to lay persons (see above, p. 159 n. and finally lists the names of monks and nuns indiscriminately together.

[2] See de Valous, op. cit. I 382 and II 221.

[3] Edited by Cucherat, op. cit. p. 233: Richard, *Cart. de Marcigny*, p. xiv, has a rather low opinion of this catalogue. One must first compare all the details of the Elsendis necrology and the necrologies of Cluniac and non-Cluniac monasteries before one can test such Cluniac traditions.

[4] See the Appendix to this article.

names entered later as well. Added to this we have the following evidence. Throughout the earlier necrology of Limoges two
headings are to be found: 'monks of our community' and 'not
of our community' (lit. 'strangers'). Under the first heading a
further distinction is frequently made between *l*, *le* (Limoges)
and *c*, *cl* (Cluny). This form of differentiation is used for bishops,
abbots and monks in the Limoges necrology and also for the
nuns mentioned in it. Of the 78 nuns' names occurring both in
Limoges and Elsendis, 26 are marked with *c* or *cl* in Limoges,
indicating that they belonged to Cluny.[1] Amongst these is a
'Bona, nun c'. In the Elsendis necrology the name Bonafemina
nun occurs once only, and that on the same day (11.4) as a later
insertion. And in the French translation of a lost original in the
reconstructed cartulary of Marcigny (no. 53) a nun called
Bonne femme is mentioned once. So 'nuns of Cluny' meant at
that time at Limoges 'nuns of Marcigny'.

Another possibility is to compare the names of nuns recorded
by Elsendis or later in the necrology with the reconstructed
cartulary of Marcigny-sur-Loire, but here one gets into
difficulties, for the obituary dates are missing in the cartulary,
and it is precisely these that are needed to make the identification absolutely certain. But if one takes the names which occur
once only in Elsendis and then looks for them in the Marcigny
cartulary, twelve are found to coincide.

Elsendis Necrology	*Marcigny Cartulary*
Agia,[2] nun 20.5 (Elsendis)	Agie (1055–96) no. 38
Aia,[2] nun 3.3 (Elsendis)	Aia (after 1065–96) nos. 55, 61
Bonafemina,[3] nun (11.4 (later hand)	Bonne femme (before 1096) no. 53
Cecilia,[2] nun 22.8 (Elsendis)	Cecilia (1088, 1055–65) nos. 2, 15, 19
Gundutta,[4] 30.6 (later hand)	Conducia (1093) no. 28
Hecelina, nun 7.10 (later hand)	Hecelina (before 1115) no. 171

[1] Ibid.

[2] Also entered on the same day in the earlier necrology of St Martial,
Limoges.

[3] Ibid.: 'Bona sanctimonialis c(luniacensis)'.

[4] Ibid.: 'Gunducia'.

Elsendis Necrology	Marcigny Cartulary
Lutia,[1] nun 11.8 (later hand)	Lucie (about 1070) nos. 6, 16
Nazarea, nun 13.3 (later hand)	Nazarée (before 1105)[2] no. 94
Pontia, nun 18.2 (later hand)	Poncie (1055–96, after 1130) nos. 31, 67, 192
Sara,[1] nun 24.5 (Elsendis)	Sara (1078–90) no. 23
Solica,[3] nun 18.2 (Elsendis)	Solicia (1063–93) no. 26
Susanna,[4] nun 13.5 (Elsendis)	Suzanne (1055–96) no. 36

So we have twelve names, each occurring once only in the obituary entries of Elsendis and her successors, all shown here to refer to nuns of Marcigny. Are there likely to be twelve accidental coincidences of that sort? There are two other names which occur once only in the Elsendis necrology: Tarasia (9.6 later hand) and Raingard (25.6 later hand). Corresponding to the first of these is an entry on the same date in the necrology of the Cluniac priory of St Martin-des-Champs: 'Tarasia, countess'.[5] Molinier, who edited this necrology, identified the countess with the Infanta Tarasia of Castile.[6] His idea that Princess Tarasia was a nun at Marcigny is confirmed by the catalogue of the community, which has under 1137 'Véraise, daughter of King Alphonso'.[7] Raingard, whose name was recorded on June 25 in the necrology by someone after Elsendis, was presumably the mother of Abbot Peter the Venerable. He wrote in a letter to Bishop Henry I of Winchester that she had been a nun at Marcigny, where she held the office of cellarer, and that she had died on the feast of St John the Baptist (24.6): he begged the bishop to have suffrages said for her throughout his diocese.[8] We started with those nuns' names which occur only once in the Elsendis necrology, and working from there

[1] Also entered on the same day in the earlier necrology of St Martial, Limoges.

[2] This document must be placed c. 1105 (Richard, Cart. de Marcigny, no. 94: 'vers 1105?') because of a document concerning the same Nazarea according to which on 3.1.1105, on the occasion of her entry to Marcigny, she made a gift to Cluny: BB v 3825.

[3] Occurs on the same day in the earlier necrology of St Martial of Limoges: 'Solicia'.

[4] Occurs on 14.5 in the necrology of St Martial of Limoges.

[5] See above, p. 164 n.   [6] Ibid.   [7] Ibid.   [8] p. 163, n. 5.

we have found that twelve of these can be proved from the Marcigny cartulary to have been nuns of that community, and it has also been shown by collating the necrology with other documents that two other names are those of particularly outstanding members of the community of Marcigny.

The series of 'coincidences' is still not at an end. One would certainly not expect to achieve any very striking results from a comparison of the necrology with the late catalogue of the Marcigny nuns, especially as the reliability of this document as a source of information is dubious, and errors have been detected in it.[1] All the same, a few simple statistical facts may be established in this way. In the necrology of Elsendis there are altogether seven nuns with the name of Ermengard recorded, and six of these occur also on the same days in the earlier Limoges necrology, two of them with the addition of *c* (Cluniac).[2] Now there are also seven nuns called Ermengard in the catalogue of the Marcigny community.[3] Elsendis recorded once only the name of a 'Goilinda, nun' (29.12), and there is no nun of this name among the later additions to the necrology. This fits in with the fact that a 'Golesne' is mentioned once only in the catalogue, and that in 1072.[4] A 'Benedicta, nun' appears once in the necrology as a later insertion on 19.3: a 'Benoîte' is mentioned once only in the catalogue, which records that she entered Marcigny in 1110.[5] The name Albereda (Albareda) occurs three times in the necrology, but only once, on 22.2, with the qualification 'nun'. The catalogue also contains only one Alberée.[6] Three nuns with the name of Petronilla are to be found in the necrology (two entered by Elsendis, one in a later hand).[7] All three recur in the earlier necrology of St Martial of Limoges, two

---

[1] Richard, op. cit. pp. xiv ff.

[2] 8 Aug. The following also occur in the earlier necrology of St Martial, Limoges: 27.12; 8.2; 19.11; 14.12; 19.8 (with the same note); 20.6 (with the letter *c*).

[3] Cucherat, op. cit. under the years 1061, 1068, 1077, 1100, 1101, 1123, 1144. The comparison is only taken as far as 1150 since thereafter the necrology was used in Münchenwiler and the entries from the nuns' catalogue end then.

[4] Ibid. p. 234.   [5] Ibid. p. 236.

[6] Ibid. p. 234 for the year 1078.

[7] Schnürer, loc. cit. under 18.7 and 17.8, both entered by Elsendis. A later hand wrote the 8.7 entry.

of them with the addition of *c* (Cluniac).[1] The catalogue testifies to the entrance of two ladies named Petronilla.[2] So in five cases the necrology corresponds with the Marcigny catalogue with regard to the number of times that a particular name occurs. Moreover the entrance date of these nuns recorded in the catalogue fits in exactly with the chronological distinction in the necrology between the entries of Elsendis herself and those added in the first half of the twelfth century.[3]

A few helpful indications can also be gleaned from a comparison of the necrology with whatever information, however slight, can be pieced together about the priors and prioresses of the monastery of the Holy Trinity at Marcigny.[4] Eight prioresses are mentioned between 1061 and 1138; after that all their names have come down to us but not their dates.[5] The names of five of them occur – some more than once – as names of nuns in the necrology.[6] For anyone unskilled in philology it is difficult to identify with certainty the Latin name corresponding to Alix. Two named Sancia (Sanctia), 1136 and 1138 respectively, and Fradeline, presumably from Spain, are not to be found in the necrology. But the Spanish Queen Sanchia is entered by Elsendis 7.11.[7] A brief of Urban II concerning Marcigny dated 1095 mentions the Prioress Agilmodis,[8] and we may presume that one of the two Elsendis entries of 'Agilmodis, nun' on 30.3 and 13.9 respectively refers to her. Both obituary entries occur also in the earlier Limoges necrology, the one on 30.3 with the addition of *c* (Cluniac).[9]

As regards the priors of Marcigny, we know the names of

---

[1] The letter *c* occurs in both entries corresponding to those of Elsendis. See n. 7.

[2] Cucherat, op. cit. p. 233 (A.D. 1064); p. 237 (A.D. 1124).

[3] In all, the entrance dates of 168 nuns are recorded in the catalogue and cover the years between the mid-eleventh and mid-twelfth centuries, whereas the names of 153 deceased nuns are recorded in the necrology.

[4] Cucherat, op. cit. p. 262 (*Index Priorum Marciniaci*) and p. 229 ('Catalogue des dames prieures de Marcigny') : see Richard, op. cit. pp. xvi ff.

[5] Cucherat, op. cit. p. 229.

[6] Ermengardis–Hermengarde; Gisla–Gille or Giselle or Ghisla or Galsuinda; Johanna–Jeanne; Agilmodis–Agilmolde; Adela–Adèle. See Schnürer's index for each of these names.

[7] See above, p. 164, n. 1, and Richard, op. cit. nos 304, 305, and p. 252.

[8] Ibid. no. 269.   [9] See Appendix.

eighteen of them between 1063 and 1156.[1] All these names appear
also in the necrology, most of them many times over.[2] However
we can be certain about four points. The first prior of Marcigny,
appointed by Abbot Hugh of Cluny himself, was Renco
(Rencho, a senior) mentioned in 1063.[3] Three monks of this
name are recorded in the necrology, two of them by Elsendis
herself.[4] One of the latter would be the right date for Prior
Renco or Rencho. Ulrich of Zell was another prior of Marcigny.
He had come to Cluny from Regensburg and was later to exert
an influence in Switzerland and the Black Forest.[5] He is best
known for the copy of the Cluniac customary which he had
made for William of Hirsau. We know the actual day of this St
Ulrich's death: July 14.[6] On that very day an Odalricus appears
in the necrology as the first entry after Elsendis, and is mentioned among the monks on the same day in the earlier
necrology of St Martial of Limoges. Godfrey III of Semur,
nephew of Hugh of Cluny, entered Cluny in 1088,[7] and his
name also appears on the list of priors of Marcigny.[8] The date of
his death is recorded in the Marcigny cartulary: 24 May 1123.[9]
On May 24 in the necrology we find among the deceased
monks a Ganfredus, written in by a later hand. The last prior
of Marcigny mentioned before 1156 was Turquillus.[10] This name
occurs only twice in the necrology, both times on 6.9 in a later
hand. It can be assumed that one of these entries refers to the
prior. Considering the number of instances already given in
which the Elsendis necrology corresponds with Marcigny's
fragmentary sources, these further points concerning the priors
can scarcely be dismissed as mere coincidences, especially in view
of the tremendous number of monks' names in the necrology.

Before leaving the series of corresponding items in Elsendis

---

[1] Cucherat, op. cit. pp. 262 ff.

[2] Using the names given by Cucherat, ibid., they can be found in
Schnürer's index.

[3] *Bibl. Cl.* 420 and 455.

[4] Schnürer, 'Das Necrologium', under 6.5 and 8.11. (Both entries may
also be found on the same dates in the necrologies of Longpont and Moissac.)

[5] *Vita S. Udalrici prioris Cellensis* (*MGH SS* 12): 'Vita prior': cap. 6 and 7,
p. 253; 'Vita posterior': cap. 20, p. 258 and cap. 34, p. 263.

[6] Ibid.   [7] Richard, *Cart. de Marcigny*, no. 2 and p. 3, n. 2.

[8] Cucherat, op. cit. p. 264; see Richard, op. cit. p. xvii.

[9] See n. 7.   [10] Cucherat, op. cit. p. 266.

and the Marcigny sources, we should recall the prayer formula in the manuscript of the necrology, which Schnürer attributed to Münchenwiler.[1] As has been shown, it dates back to before 1048 and actually comes to us from Cluny via the Farfa customary.[2] Instead of mentioning our Lady, patroness of Farfa, it invokes the patronage of the Blessed Trinity, to whom Marcigny-sur-Loire was dedicated before Münchenwiler was even founded.[3]

A certain amount of correlating of supplementary facts remains to be done on the subject of the origin of the Elsendis necrology, but the evidence we have pieced together so far does at least support our theory that Elsendis used a Cluny necrology, which has since been lost, as model for her own, and that she adapted this for the monastery of Marcigny-sur-Loire with the help of some records there. The whole layout of the manuscript, with its lessons, martyrology, Rule of St Benedict and necrology, points unmistakably to the fact that the Elsendis necrology was part of a book intended for daily use in chapter by the community at Marcigny.[4]

So far we have not attempted to suggest how the manuscript came from Marcigny to Münchenwiler. The most likely explanation is that there was some connection between Marcigny and the descendants of the family which founded Münchenwiler or of some other noble line which had links with it: such a connection might easily have arisen through someone entering Marcigny. But even though this question must remain unanswered, the necrology corresponds with the Marcigny sources. The first hint of the manuscript having been used at Münchenwiler is the deed on fol. 43 dated 1146, though we cannot be sure that it was actually recorded in the manuscript at that date.[5] The later entries in the necrology refer without any doubt to Münchenwiler. In some cases they were written in last on the list for the particular day, when there was scarcely any space left.[6] They occur well within the second half of the

---

[1] Schnürer, loc. cit. p. 109.   [2] See above, pp. 161 nn. 6–8 inclusive
[3] Richard, op. cit. nos 2 and 288.   [4] Schnürer, loc. cit. pp. 1 f.
[5] See above, p. 148.

[6] It would be possible to conclude from the fact that there was so little space left in the necrology that, since it was copied from the more comprehensive commemorations of Cluny itself, it was used for a time at Marcigny and then became dispensable.

twelfth century.[1] So we can fix the date at which the necrology and the whole manuscript were used at Münchenwiler as rather later than the middle of the twelfth century. It is significant that none of the dated documents in the Marcigny cartulary are later than 1144, and that the entries come to an end at about 1150.[2] The rent-rolls in the cartulary do not go any further either.[3] The last date given in the catalogue is also 1150.[4] In the list of prioresses only seven names are given for the period from 1138 to 1370, and there are no dates at all between 1138 and 1370.[5] About the middle of the twelfth century written tradition, hitherto obviously such a living thing at Marcigny, faded out. After existing for about a hundred years the monastery may well have entered upon its first stage of stagnation. This would have coincided with the last years of Peter the Venerable, when Cluny too was on the decline from its unique historical significance.[6] Added to this is the fact that Marcigny's sources tend to run dry from about 1150, and the obit book, now recognised as the Marcigny necrology compiled by Elsendis, also shows the first signs of use at Münchenwiler about the middle of the twelfth century. We must conclude that the great necrology, already nearly full by 1150, was no longer used at Marcigny but could still serve a useful purpose in the little priory in the district of Murten: this would accord with the impression that we get of Marcigny in the middle of the twelfth century and with what we know of Cluny too.

We have now arrived at our goal. We set out to discover in which community the Elsendis necrology was compiled and where it was intended for use before it was actually used at Münchenwiler in the second half of the twelfth century. Even though Cluny's own necrologies are lost and forgotten, we know that we still have the necrology used for chapter in Marcigny-sur-Loire, the Cluniac nuns' monastery, founded by Hugh of Cluny as the first of its kind, and forming a single community with Cluny itself. Further possibilities of research lie open to us.

Molinier was anxious that the necrologies of all Cluniac monasteries should be collated, so that all the names they had

---

[1] See above, p. 149. [2] Richard, op. cit. pp. ii and vii ff.
[3] Ibid. p. xiv. [4] Cucherat, op. cit. p. 238. [5] Ibid. p. 229.
[6] See Tellenbach, 'Der Sturz des Abtes Pontius' (See above, p. 157n).

in common could be extracted to form a partial reconstruction of the 'lost necrology of Cluny'. The remaining names which occurred in only one of the necrologies were supposed to belong to Limoges, St Martial-des-Champs, Longpont etc. This would have been a simple method and a step in the right direction, but knowing where the Elsendis necrology originated, we can follow a safer course and get still further. Collating Cluniac necrologies no longer leads to the dead end of a lost source, but can now be referred back to a definite point in the tradition of Cluny's commemoration of the dead – to the necrology used at Marcigny with its list of Cluny's deceased members. The monks and nuns at Marcigny were brothers and sisters of the community of Cluny Abbey itself. The men's names entered in the Marcigny necrology under the heading 'monks of our community' and the nuns' names interspersed amongst them referred to the community of Cluny Abbey, consisting of both Cluny and Marcigny together. Admittedly we can find a thousand names coinciding with those in the Marcigny necrology in two other Cluniac necrologies alone, but even if we extend the comparison to the necrologies of other Cluniac houses as well, the number of names in common certainly does not come up to the 9000 names of monks of the community of Cluny inscribed in the Marcigny necrology. The latter contains under the heading 'monks of our community' something like twice the number of the common entries found in other necrologies referring to Cluny. All that Cluniac necrologies have in common is reflected in the Marcigny necrology, but it surpasses the others in the extent of its contents and approximates most closely to the necrology in use at Cluny at the end of the eleventh century: indeed one might say that the latter has come down to us in revised form from the hand of Elsendis.[1]

Of course it may be objected that this category of deceased monks in the Marcigny necrology perhaps refers to something more than the actual community of Cluny Abbey, possibly to the whole Cluniac 'congregation',[2] in which case the entries

---

[1] Thus the remark of Schnürer ('Das Necrologium', p. xxxiii) about the necrology – 'in its oldest part it gives us essentially the lost necrology of Cluny' – can now be understood in a finer and more precise sense.

[2] Before the time of the Cistercians a constitutional code concerning affiliation did not exist. The meaning of the term congregation used in the

over and above those common to the other necrologies would refer to the community's own members. This point can be settled definitively only when the Cluniac necrologies have been collated in detail with one another, each of them checked against the Marcigny necrology as well as against those of non-Cluniac monasteries, and all this done in the light of historical evidence.

Meanwhile we can be certain of this much: documentary evidence from Cluny and Marcigny shows that up to the middle of the twelfth century Marcigny had no independent life of its own. From both the legal and economic point of view Cluny and Marcigny formed one monastery.[1] Donors and witnesses for Marcigny, mentioned in deeds, were such for Cluny too.[2] The evidence of the Marcigny necrology fits in with all that can be gathered from deeds as well as from the list of priors and prioresses of that house, provided that monks and nuns there formed a single community. The extensive compass of the necrology itself could hardly be explained except as being derived from Cluny. But there is other supplementary evidence as well, to be found by collating the Marcigny necrology with those of other Cluniac monasteries.

In the earlier necrology of St Martial of Limoges entries are divided, as we have seen, into 'monks of our community' and 'not of our community' (lit. 'strangers').[3] By far the greater number of names come under the first heading, and it is here that the names occurring also in the Marcigny necrology are to

necrology would mean all the monks who had made profession at Cluny whether they lived at Cluny or elsewhere. This meaning is reflected in the words of Peter and Venerable (*Dispositio rei familiaris Cluniacensis*: *PL* 189, 1050): 'nomina fratrum defunctorum congregationis nostrae, hoc est professorum'; and statute xxxii: *PL* 189, 1034: 'defunctis fratribus nostris universis scilicet professis'. From the point of view of the commemoration of the dead this concept of *congregatio nostra* had remained unchanged since the time of St Odilo: see *CF* ii 63, p. 205. On the interpretation of *ecclesia Cluniacensis* and the *corpus ecclesiae Cluniacensis* in the eleventh and twelfth centuries, see Wollasch, 'Mönchtum des Mittelalters' (See above p. 143, n. 2). [See also Hunt, *Cluny under St Hugh*, pp. 154 ff. for an analysis of the concept of the order and congregation. Ed.]

[1] See above p. 165 [and Hunt, op. cit. pp. 186 ff.: chapter on Cluniac nuns. Ed.].

[2] See Richard, *Cart. de Marcigny*, pp. 232 ff.: 'Répertoire biographique'.

[3] See above, p. 159, n. 4.

be found.[1] Many of the hands in which names are entered in the Limoges necrology make a further distinction under the heading 'monks of our community', as stated above, between those marked with *l, le* (Limoges) and those with *c, cl* (Cluny). Even if the heading in this case does include both Cluny and St Martial of Limoges, they are still differentiated from each other by these abbreviations. Further examination shows that only a negligible proportion of the entries marked with *l* recur in the Marcigny necrology, whereas practically all those marked with *c* are to be found in it. Even in cases where a whole series of names correspond in the Limoges and Marcigny necrologies, the ones marked with *l* in Limoges are generally missing in Marcigny. It is obvious from this that the monks (or nuns) of St Martial did not have their names inscribed in the Marcigny necrology unless they had been professed at Cluny, and so counted as members of that abbey.[2]

A comparison of the Moissac necrology with that of Marcigny points in the same direction. Though in many instances they correspond even down to the order of the entries for a particular day, yet in these cases it often happens that the first names given for the day in the Moissac necrology are missing from the Marcigny list. The only explanation can be that the earliest entries in the Moissac necrology refer to monks who lived in this Gascon monastery before it passed over to Cluny in the second half of the eleventh century,[3] and that the Marcigny necrology did not register the names of any Moissac monks save those who served in this southern monastery under abbots from Cluny itself. This conclusion is supported by the martyrology which has come down to us with the Moissac necrology. All notes in it referring to Cluny and its abbots are later marginal additions.[4]

As a result of these preliminary investigations one can say that the Marcigny necrology in the first place gives the names

[1] See the provisional list in the Appendix, pp. 183 below, and the photographs in *Frühmittelalterliche Studien* (see above, p. 143, n. 1) p. 405.

[2] See above, p. 175 n. 2.

[3] See J. Hourlier, 'L'Entrée de Moissac dans l'ordre de Cluny', in *Annales du Midi*, 75 (Toulouse, 1963) 25 ff.

[4] L. d'Alauzier has already proved this (see above, p. 160, n. 2).

of the monks of Cluny from the tenth and eleventh centuries.[1]
Their number suggests an average of about 300 monks in the
community, which tallies with the figures given in the sources.[2]
Over and above those monks, the necrology evidently includes
some from monasteries dependent on Cluny, but only selected
members of such communities. Some abbeys and priories,
founded or reformed by monks from Cluny, later broke away,
and so came to have members of their communities who had no
longer been professed at Cluny.[3] The Marcigny necrology may
well have reckoned as members of the community of Cluny priors
who had been sent out from there to Cluniac houses, revered
seniors, professed at Cluny but living elsewhere. A number
of entries in the Marcigny necrology confirm this impression.[4]

---

[1] See p. 142 above and n. 2.

[2] See Peter the Venerable's reference to the beginning of his abbacy
(*Dispositio*: *PL* 189, 1047): 'Trecenti erant vel eo amplius fratres'; also *PL*
189, 1051.

[3] For example St Maur-des-Fossés: Sackur, *Die Cluniacenser*, 1 247 ff., esp.
p. 249 and note; Hallinger, *Gorze–Kluny*, 11 751; on Longpont, see J. Marion,
Le cartulaire du prieuré de Notre-Dame de Longpont (1879) no. 51.

[4] Roclenus (5.1): the only Roclenus in the Marcigny necr., entered by
Elsendis; also noted on the same day in the necr. of Moissac; a Prior
Roclenus of Romainmoutier is documented for 1041 and 1050: see Egger,
Gesch. d. Cluniazenser-Klöster i.d. Westschweiz, p. 237.

Teobaldus (8.1): entered in the Marcigny necr. by a later hand; necr.
St Martin-des-Champs (*RHF Obit.* 1, 1, 421): 'Depositio domni Theobaldi
huius loci prioris' (d. 1158): see also p. 481.

Petrus (25.1): entered by Elsendis in the Marcigny necr.; entered on the
same day in the earlier necr. of St Martial, Limoges; necr. St Martin-des-
Champs, p. 424: 'Petri prioris de Insula' (= L'Isle-Adam? see de Valous,
op. cit. 11 196).

Petrus (4.2): entered in the Marcigny necr. by a later hand; in the old
necr. of St Martial, Limoges; St Martin-des-Champs, p. 425: 'Petrus prior
de Capi' (Cappy, see de Valous, op. cit. 11 191).

Henricus (20.2): entered by a later hand in the Marcigny necr.; Longpont
necr. under 21.2 (*RHF Obit.* 1, 1, 521): 'Dep. domni Henrici prioris et
fundatoris hujus ecclesiae' (d. after 1125).

Lanzo: (1.4): entered by a later hand in the Marcigny necr.; appears
in the earlier necr. of Limoges with *c(luniacensis)* added; necr. St Martin-des-
Champs, p. 432: 'Deposicio domni Lanzonis'.

Borcardus (24.6): entered by a later hand in the Marcigny necr.; necr.
St Martin-des-Champs, p. 443: 'Burchardus prior de Caritate' (La Charité.)

Vdo (2.8): entry by Elsendis; Longpont necr. under 3.8, p. 525: 'Oddo
prior de Longoponte (d. after 1076).

The heading 'monks of our community' in this necrology really did refer to the abbey of Cluny, only it is not always easy to see how far it was extended to include other Cluniac communities. Of course we must not jump to conclusions, but after comparing the Marcigny necrology with those of Cluniac and non-Cluniac monasteries, and taking historical evidence into account, we certainly realise that the Marcigny necrology was drawn up with a quite definite idea as to who could be reckoned a member of the community of Cluny. And that brings us within reach of the answer to a question of general historical significance which has so far eluded us in our research.

A considerable proportion of all that is written about the middle ages is devoted to the subject of the abbey of Cluny, the Cluniac congregation and the religious and intellectual

---

Landricus (2.9): entered by a later hand in the Marcigny necr.; Longpont necr. p. 526: 'Landricus prior' (d. after 1136).

Johannes de sancto Albano prior Paredi (15.9): entered by a later hand in the Marcigny necr.; Schnürer, loc. cit. p. 69, n. 3: 'a prior John of St Alban's, Basel, appears in a document of 1184 (Trouillat, 1 394)'. But 'prior Paredi' means prior of Paray-le-Monial. The John named here could have come from a church of St Alban (perhaps in Basel) and became prior of Paray-le-Monial. In the cartulary of P.-le-M. ed. Chevalier, nos 221 f., a Prior John of Paray is documented for the year 1180.

Arleius (1.10): entry by Elsendis; in the later necr. of St Martial, Limoges: 'Arleius prior'.

Gemmo (11.10): entry by Elsendis; in the earlier necr. of St Martial, Limoges, and in the Moissac necr.; in the necr. of St Martin-des-Champs, p. 462: 'Gamo prior de Gornaio' (Gournay-sur-Marne: see de Valous, op. cit. p. 195).

Rotbertus (16.10): entry by Elsendis; in the earlier Limoges necr. and in that of Moissac; necr. of St Germain-des-Prés – not Cluniac! (*RHF Obit.* 1, 1, 275): 'Rotbertus congregationis Majoris Monasterii' (Marmoutier near Tours) 'prior sacerdos' (an eleventh-century entry). In the St Germain necr. several entries for the end of the tenth and beginning of the eleventh centuries coincide with Cluniac entries. It is known that Marmoutier was influenced by Cluny under Mayeul: see Sackur, *Die Cluniacenser*, 1 246.

Wilelmus (1.11): entered in Marcigny necr. by a later hand; towards the end of the twelfth century Bernard Iterius wrote in a later Limoges necr.: 'Guillelmus Fabri prepositus de Rossac.

Bernardus (4.12): Elsendis entry; occurs in the necr. of Moissac; and in the later Limoges necr.: 'Bernardus prior'.

Hugo (21.12): entered in the Marcigny necr. by a later hand; in the old Limoges necr. with *c(luniacensis)* added; in the later Limoges necr.: 'Hugo prior'.

monastic movement of the early middle ages which goes under the name of Cluny. 'Cluny' was related in a special way to the German empire,[1] to culture,[2] to the papacy and to the investiture contest.[3] Questions have even been asked about Cluniac poetry,[4] Cluniac architecture[5] and Cluniac sculpture.[6] People have tried to define Cluniac historiography[7] and to discern Cluniac spirituality.[8] But in all these spheres there seems to be difficulty and uncertainty in distinguishing the characteristics of Cluniac monasticism from those of monastic life in general.[9] Even investigation of the internal affairs of the monastery, such as its government, daily life and the habit worn, failed to lead to a clear distinction between Cluniac and non-Cluniac monasticism.[10] The fact that after the rise of the Cistercians there was a tendency in the twelfth century to call all Benedictine monks Cluniacs[11] shows how many difficulties lie in the way of that kind of research. All attempts come up against the question: 'Who were the Cluniacs?' Who were

[1] See Hallinger, *Gorze–Kluny*, II, index: *Reichsgedanke, Reichsmönchtum, Kluny*, (pp. 1035 and 1018 f.).

[2] On Hallinger's position with regard to culture, see J. Leclercq, 'Spiritualité et culture à Cluny', in *Spiritualità*, pp. 385 ff., and 'Pour une histoire de la vie à Cluny', in *RHE* LVII(1962) 385 ff.

[3] See H. Hoffmann, 'Von Cluny zum Investiturstreit', in *Arch. f. Kulturgesch.* 45 (1963) 165 ff.

[4] H. Rupp, *Deutsche religiöse Dichtungen des 11. und 12. Jahrhunderts* (1958) is rather sceptical on the subject.

[5] On the problem of a school of architecture springing from monasticism, see W. Hoffmann, *Hirsau und die 'Hirsauer Bauschule'* (1950); on building at Cluny, see K. J. Conant, 'Cluny 1077–1088' and J. Stiennon, 'Hezelon de Liège, architecte de Cluny III', in *Mélanges offerts à René Crozet* (Poitiers, 1966). [See also K. J. Conant, *Cluny, Les Églises et la maison du chef d'Ordre* (Mâcon, 1968) and his article in the present volume, pp. 77 ff. Ed.]

[6] See D. Grivot and G. Zarnecki, *Gislebertus Sculpteur d'Autun* (Paris, 1960).

[7] H. Wolter, *Ordericus Vitalis. Ein Beitrag zur kluniazensischen Geschichtsschreibung* (Inst. f. europ. Gesch. Mainz, 7, 1955) and P. Lamma, *Momenti di storiographia Cluniacense* (1961).

[8] *Spiritualità*.

[9] See G. Tellenbach, 'Zum Wesen der Cluniacenser', in *Saeculum*, 9 (1958) 370 ff.; see also Leclercq, 'Pour une histoire', as in n. 2 above.

[10] See Hallinger, *Gorze–Kluny*; and, using his method to take the subject further, J. Semmler, 'Die Klosterreform von Siegburg', in *Rhein. Archiv*, 53 (1959) and H. Jakobs, 'Die Hirsauer', in *Kölner Histor. Abhandl.* 4 (1961).

[11] See the work of Wollasch mentioned in n. 5, p. 143 above.

responsible for this thing known to us as 'Cluny'? Of course research work has already been done with this constantly recurring question in mind.[1] But although the right methods were used for identifying individuals, the historians in question lacked access to liturgical manuscripts which, coming as they do from the very heart of the monastic communities of the middle ages, would have answered the question: 'Who were the Cluniacs?' Of course there are many aspects to the problem of who they were and who belonged to them or wished to do so. But if we want to know which individuals were reckoned as members of Cluny according to the judgement of the tenth, eleventh and twelfth centuries up to the rise of the Cistercians, or if we wish to clarify the boundaries between Cluniac and non-Cluniac and know whether the members of Cluny regarded themselves as a self-contained unit within the general monasticism of their age, then there is nothing for it but to collate the necrologies which have survived. What we have learnt from the Marcigny necrology shows that this is the way to find a satisfactory answer to those questions still confronting us. By first collating necrologies, then narrowing this down to Cluniac necrologies and finally concentrating on the one from Marcigny-sur-Loire, we can gain direct insight into the part played by Cluny at the highest level in the church and in secular society.

Among the deceased registered in the Marcigny necrology under the heading 'monks of our community' there are 76 archbishops and bishops; going by the evidence set out above, we may assume that most of them had come from Cluny itself, some of them from other Cluniac houses, and that their contemporaries regarded them all as members of Cluny.[2] In the same way one could show that at least 200 abbots in the earlier middle ages had endeavoured to introduce the monastic life of Cluny elsewhere, and one could tell when and where they had

[1] E.g. Sackur, *Die Cluniacenser*; *NF*; the summary of Leclercq, 'Pour une histoire' (see p. 180, n. 2 above).

[2] As most of the bishops are named without reference to their sees it is necessary to do more research in order to determine the sphere of influence of the ecclesiastics of Cluniac origin. One must start first with the valuable research of H. Diener, 'Das Verhältnis Clunys zu den Bischöfen', in *NF* pp. 219 ff. and build on that. This would probably mean that the number 76 quoted above would rise to nearer 100 when the other Cluniac necrologies are compared with the Marcigny necrology.

laboured.[1] Then, too, by collating the Marcigny necrology with those of other Cluniac and non-Cluniac monasteries, it is possible to ascertain which historical figures in the secular world exerted their influence on behalf of Cluny, whether they were emperors, kings, empresses, queens or members of the higher or lesser nobility. An especially fruitful line of research would be to compare necrologies with charters and chronicles.

The way now lies open before us. The community at Marcigny included female relatives of abbots, priors and monks of Cluny, as well as of its dependent monasteries. Some of the families from which monks at Cluny and nuns at Marcigny came were associated with Cluny and numbered amongst the benefactors of its community of brothers and sisters. Such families certainly formed the closest circle of Cluny's connections in the secular world. For an introduction to them we need not rely entirely on the ill-preserved cartulary of Marcigny, as we have at our disposal the unique collection of documents from Cluny. Actually what has been preserved at Cluny provides the main sources for a history of Marcigny. Our necrology, with its 10,000 names, can now join these extensive and well-documented sources.

Even the late catalogue of the Marcigny community can be of value in carrying out this project of identifying families linked with Cluny and Marcigny through relatives in the community. Such a project would throw light on both the social and geographical backgrounds of members of the community. Although the catalogue is full of errors, the original nucleus is recognisable when compared with the Marcigny necrology. As in the eighteenth century, notes have been added giving details about the noble lineage of the nuns whose names and entrance dates appear in the catalogue. These notes can for the most part be checked against documents from Cluny, and so it really is possible, by collating all available sources, to get a general idea as to which families had the closest and most lasting con-

---

[1] This would be possible because so many abbots are listed in the Marcigny necrology under the rubric *nostrę congregationis monachi* and most of them are also mentioned in the necrologies of other Cluniac monasteries. But, as with the bishops and archbishops, they must first be identified by the systematic comparison of the necrologies themselves and by the further comparison of necrologies with other historical evidence.

nections with Cluny, had provided abbots, priors, monks and nuns for it and for its dependent abbeys and priories, and were, in short, the families from which the Cluniacs came.

And so by means of research on Cluniac necrologies, and thanks to the discovery that the most outstanding necrology of the middle ages comes from Marcigny-sur-Loire, we can at last submit an incomplete but valid answer to the question: 'Who were the Cluniacs?'

APPENDIX: NUNS (*SANCTIMONIALES*) OF CLUNY AT MARCIGNY

The following list consists of the names of those women who appear in the necrology (Bibl. Nat. Paris, MS. nouv. acq. lat. 348; Molinier no. 348; ed. Schnürer in *Collectanea Friburgensia*, n.s. 10 (1909)) with the note *sanctimonialis* or *monacha* or *conuersa*. They are given in alphabetical order and the entries by a later hand are placed in square brackets to distinguish them from the Elsendis entries. The date of decease is placed in round brackets after each nun so that it is possible to find the entries in the necrology and cross-check them with other necrologies and historical evidence. The cross-references given here to the necrologies of St Martial of Limoges and Moissac are complete; references to other necrologies are incidental and not necessarily complete. References to Marcigny documents and the catalogue of nuns is only made when it is very clear indeed that persons mentioned there are the same as those occurring in the necrology. Footnote references are only given where comparison proves that names exactly correspond.

ABBREVIATIONS

SML = occurs in the necrology of St Martial, Limoges.
SMC = occurs in the necrology of St Martin-des-Champs.
  L = occurs in the necrology of Notre-Dame de Longpont.
  M = occurs in the necrology of Moissac.
  [ ] = entry by a later hand than that of Elsendis.

Adaleida	(9.2)	SML: Alaidis sanctimonialis
Adaleida	(24.6)	SML

G

[Adaleida]	(26.9)	SML
[Adaleidis]	(11.8)	SML
[Adeleyda]	(16.1)	SML with *c(luniacensis)* added; M
Adeleyda	(29.8)	SML with *c(luniacensis)* added; M
Alaida	(27.7)	
Adalgardis	(25.6)	SML
[Adalgardis]	(28.7)	
Adalgardis	(11.8)	
[Adalmodis]	(23.4)	SML: Agilmodis sanctimonialis
[Adaltrudis]	(24.4)	SML with *c(luniacensis)* added
Adaltrudis	(12.5)	M
[Adela]	(21.10)	L
Elsendis	(no date)	
Agia	(20.5)	SML; *Cart. de Marcigny*, no. 38[1]
Agilmodis	(30.3)	SML with *c(luniacensis)* added; *Cart. de Marcigny*, no. 269[2]
Agilmodis (see A. under 30.3)	(13.9)	SML; M (under 12.9)
Agina	(20.10)	SML with *c(luniacensis)* added; L
Aguina	(9.1)	
[Agnes]	(22.4)	SML
Agnes	(18.8)	
Aia	(3.3)	SML; *Cart. de Marcigny*, nos. 55 and 61[3]
[Aya]	(27.12)	
[Albereda]	(22.2)	Catalogue of the nuns of Marcigny under A.D. 1078[4]
Aldegardis	(14.7)	SML
[Alexandra]	(27.3)	*Cart. de Marcigny*, no. 266[5]

[1] Only one Agia appears in the necrology, only one in the Marcigny cartulary, and the dates of the two references overlap.

[2] Of the two nuns entered by Elsendis named Agilmodis it may be assumed that one can be identified with Agilmodis, prioress of Marcigny *c.* 1100, who is named in the cartulary. See Richard, *Cart. de Marcigny*, p. 237: 'Aumode'; see also above, p. 171.

[3] On Aia, see above, p. 163, n. 6.   [4] See above, p. 170 and n. 1.

[5] There is only one Alexandra mentioned in the Marcigny cartulary who had a definite connection with Marcigny at the time of Elsendis: the request of the dying Alexandra, wife of Stephanus Buterius, to be remembered in the prayers of the community of Marcigny. The ascribing of the document to 1139 agrees with the above entry by Elsendis. Alexandra is

[Alleldis]t[1]	(14.3)	
(marginal)		
Amelia	(18.8)	SML with rubric *officium*
Amiza	(13.9)	SML with *c*(*luniacensis*) added
[Ancilla]	(16.5)	
[Anna]	(23.8)	SML with *c*(*luniacensis*) added
Anna	(6.12)	M
[Aresta]	(4.7)	SML
Arsenia	(10.1)	SML; M: Arsena deuota
[Atila]	(7.8)	
[Atila]	(8.8)	SML
[Attila]	(10.8)	
[Aufrisa]	(8.1)	SML; M (under 7.1: Auria sanctimonialis)
Auxilia	(12.7)	SML
Aua	(10.1)	
[Aua]	(8.2)	
(see also under Eua)		
[Beatrix]	(22.4)	SML (under 21.4)
[Beatrix]	(2.9)	L: Beatrix comitissa
conuersa		
Beatrix	(16.9)	SML
[Benedicta]	(19.3)	Catalogue of the nuns of Marcigny under A.D. 1110[2]
[Benefacta]	(18.4)	SML with *c*(*luniacensis*) added
[Benefacta]	(19.5)	
[Berta]	(22.4)	
Berta	(5.7)	
[Berta]	(27.10)	SML (under 26.10) with *c*(*luniacensis*) added
[Bligardis]	(20.1)	SML (under 19.1: Blitgardis) with *c*(*luniacensis*) added

described in the necrology as *monacha*, not *sanctimonialis*: perhaps this is connected with the fact that the reference in the cartulary makes no mention of Alexandra actually entering Marcigny.

[1] Because of the way this record is placed among the names for that day, and because of the attached *t*, it is known that this entry was made at Münchenwiler in the second half of the eleventh century.

[2] See above, p. 170 and n. 6.

[Bonafemina]	(11.4)	SML: Bona sanctimonialis with *c(luniacensis)* added; *Cart. de Marcigny*, no. 53: Bonne femme[1]
Cęcilia	(22.8)	SML; *Cart. de Marcigny*, nos 2, 15, 19[2]
[Christina]	(6.4)	
Chunigundis	(20.8)	
Constantia	(20.6)	
Constantina	(10.11)	
Diua	(11.5)	SML on the *peregrini* page[3] (under 12.5: Dina sancti-monialis)
[Domnamaior]	(5.10)	SML: maiori sanctimonialis
[Eica]	(9.1)	SML: Eyca
[Elca]	(5.6)	
[Eldeburgis]	(29.10)	SML (under 28.10) with *c(luniacensis)* added; M: Adalburgis

(Elisabeth: see under Helisabeth)

[Emelina]	(30.3)	
[Emma]	(24.3)	
[Emma]	(21.4)	
[Ermengardis]	(8.2)	SML
[Ermengardis] conuersa (marginal)	(19.3)	
[Ermengardis]	(20.6)	SML with *c(luniacensis)* added; L
Ermengardis	(19.8)	SML with *c(luniacensis)* added
Ermengardis	(8.10)	
[Ermengardis]	(19.11)	SML

[1] See above, p. 168; the document is one of the charters of the Marcigny nuns: see Richard, *Cart. de Marcigny*, no. 16, and p. v f.

[2] This entry by Elsendis could refer, as regards time, to Cęcilia, daughter of Godfrey III of Semur and great-niece of Hugh of Cluny, who with her mother and sisters became a nun at Marcigny in 1088 (*Cart. de Marcigny*, nos 2 and 15); or to Cecilia, daughter of Guichard de Bourbon-Lancy (*Cartulaire*, no. 19), who was descended on the maternal side from the house of Semur (see Richard, *Cart. de Marcigny*, p. 243 under Guichard I de Bourbon-Lancy) and who entered Marcigny in the second half of the eleventh century.

[3] See above, p. 168.

[Ermengardis]	(14.12)	SML
Ermengardis	(27.12)	SML
[Ermentrudis]	(9.11)	
[Eua]	(4.5)	SML on the *peregrini* page:[1] eua
(see also under Aua)		o(*biit*)
Fascia	(11.2)	
[Florentia]	(23.12)	
(marginal)		
[Fredeburgis]	(8.6)	
(marginal)		
Fulcheldis	(21.6)	SML;M
[Gandalmodis]	(30.4)	
(see also under Wandalmodis)		
Geretrudis	(4.6)	SML
[Girberga]	(6.1)	SML
Girberga	(12.7)	
[Gireldis]	(5.1)	
[Gisela]	(7.2)	
(marginal)		
[Gisla]	(12.8)	
conuersa (marginal)		
[Gisla]	(28.11)	
[Gisloara]	(31.12)	SML: Gislouara
[Gŏda]	(29.3)	
(marginal)		
[Goda]	(29.10)	SML (under 28.10) with *c*(*luniacensis*) added; L
Goilinda	(29.12)	Catalogue of the nuns of Marcigny under A.D. 1072[2]
[Guinberga]	(12.10)	SML (under 13.10)
[Gundutta]	(30.6)	SML: Gunducia; *Cart. de Marcigny*, no. 28: Conducia[3]
[Hazika]	(13.6)	

[1] See above, p. 168.

[2] See above, p. 170 and n. 6.

[3] The name Gundutta occurs only once in the necrology; the name Conducia only appears once among the nuns' names in the cartulary, and once in the catalogue of nuns – under the year 1093: it is misrepresented as N. de Conducie. The necrology of St Martial of Limoges names on 27.6 a 'Gunduncia c(luniacensis) sanctimonialis'.

[Hecelina]	(7.10)	*Cart. de Marcigny*, no. 171[1]
[Helisabet]	(16.1)	SML
Helisabeth	(22.7)	SML with *c(luniacensis)* added; M
[Helisabet]	(2.11)	
[Hresendis]	(7.1)	
(marginal)		
Humberga	(12.4)	SML with *c(luniacensis)* added
[Hvnberga]	(20.3)	SML with *c(luniacensis)* added
(see also under Vberga)		
Hymineldis	(19.4)	
[Ita]	(13.4)	
(marginal)		
[Itta]	(7.3)	
[Itta]	(11.8)	
[Iniuliardis]	(30.3)	SML: Ingilgardis with *c(luniacensis)* added
[Isingardis]	(15.9)	SML with *c(luniacensis)* added
Joceldis	(8.3)	
[Judinta]	(24.8)	
[Jutta] t[2]	(28.5)	
[Lutia]	(11.8)	SML; *Cart. de Marcigny*, nos 6 and 16[3]
[Mathildis]	(20.5)	
[Mathildis] t[2]	(14.8)	
Mathildis	(25.8)	
[Matildis]	(11.1)	
[Nazarea]	(13.3)	*Cart. de Marcigny*, no. 94; BB v 3825[4]

[1] The single appearance of the name Hecelina in the necrology points to the single mention of a Hecelina in the cartulary of Marcigny. The latter refers to the mother of Archbishop Hugh d'Amiens of Rouen, who became a monk of Cluny. There is a coincidence, time-wise, between the necrology entry and the cartulary reference.

[2] Because of the way this record is placed among the names for that day, and because of the attached *t*, it is known that this entry was made at Münchenwiler in the second half of the eleventh century.

[3] See above, p. 169. The Lucia in the cartulary was the daughter of Godfrey II of Semur, niece of Abbot Hugh of Cluny.

[4] See above, p. 169 and n. The name Nazaria occurs twice in the Marcigny cartulary: nos 90 and 94. As Elsendis entered the Nazarea of the necrology, it is likely that the latter corresponds to the Nazarea named in

[Oda]	(14.7)	
Odila	(28.2)	SML
(see also under Vtilia)		
Ozin	(12.4)	
[Petronilla]	(8.7)	SML
Petronilla	(18.7)	SML with c(*luniacensis*) added
Petronilla	(17.8)	SML with c(*luniacensis*) added; M (under 18.8)
[Pontia]	(18.2)	
Raina	(16.5)	SML; BB v 3734[1]
[Ráina]	(1.8)	
(see above under Raina)		
[Raingardis]	(25.6)	Letter from Peter the Venerable in Jorden, loc. cit. p. 116 and catalogue of the nuns of Marcigny A.D. 1114[2]
[Rangisia]	(7.8)	SML with c(*luniacensis*) added
Reginlindis	(3.6)	SML
[Restibilia]	(21.4)	SML: Restabilia sanctimonialis
[Rixendis]	(29.9)	
[Rotoldis]	(21.7)	SML
[Rotrudis]	(20.7)	
Rumodis	(22.8)	SML: Raimodis with c(*luniacensis*) added
Sara	(24.5)	SML: Sarra; *Cart. de Marcigny*, no. 23[3]
[Sofia]	(20.6)	

charter no. 94, who seems to be identical with the Nazarea named in BB v 3825 (A.D. 1105), since in both documents Nazarea's son Bernard is referred to; both documents mention the donation of property *in Culmines* and Agano of Charolles appears in both lists of witnesses. I am therefore inclined to retract what I said elsewhere (*Annales du Midi*, 75 (1963) 19, n. 16) about the Nazareas mentioned in nos 90 and 94 of the cartulary not being identical.

[1] We learn from this charter that 'Raina' wanted to become a nun at Marcigny. It is likely, therefore, that she can be identified with one of the two Rainas mentioned in the necrology.

[2] See above, p. 163, n. 5.

[3] There is only one Sara in the necrology and one in the Marcigny cartulary (in a document belonging to the nuns' charters). Both references come from the same period.

Solica   (18.2)   SML: Solicia sanctimonialis;
                                       Cart. de Marcigny, no. 26[1]

Stephana   (24.4)   SML with *c(luniacensis)* added; M
[Stephana]   (6.8)
[Stephana]   (24.10)   SML with *c(luniacensis)* added
Susanna   (13.5)   SML (under 14.5); *Cart. de*
  (see also under Usanna)   *Marcigny*, no. 36[2]
[Tarasia]   (9.6)   SML, SMC: Tarasia comitissa;
                                       catalogue of nuns of
                                       Marcigny under A.D. 1137[3]

[Tetcelina]   (13.10)   SML
Vberga   (10.12)   SML
  (see also under Humberga)
Vfficia   (9.10)
[Vlgardis]   (12.5)   SML
Usanna   (9.10)
  (see also under Susanna)
Vtilia   (28.4)
  (see also under Odila)
Wandalmodis   (16.9)   SML
  (see also under Gandalmodis)
Wandalmodis   (26.9)
[Willelma]   (20.8)
Williza   (13.2)
[Witburgis]   (1.3)
  (marginal)

---

[1] The single mention of a Solicia in the necrology corresponds with the single reference to a Solicia in the cartulary: the references belong to the same period, and the charter belonged to the nuns.

[2] What has been said of Sara and Solicia on p. 189 nn. 3 and 1 above is true also of Susanna.

[3] See above, p. 164, n. 1.

10 The Crusading Idea in Cluniac Literature of the Eleventh Century[1]

E. DELARUELLE

Noteworthy as Cluny's role may have been in the eleventh century as far as strictly religious history is concerned, it is possible that it has been overestimated in the fields of political, social and literary history. For the last thirty years certain historians have been infected with what one can only call 'panclunism'. Cluny has been given the credit for the creative vitality of the age, and to her has been attributed a decisive influence over the 'Gregorian reform', the development of the pilgrimage to St James of Compostela and the redaction of the epic songs and heroic poems of chivalry. Just as there has been a tendency to represent the church as hitherto a spiritual society but now organising herself into a juridical and political entity, or to portray a holy pope like Gregory VII as evolving

[1] [Translated from 'L'idée de croisade dans la littérature clunisienne du XIe siècle et l'abbaye de Moissac', in *Annales du Midi*, 75 (Toulouse, 1963) 419–39. Ed.]

Sources. On St Mayeul, *De vita b. Maioli Libellus*: *PL* 142, 943–62, is the most interesting, not only as regards its subject but also from the point of view of hagiography. *PL* 142 contains the main material on St Odilo: the life by Jotsald, cols 895–912; his letters, 939–42; his poems, including the *Epitaphium Ottonis I magni imperatoris*, essential to our inquiry, 961–8; his sermons, 991–1036, which were written, it seems, for the community at Cluny and which have been partially translated in Raymond Oursel, *Les saints abbés de Cluny* ('Coll. Les écrits des saints', Namur, 1960) pp. 89–161. Several lives of St Hugh were produced: most of them are edited in *AA SS* April III 641–65; most relevant are, perhaps, the *Analecta*, pp. 665–70. All this material is also in *PL* 159, 845–928, plus the correspondence of Hugh (cols 927–46), with many references to other works. Beside the history of the great abbots and their work must be set the daily life of the monastery by a scrutiny of the charters, especially BB IV. R. Glaber, *Historiarum libri V*: *PL* 142, 611–98, is particularly significant because of his one-time connections with Cluny, where he stayed. On the problems of whether Glaber was

into an expert on war and finance,[1] so too, we are told, did the
monastic institution, pressurised by circumstances and attempting to meet a variety of demands, become more and more
involved with the world.

Cluny has appeared along with other candidates for the
honour of having originated the crusades. The case in favour of
this theory has been made out at its strongest by the historian
Anouar Hatem, and it will be useful to quote him in order to
show the opportuneness of the critical investigation on which
we are embarking. 'Another factor which contributed even more
than did the papal pronouncements to the realisation of the
crusades', he writes, 'was the influence of Cluny . . . the holy

a Cluniac, what is meant by Cluny, what was the difference between the
Burgundian abbey and other Benedictine monasteries, what was the spirit
of Cluny, see J. Leclercq, 'Pour une histoire de la vie à Cluny', in *RHE*
LVII (1962) 786 ff.

Secondary Works. Unfortunately no work has been specifically devoted
to our theme. One can have recourse to the general histories of the
Benedictine order, notably E. Sackur, *Die Cluniacenser*, II 101–13; Dom P.
Schmitz, *Hist. de l'Ordre de saint Benoît*, I, 2nd ed. (Maredsous, 1948) pp.
234–46, with a map in addition to the text: no. 6; P. Jardet, *Saint Odilon,
sa vie, son temps, ses oeuvres* (Lyons, 1898) is still useful. More recent is the
work of G. Gaillard, 'La pénétration clunisienne en Espagne pendant la
première moitié du XIe s.', in *Bull. trimestr. du Centre internation. d'études
romanes* (1960) 8–15; similarly 'Cluny et l'Espagne dans l'art roman du XIe
s.', in *Bull. hisp.* LXIII (1961) 153–60; E. Magnien, 'Le pèlerinage de Saint-
Jacques de Compostelle et l'expansion de l'ordre de Cluny', ibid. (1957)
III 3–17. The article by R. d'Abadal i di Vinyals, 'L'esperit de Cluny i les
relacions de Catalunya amb Roma i la Italia en el segle X', in *Studi medievali*,
3rd ser. II 3–41, does not touch at any point on the problem of the crusades.

On Spain at this time, see the important work by R. Menendez Pidal,
La España del Cid, 4th edition, completely revised, published in *Obras
completas* (Madrid, 1947) esp. vol. I, and in II the genealogical table of various
Spanish dynasties, and maps. On the idea of the crusade, see the remarkable
work by Carl Erdmann, 'Die Entstehung des Kreuzzugsgedankens', in
Forschung z. Kirchen- u. Geistesgesch. VI (Stuttgart, 1935), where the gradual
emergence of the idea in the west is examined together with the rise of a
new spiritual consciousness and the Christianisation of war in a society
transformed by the Gregorian reform: esp. pp. 60 ff. on the Cluniacs before
the holy war, pp. 88–91, 124–7 on the Spanish crusades. Reference will also
be made to the present writer's article 'Essai sur la formation de l'idée de
croisade', in *Bulletin de littérature eccl.* (=*BLE*) (1941).

[1] As does Erdmann, loc. cit. pp. 161 and 141. We are not concerned here
with the veracity of these particular views.

war was the constant preoccupation (of the Cluniac abbots)'
who incited the whole of the west to attack the Moslems, particularly in Spain, where Cluny 'was to play a major part in the
liberation' of the country.[1] Cluny's activity in the matter, the
historian continues, was not confined to exhortation from the
monks designed to inspire the lords and knights of their
acquaintance to take the crusaders' vow: Cluny was responsible
also for maturing the very idea of the crusade, for it was in the
course of visiting Cluniac houses that Pope Urban II consecrated
at Clermont 'the ecclesiastical doctrine maintained by Cluny
from her foundation'. Thus Cluny 'prepared the way for the
holy wars in a sense analogous to that in which the Encyclo-
pedists prepared the French Revolution', by a thoroughgoing
education of minds.[2]

Exaggerated as these ideas may seem at first sight, they
reappear, sometimes in attenuated form, in the works of other
experts in the field: Chalandon[3] and Boissonnade,[4] not to
mention Joseph Bédier, who associates the crusades in Spain

[1] Anouar Hatem, *Les poèmes épiques des croisades, genèse, historicité, localisation,
Essai sur l'activité littéraire dans les colonies franques de Syrie au Moyen-Âge*
(Paris, 1932) pp. 43, 45, 52. These views on the origin of the crusades
occasionally further the 'panclunism' referred to above: 'for two centuries
this Burgundian institution ruled the papacy unceasingly' (p. 45). The truce
of God was 'par excellence a Cluniac institution' (p. 76).

[2] Ibid. p. 71. Crusade specialists as informed and sound as P. Rousset,
Les origines et les caractères de la première croisade (Neuchâtel) p. 16, have felt it
necessary to discuss these theses, which we also have to consider to begin with.

[3] Ferdinand Chalandon, *Histoire de la première croisade* (Paris, 1925) pp.
12, 14.

[4] P. Boissonnade, *Du nouveau sur la Chanson de Roland* (Paris, 1923) p. 11.
It is at the point where he makes the most decisive and delicate statements
that he too often fails to give references. On p. 12, for example, he says that
'monks and clerks encouraged these matrimonial alliances' between France
and Spain, which were decisive in the idea of a holy war. On p. 22 he refers
to the crusade of Barbastro as the 'first that the papacy organised under the
influence of French monks'. The same author returns to the problem and
underlines even more heavily the role of the Cluniacs in 'Cluny, la papauté
et la première grande croisade internationale contre les Sarrasins d'Espagne,
Barbastro (1064–1065)', in *Rev. des questions hist.* CXVII (1932) 257–301. His
conclusions have been challenged by A. Fliche, *Histoire du Moyen Âge*, II:
L'Europe occidentale de 888–1125 (G. Glotz, 'Histoire générale', Paris, 1930)
p. 551, n. 12 and by Erdmann, op. cit. p. 61, who speaks of 'pure fantasy'.
But neither of these specialists discusses the subject at any length.

with *Turpin's Chronicle* and with the pilgrimage to Compostela, for both of which Cluny is held responsible.[1]

There can be no denying that Cluny was deeply implicated in the affairs of the day and that her great abbots did sometimes intervene in politics. It is moreover incontestable that plenty of individual crusaders in Spain, particularly those who came from Burgundy and Poitou, kept up friendly contacts with monks at Cluny and elsewhere, and it is probable that in many cases, even if we cannot point to a definite example, monks may have been responsible for a knight's decision to go to Spain, or later to the Holy Land. Further, we know that monasteries benefited from the booty brought back from these expeditions; a special study has been made of the case of the Moslem gold at Cluny.

It is equally clear that we must avoid the error of attributing to the Cluniac monks at this time the ideas of a different age by taking it for granted that they would on conscientious grounds have condemned the holy war in the name of the gospel. The *Libellus* that tells the story of how Mayeul was taken prisoner by the Saracens is in no way shocked by the fact that this misfortune on the part of the man of God led to the launching of a small military expedition.[2]

We may even go further and concede that Cluny contributed powerfully to the formation of the typical Christian soldier, a new figure on the stage of history and soon to be the hero of the crusades. Far from regarding secular warfare with disapproval, as earlier monks had done with their pun on *militia* ('military service') and *malitia* ('wickedness'), Cluniac writers extolled the virtues of the knight who used his sword in the service of the church, and even praised his prowess or his worldly accomplishments: to the examples already given could be added the *Libellus* eulogising Mayeul's father and the *Deploratio* of Jotsald.[3] The more fundamental question, however, is this: did

[1] J. Bédier, *Les légendes épiques, Recherches sur la formation des chansons de geste*, III (Paris, 1912) pp. 368–72, 384. See also IV 462, which inspired E. Petit in his *Histoire des ducs de Bourgogne*.

[2] *De vita b. Maioli Libellus: PL* 142, 959–60.

[3] Ibid. cols 947, 951, 960; *De vita S. Odilonis*, col. 897, and I, II. See *BLE* (1944) 24–8, where I have studied the new kind of warrior, very different from the plundering baron. A biography such as the *Vita Geraldi Auriliacensis* of St Odo contributed to the new concept. Here one ought to add a note on the famous satirical poem by Adalbert of Laon on Cluny and Odilo: it has

Cluny play a part in that amazing evolution of minds and of spiritual outlook which made secular warfare acceptable to clerics and monks hitherto dedicated to peace, which indeed went further and regarded war as a holy enterprise harking back to the Old Testament, and saw the warrior as the typical Christian hero, heir to the martyr of the primitive church and to the ascetic of the early middle ages?

I. THE CONSTANT SILENCE OF THE TEXTS

Tempting as it may be to assign to Cluny the role for which she has been cast by the historians just mentioned and so to give a more satisfactory account of the profound unity and efficacy of the Gregorian reform, the fact remains that the texts alone can provide evidence as to the true place the crusade occupied in Cluniac thinking. Abundant as they are at this period, however, the texts maintain persistent silence on this question.

CORRESPONDENCE BETWEEN ABBOTS AND SPANISH KINGS

Boissonnade laid considerable stress on the contacts between the Spanish monarchies and Cluny, particularly in the time of Sancho the Great, who sent Paternus to Burgundy to be trained with a view to his transforming San Juan de la Peña into a sort of seminary for Spanish clergy on his return. After detailing the

been edited and translated with a commentary by G. A. Hückel, 'Les poèmes satiriques d'Adalbéron', in *Mélanges d'Histoire du Moyen-âge* (published under the direction of Luchaire, 'Bibl. de la Faculté de lettres de Paris', XIII, Paris, 1901) pp. 49–184. For Hückel, the appearance of Robert the Pious marked a new monastic policy: the king calling into public life the monks, whose numbers were increasing, especially the Cluniacs; the *Carmen ad Robertum* denounced this policy, condemning at the same time Odilo and the new style of life at Cluny: 'I am a soldier now. . . . No, I am no longer a monk but I fight under the orders of a king, Odilo, king of Cluny' (vv. 113–15). But this poem is too old – the MS. comes from the early part of the eleventh century (p. 124) and the satirical character is too marked for us to be able to find in the extract evidence relating to the idea of a crusade in Cluny: if the Saracens are involved (vv. 120 ff.) it is in connection with a raid in the diocese of Tours and the inspiration is burlesque, which affects the way this pamphlet must be interpreted: not too seriously.

foundations made at the time in Spain for the benefit of Cluny, the historian continues: 'the French clergy used their institutions in France as so many propaganda centres for the Spanish crusades'.[1] But this is jumping to conclusions, for in the famous privilege of 1033 only a vague reference is made to the Spanish crusades.[2] The king claims the right to 'care for ecclesiastical affairs' (which is a strikingly un-Gregorian notion: we will come back to the point later) and goes on to list his conquests: 'I have to a great extent overcome and reduced the despicable race of Saracens and suitably enlarged the limits of our domains.' Yet this hero of the reconquest, far from dwelling on these glorious claims which could have been the starting point for an epic celebrating the valiant knight as the supreme embodiment of Christian holiness, turns rather to consider evangelical perfection, and on learning that it is pursued at Cluny sends Paternus there to study monastic customs. Throughout this long document there is no further mention of the crusade.

The same is true of the letter from Alphonsus, king of Spain, to Hugh the Great.[3] The king expresses his gratitude to Hugh not for having inspired the wars of reconquest in Spain, nor for sending him numerous crusaders from Burgundy or Poitou, but for sending him monks.[4] He will double his alms to Cluny in future and he makes testamentary provision for this, but all his

---

[1] Boissannade, *Du nouveau*, p. 12.   [2] BB IV 2891.

[3] *PL* 159, 938. One could cite numerous examples: BB 3441 and 3562, where the friendship between King Alphonsus and St Hugh is referred to and which makes these letters something very different from a political correspondence. 3442, 3452, 3492, 3507, 3508, 3533, 3540, 3541, 3554, 3582, 3623: all from a great variety of benefactors, Countess Tarasia, Urraca, viscount of Cardona, to say nothing of King Alphonsus himself, who seem not to dream of linking their donations to political or military considerations. No. 3509 deserves special mention because of its interest for Moissac iconography, since the preamble of the document contains a long eulogy in honour of the triune God, 'quem viginti et quatuor seniores ter sanctificant'. The text is taken almost exactly from the Apocalypse.

[4] Boissannade, 'Cluny, la papauté', p. 258, assigned an exceptional role to St Hugh, saying he had influenced his own family in the direction of a Spanish crusade. Ibid. p. 274 for a lengthy study of the provenance of the French contingents in the Barbastro expedition, drawing attention to Guy Geoffrey and the presence of Hugh of Cluny in districts of the west: all this is quite useful in modifying the thesis of E. Petit, who tends to attribute the Spanish crusades above all to the Burgundians.

generous conduct has no motive other than a religious one.[1]

CORRESPONDENCE BETWEEN ABBOTS AND POPES

The same impression is given by the correspondence between Hugh and Gregory VII, which is of greater importance because more abundant. Not merely does Hugh fail to appear in these letters as the man who inspires the papal policy, who shares all his friend's preoccupations and who is ready for continual collaboration particularly in the matter of the holy war; he even finds himself being reproached several times for his lack of interest in the cause of the church. As far back as 1074 Gregory expresses his surprise that Hugh has not yet come to Rome, reminds him of the matters for which he, Gregory, is responsible, and says how much he relies on Hugh – but what he relies on is his prayers.[2] When the question of the consecration of a Spanish bishop at the request of the king of Spain and on Hugh's recommendation comes up again, it is dealt with simply in the perspective of religious reform.[3]

In this connection, however, the characteristic letter, most telling both for the subject of our investigation and for the psychology of the two persons involved, belongs to 1079.[4]

[1] It could be that the word *census* has deceived certain historians into thinking in terms of the famous tributary kings of the Gregorian era. As a result, such writers see in the *cens* paid by the Spanish kings the acknowledgement of suzerainty and evidence of political and military co-operation. In the testament of Alphonsus (*PL* 159, 973) the mention of the *census* is linked with a *pactum fraternae societatis*. Elsewhere it is viewed as a kind of fortuitous liturgical offshoot aimed at subsidising the monks in return for their prayers on behalf of their benefactors. In neither case has the least connection between this *census* and that of the pope been established, in contrast with the donation to Cluny of the *abbatia sancti Aegidii*: BB 3410.

[2] *PL* 148, I 62, which should be compared with *PL* 148, II 49, where Gregory begs Hugh not so much for collaboration as for compassion. It cannot be concluded from the fact that he asks him to preach to the *milites* on the subject of holding St Peter in the highest regard that Hugh is being asked to enlist them in the holy war.

[3] *PL* 148, V 21.

[4] *PL* 148, VI 17. I have already drawn attention to this letter in *BLE* (1944) 74 ff. in studying Gregory VII's concept of the role of the laity. His concept seemed to me to differ from that of the abbots of Cluny, at least at that time and on the question of the crusade. This pope had a conscious and consistent political programme of which I can find no trace at Cluny.

Gregory is beset with all kinds of difficulties in his church reform, and aware at this juncture that its success depends not merely on goodwill but on sound policy and definite relations with monarchs. He complains of lack of understanding on the part of the abbot of Cluny, who is so preoccupied with his monastery and his congregation that he has forgotten about the church. As evidence Gregory adduces the fact that Hugh has approved the duke of Burgundy's entry into his monastery, as though the church had not even greater need of truly Christian princes than of monks: 'You have enticed or at any rate received the duke into the peace of Cluny, leaving a hundred thousand Christians bereft of their protector.' So far from having propagated the idea of the holy war, Hugh is categorically accused of having failed to understand its urgency and of being tied to a concept of monastic life that would confine the monk to contemplation.

Pope Urban II took the same line; his correspondence with Hugh deals with ecclesiastical affairs in Spain but never with the crusade.[1] On the occasion of the famous Council of Piacenza, when he launched the idea of an expedition to the Holy Land, Urban found time to confirm Cluny's privileges, but breathed not a word about any collaboration he expected from her in return.[2]

THE LIVES

The biographers of the two great abbots Mayeul and Hugh, well informed as they are on the activities and policies of their

[1] *PL* 151, 291: *Epist.* 8 (A.D. 1088). *Epist.* 9 enumerates the privileges of Cluniac monasteries, and they are those of the Pyrenean Midi. From this one could perhaps deduce that Pope Urban II had a Mediterranean and Spanish policy in which he relied specially on Cluny. It is a great pity that Fliche never developed the highly suggestive hypotheses concerning these problems that he referred to in vol. VIII of the *Histoire de l'Église* which he edited. He showed there that this pope wanted to establish in the west Mediterranean a sphere of influence conducive to the *reconquista* (pp. 115–16, 124–7, 229–32); at the same time Fliche insists on the alliance of the holy see and Cluny during this pontificate (pp. 200, 223, 334). One can see the implications of these views for an understanding of Moissac, which would have been deliberately favoured by Urban II as part of such a policy. But all this is mere hypothesis and none of our texts indicate such motives.

[2] *PL* 151, *Epist.* 137; *epist.* 196 relating to Moissac; *Epist.* 197 dated at Moissac and referring to St Orens in the diocese of Auch.

subjects, know nothing of this crusading project alleged to be theirs. Jotsald, certainly, takes pride in enumerating the friendships Mayeul enjoyed in royal circles, and in addition to Robert the Pious, Adelaide and the Emperor Henry he mentions Sancho, 'king of the peoples of the Hesperides',[1] but he never seems to consider what form such a friendship beyond the Pyrenees might assume. The lives of St Hugh are also significantly silent on the point: on learning that King Alphonsus has been taken prisoner by his brother Sancho, Hugh immediately orders prayers to be offered for him by the community at Cluny, which could do no less in view of the generosity of their father Ferdinand towards the monastery.[2] But where is the political complicity? Hildebert knows nothing of it.

THE CHARTERS

The foregoing conclusions are confirmed by a study of Cluny's charters.[3] Innumerable donations were made at this period by counts or other powerful personages involved in contemporary politics or wars, yet never is the slightest allusion made to any military task being entrusted to these friends of Cluny.[4] The collection contains numerous acts of donation

[1] Jotsald, cap. VII.

[2] *PL* 159, cols 945–6, where this prayer for Alphonsus is carefully arranged for because he was a *fidelis amicus* and benefactor.

[3] Here I will do no more than examine the collection of documents in BB IV, and those in particular which relate to the famous Barbastro expedition to which Boissannade attached such importance.

[4] 2845, 2846, 2852, 2855, 2888, 2977, etc., and for the end of the period with which we are concerned, 3600 (A.D. 1083), 3601, 3610, 3614, 3615, 3626, 3652. For the region we are dealing with, see no. 3410: donation by Almodis and Raymond de St Gilles; 3454 and 3500: donation by Roger de Foix. There is only one case of a Holy Land pilgrimage, 2922: Archimbald viscount of Mâcon, written before going to Jerusalem. On the composition of the Cluniac domain in the Pyrenean Midi, see nos 3410, 3414, 3416, 3419, 3454, 3457, 3471, 3480, 3500, 3514 (la Daurade de Toulouse), 3515 (Camprodon). Among these donations we have already noted the one made by Almodis, even though it does not exactly relate to this region; but Raymond de St Gilles associates himself with his mother in this deed, and one wonders where he got the idea of the crusade from: may one suppose he had actually fought in Spain? See Laurita and John Hill, 'Raymond IV de Saint-Gilles, comte de Toulouse', in *Bibl. méridion.* 2nd ser. XXXV (Toulouse,

made by soldiers,[1] and we are dealing here with precisely that
period when the holy see took this new class under its care,
recognised it as having a true vocation and assigned to it a
mission in the church, that of putting its arms at the service of
the cause of religion, whether it be the peace of God, ecclesiastical reform or the holy war. Yet for all that not one of the
extant charters reflects the slightest preoccupation of this kind.
The fact is all the more significant since the charters are often
introduced by stylised preambles, probably drawn from
common formularies since many texts follow the same pattern,
but sometimes dictated by the monks, which would have
provided the opportunity for diffusing the monastic 'doctrine'
of the holy war had there been one, yet the sentiments expressed
in these preambles are purely religious. Often indeed we find
these soldiers whom Gregory VII would have liked to keep in
the world renouncing it to become monks[2] and thus proclaiming
that, inspired by their Cluniac directors, they held firm to the
old idea of hierarchical ordering: above the layman, even
though he were a knight called to the service of the church and

---

1959) 7, where the authors quite rightly point out our ignorance of the precise relationship between Raymond and Cluny with regard to the crusading
idea. The problem has been treated by A. Fliche, 'Urbain II et la croisade',
in *Rev. d'hist. de l'Égl. de Fr.* XIV (1927) 296 ff.

[1] BB IV 2815, 2823, 2870, 2884, 3017, etc. In no. 2950 the initiative was
not taken by the *miles*: it was Odilo who made a conditional grant to a
miles, but without attaching any condition of a military character or anything touching the question of serving the church in a crusade.

[2] 2994, 3002, 3030, 3031, 3045, etc. Occasionally one even comes across
the ancient formula 'Ego . . . secularis hactenus miles, ab hac die in antea
soli Deo militare desiderans': the *militia saecularis* is thus inferior to the
militia Christi; the monk is placed at the summit of the hierarchy of *ordines*,
well above the knight; one can only pity those who remain in the world
and are involved in its affairs (3301). There is no question of presenting to
them the idea of a holy war as a service sanctifying in itself. There is nothing
for the *milites* to do but leave the world and become monks: as was the case
with the count in no. 3528. We have already noted the different attitudes
of Hugh and Gregory VII on the subject of the duke of Burgundy. Similarly,
there is a letter from Hugh to King Philip I of France, who wanted to enter
Cluny and whom the abbot, a little naïvely on this occasion one feels, did
not discourage: *Epist.* 8 in *PL* 159, 930. By contrast Hugh dissuaded
Alphonsus VI from entering the cloister, according to Bernold of Constance:
see Erdmann, op. cit. p. 61.

the witness of bloodshed, ranked the monk who was dedicated entirely to prayer.

Among these benefactors were heroes of the war in Spain, and their charters make proud mention of the fact. Yet while this may prompt them to make over to Cluny a part of the booty, it is never an occasion for acclaiming the monks as advisers in their military undertakings or as directors of their political consciences. Garsia dedicates a tithe of his conquests, but renders thanks for what has fallen to him 'of Saracen territory' to God alone.[1] In similar circumstances Arnaldus Miro sings of the power of God,[2] while Ermengarde, daughter of a count returning from Spain, can find no better way of showing her gratitude to God than to offer her son to the monastery, choosing for him a life of prayer withdrawn from the world in preference to a military career.[3]

II. THE NOTION OF THE CRUSADE AND THE CLUNIAC MENTALITY

Our next task is to examine modes of thought during the period we are studying in order to show that the absence of references to the crusading idea in Cluniac literature is due to the fact that the mystique of the holy war then developing was foreign to the spirit of Cluny.

Discussion of the crusades conjures up not merely the idea of military enterprises dependent on vast political, diplomatic and technical preparations, but also a mentality characteristic of the Christian at this time. It is strange that a religion essentially pledged to peace should from a certain date have grown used to fermenting wars and should have justified its practice doctrinally. Such an attitude presupposes a definite concept of man, of society and of the church. The era of the Gregorian reform not only saw the correction of abuses and a renewal in the traditional structures of the church; it was also a time for questioning accepted ethical norms, for new ecclesiology, for

[1] BB IV 3343.
[2] 3409, in A.D. 1066: the year after the taking of Barbastro. See no. 3623 (A.D. 1087).
[3] 3602 (A.D. 1083).

new theories, ideals and myths. While, however, certain social groups at once made this new way of looking at things their own and in this sense became pioneers of the reform, it seems that the Cluniacs remained attached to the old Carolingian and Ottonian world, either because their spirituality was incompatible with the new ways or because they were held back by mere inertia.

THE CLUNIAC IS A MAN OF PRAYER

A new order is usually adaptable, and such proved to be the case with the religious orders which, born with the new century, spontaneously adjusted themselves to the Gregorian reform and to its various developments. The most typical case is that of the Templars, monk-soldiers who made the holy war their work and the cornerstone of their spirituality. Similarly the Dominicans would, later on, be at home not only in the universities (which in their own way also stemmed from the Gregorian reform) but in the inquisition too, and in the crusades of which they would often be the official preachers. It was otherwise with the Cluniac, as has already become apparent from two or three of our texts. He continued to be a man of the cloister, of penance, of liturgy and of contemplation. None of the great abbots of the period made any attempt to substitute the promotion of a holy war for this traditional ideal.

We have already seen how the Cluniacs propagated the idea that it is better to be a monk than a soldier and preached flight from the world. Thus Odilo takes it for granted that in face of Christian calamities and Saracen invasions his brethren's role can be none other than prayer. When writing to Abbot Paternus, whose mission has already been mentioned, on the latter's return to Spain from Cluny, Odilo, instead of urging him to be the moving spirit in the reconquest, mentions prayer alone 'for the good estate of the realm, that it may be free from pagan invasion'. It is clear that Odilo does not condemn those who fight in this holy war, but the task of monks is different.[1]

[1] *PL* 142, 941, *Epist*. 2. In *Epist*. 3 Odilo addresses Garcia, wishing him *pacem et victoriam* but without promising him any other help than that of prayer. It is doubtless the same Garcia that we meet in BB IV 3343, victorious over the Saracens. If the vocation of the Cluniacs differs from that of the *milites* it, too, can be seen in a heroic light: but its struggle is against

This minimising interpretation of Odilo's letter is proved sound by the fact that the saint's biographer Jotsald viewed his hero in this way too, and his testimony is the more significant because Jotsald was by no means insensitive to the glories of his age. He sincerely sings the praises of Odilo's noble birth: the saint's father was 'a might warrior who had other strong and noble sons'; Mayeul had been aware of the 'outstanding physical beauty and the noble lineage' of the young man who offered himself to the monastery, but for all that Odilo, the 'young soldier', renounced the world. The portrait drawn by his disciple is not that of a ruler with a will to power and ambitious for political influence, but that of an austere monk. Fortitude was certainly among his virtues, but Jotsald means by this not the courage of the reconquering knights but that of the martyrs who had chosen to suffer rather than defend themselves.[1]

Abbot Hugh's role was similarly understood, and primarily so by the Spanish kings, as appears in the will of Alphonsus:[2] the trust his father Ferdinand had placed in Cluny derived principally from his admiration for the Cluniac way of life, and in order to benefit from the monks' merits Ferdinand had made a 'pact of brotherly fellowship' with them. This kind of alliance is indicative of what the kings of Spain expected of Cluny. Each party was to make its proper contribution, Cluny that of prayer, Ferdinand and Alphonsus the donation necessary for the maintenance of the men of God, for Ferdinand had hoped that 'he would share in their spiritual goods if he had been generous in supplying the needs of God's servants from his own temporal wealth'. So far from confusing the role of princes with that of the religious, Alphonsus is careful to distinguish them, and in this is simply following the traditional doctrine of the 'orders' which divided the varied and providential functions in society among monks, priests, princes or knights and labourers, never assuming that any one of these would wish to step outside his own province under pretext of spiritual enrichment.

Satan. The *Vita Maioli* (*PL* 142, 952) describes as one of Mayeul's virtues the power he brought to bear in the spiritual combat. On the heroic ideal, see E. Delaruelle, 'La pietà popolare nel sec. XI', in *X Congresso internaz. di sc. stor.* (Rome, 1955) *Relazioni*, III 322–5.

[1] *PL* 142, *Vita*, cols 895–912, cap. 1, 5, 12 and the *Deploratio*.
[2] *PL* 159, 973, no. 18.

The doctrine appears again at the same period in a letter from
the Emperor Henry III (the Black) to Hugh the Great, asking
him to pray 'for the prosperity of the state and the honour of the
whole kingdom . . . that there may be peace for the churches
and the entire people'. So categorical is this letter in restricting
Cluny to the task of intercession that if one were to admit
Hatem's theory of an earlier preoccupation on the part of the
Cluniac abbots with politics this letter could be seen as a tart
reminder to the monks of their true vocation. Indeed, it goes
on to remark that 'prayer is pure in the measure that it is
remote from worldly affairs'. Such a statement is in no way
remarkable for it echoes letters from Charlemagne to the pope
or the imperial chancellery, but we have every reason to think
that it corresponded to Hugh's religious ideal.[1]

THE OTTONIAN THEORY OF THE EMPEROR'S RELIGIOUS ROLE

Cluny is dedicated to prayer. To say this is to assert that the
running of the world is the business of the emperor in an age
when men have not yet assigned it to the pope. This doctrine,
first Carolingian and then Ottonian, of the relationship between
church and state is constantly to be found in the Cluniac writings
of the time; one need only study the great abbots of the eleventh
century to demonstrate the fact.

The life of Mayeul as written by Odilo, his successor, makes
a point of mentioning the honoured relationship in which
Mayeul stood to his royal friends Otto, Adelaide and Conrad,
but never attributes to him the slightest political influence over
these noble personages.[2] On the contrary it recalls the gospel
precept 'Render to Caesar what belongs to Caesar', and St
Peter's injunction 'Honour the king'. Moreover this is not a
matter of principle only but must be translated into practice,
and hence Mayeul awaited the king's invitation before undertaking the reform of the monastery of St Denis. Mayeul in fact

---

[1] *PL* 159, 931, *Epist. ad Hugonem*, VI. This did not prevent Hugh from
acting as a political mediator when asked: see *Epist.* X and XVIII; but here
again Hugh is reflecting the role of a church which is the church of the
peace of God: a concept more Carolingian and Ottonian than Gregorian.

[2] *PL* 142: the passage concerned begins in col. 956.

was a new Moses, and Odilo cites Ecclus. 14:3: 'He gave him
glory in the presence of kings', a passage which represents
Moses as a saint, a wonder-worker, a prophet and a man of
God, but never assigns to him a temporal mission.

Jotsald's assessment of Odilo is patterned on the one that
Odilo had made of Mayeul.[1] Jotsald commends particularly
Odilo's virtue and just dealing in never opposing kings: 'according to the apostle's command he offered no resistance to Christian princes and rulers'. The biographer's assertion on this point
is confirmed by the testimony of the 'Epitaph of the Emperor
Otto I, the Great', which echoes the full political doctrine of
the old Carolingian theorists even to the point of imitating
their biblical style in eulogies: thus Otto is David, Solomon,
Hezekiah or Josiah.[2] His functions are those which earlier
theorists had reserved to the emperor, excluding the pope; we
are therefore in an epoch prior to the Gregorian reform and so
also anterior to any crusading mystique which in its essence
presumes that to the pope alone, and not to the emperor or any
other prince, belongs the initiative in the holy war:

> Taming Slavs, Christ's slaves he made them,
> Drove the demon from among them,
> Raised for them the glorious cross.
> Warring Magyar hordes he routed. . . .

But Otto not only defended Christendom and spread the
gospel, he also made himself responsible for maintaining peace.
He was, says the poet, 'the friend of peace' and absolute master
in the making of laws:

> True and just the laws he issued
> Peacefully to rule his peoples. . . .

Ralph Glaber's 'Histories', which can in many respects be
taken as representative of the Cluniac outlook, testify to the
same ideas. In recording the Saracen invasion of Italy Glaber
notes that the counter-attack was launched on the initiative of
the lords, not on that of the pope, and gives no indication that
the ensuing struggle took place in an atmosphere of holy war.[3]

---

[1] *PL* 142, 895–912, *De vita S. Odilonis.*   [2] *PL* 142, 967.

[3] *PL* 142, 611–98, 15: 'De paganorum plagis'. Mention of the Normans is
made alongside the statement that, having been converted, the dukes
became the guardians of pilgrims to the Holy Land. On this theme see

He is of course a historian of integrity and is confining himself
to recording events. But the context into which he inserts his
account is suggestive: the war with the Moslems is put on the
same level as those waged against the Normans and the
Hungarian invaders. Glaber does not think of it as a collision
between Christianity and Islam that dwarfs the other conflicts;
nor does he represent the Saracens as the supreme enemy, as
Moslems pitted against Christians, and his failure to do so
betrays the mentality of a time earlier than the crusades. He
significantly concludes his description of the wars and suffering
of the Christian world with an account of the imperial corona-
tion, at which the cross surmounting the globe symbolises the
protection the emperor can count on in his military enterprises.
This leaves us fully within the Carolingian milieu, where minds
are still unaware of problems that will be brought to the surface
by the Gregorian reform.

There is no need to return to the case of St Hugh since the
very traditional type of letter sent to him by Henry III has been
cited already. The action of the Emperor Henry IV in making
Hugh the arbiter between himself and the holy see was
equivalent to a refusal to admit the evolution that had taken
place, an evolution that had put the guidance of the Christian
world into the hands of the pope. Henry was clinging to an
older regime, charismatic rather than juridical, under which it
had been men of God, rather than institutions as the Gregorian
movement was to reform them, who were relied on to ensure
peace and the reign of law.[1]

THE PHILOSOPHY OF HISTORY AS UNDERSTOOD
AT CLUNY[2]

Political views of this kind are part of a vast philosophy of

P. Lamma, 'Su alcuni temi di storiografia cluniacense', in *Spiritualità*, pp.
262 ff.

[1] *PL* 159, 934 and 937, *Epist. ad Hugonem*, IX and X. See also *Epist.* VIII
for the emperor's project of going to Jerusalem, though there is no question
of Henry IV consulting his godfather (St Hugh) about a military expedition
to the Holy Land, for this pilgrimage was to be a wholly peaceful pilgrimage
in line with the pilgrimage tradition prior to the crusades.

[2] See Lamma, loc. cit., and 'Momenti di storiografia cluniacense', in
Istituto stor. ital. per il M. Evo, 42–4 (Rome, 1961).

history of which Odilo is the exponent and which is incompatible with the philosophy that was to be born of the crusades.

Speaking only of the crusades in the Holy Land, we can assert that both the crusaders and their chroniclers soon became aware of the Christian army as a new people of God on the march towards the promised land. Sacred history was beginning anew; the same wonders would carry it forward and the same Providence would direct it. Hence the same virtues that were needed then were demanded now: simple virile faith and fortitude, showing itself above all as military courage that would go to the length of sacrificing one's life. Such a sacrifice would be freely made by the warrior who could thereby win a martyr's crown. Thus the crusading era was a new age of martyrs, in succession to the early medieval period which had been the age of monks. St Bernard would go so far as to say that the crusade was successful in the measure that those who fought in it, sinners though they had been until yesterday, were transformed into victims and so into God's elect.

This grandiose vision of history, however, completely cuts across that put forward by Odilo in his life of Mayeul.[1] Even in his opening lines he distinguishes with admirable clarity three ages in the church's life: the first is the era of the apostles and evangelists, the second that of the martyrs and the third that of the priests. Hence the age of the martyrs is now closed, and one might almost say that the sole business of the priests is to celebrate their triumph in order to reap the fruits of their sacrifice. To the eloquence of blood heroically shed now succeeds the eloquence of the prophetic word. The Christian saint appears in different

---

[1] *PL* 142, 943, *De vita b. Maioli Libellus.* Remarkable though it is, this page of Odilo raises a question: where exactly do the monks stand with regard to the third age, which is the age of the priests? Are we still in the third age or are we entering a new era, that of the *ordo monasticus*? 'Deinde coepit monasticus ordo pullulare.' Perhaps one may look for at least a partial solution in the fact that Odilo, unlike the previous abbots of Cluny, who had only been monks, was also a priest and always showed himself proud of this dignity: in one charter (2888) he is mentioned under the designation 'Odilo, cluniensis monasterii presbiter et monacus'. One can thus understand that he would not differentiate between the *ordo clericorum* and the *ordo monachorum* in the same way that others would want to. On all these questions, see Dom J. Leclercq, 'Le sacerdoce des moines', in *Irénikon*, XXXVI (1963) 15 ff.

guise, for after the 'mighty and noble' come the 'humble and innocent, the men who pray'.

A sharper antithesis would be difficult to imagine. Obviously Odilo is not belittling the heroic virtue of the Christian martyr: on the contrary he can almost be said to make it the core of Christian preaching in his own day and the condition for the efficacy of that preaching, but he does think that the epic age of heroes and the time for witnessing by blood is over, and that the hour has come when other virtues are called for. The church still has to confront schismatics, idolaters and unbelievers, and to meet them Odilo summons not an army of knights equipped for the holy war, successors to the martyrs, but rather the poorest of preachers, the 'humble and innocent, the men who pray'. By such as these alone will the 'savagery of the Gentiles be conquered'. This is a far cry from the mentality of the crusaders of 1096, but very near to that of St Francis of Assisi.

The term 'innocent' opens up an interesting line of study, revealing as it does a traditional way of thought diametrically opposed to the themes Bernard was to develop in his work 'In Praise of the New Army'. The 'innocent' were those Christians who had let themselves be killed without attempting self-defence, motivated not so much by love of peace in itself as by the desire for a mystical sharing in the saviour's passion. Typical examples are those 'blameless kings' venerated in the early middle ages, like St Sigismund.[1] The tradition concerning these 'innocents' had not yet been lost in the period we are dealing with, for the second half of the tenth century produced a lament on the death of William Longsword.[2]

Ralph Glaber's ideas on this subject are much less fully developed than those of Odilo, and it would be an exaggeration to speak of a philosophy of history in his case. He remains, for all that, remarkably representative of the religious sentiments

[1] H. Marrou, 'Ammien Marcellin et les *Innocents* de Milan', in *Mélanges Jules Lebreton* II ('Recherches de sciences religieuses' XL, 1952) pp. 179–90. Jotsald, cap. xii, describing the virtue of strength in Odilo, tells us that he had dreamed of martyrdom.

[2] P. Lauer, 'Le règne de Louis IV d'Outremer, Annales de l'histoire de France a l'époque carolingienne', in *Bibl. de l'École des Hautes-Études, sc. philol. et hist.* 127 (Paris, 1900) 281–2; edition of the text pp. 319–23, where the following passage occurs: 'cuncti flete/pro Willelmo/innocente/interfecto'.

typical of Cluny – or perhaps simply of Benedictines – before
the crusades. One need only recall the famous picture he gives
of the pilgrimage to Jerusalem headed not by kings and noblemen, who tomorrow would be enrolled for the holy war, but by
'people of the lower sort'. Though many, he said, desired to die,
what they had in mind was not a death in battle against the
infidel but the consummation of their pilgrimage through a
real entry into the promised land. Lethebald, who died on the
Mount of Olives contemplating the Lord's ascension, is the
antithesis of a crusader.[1]

CLUNY'S RESURRECTION-CENTRED SPIRITUALITY

The spirituality associated with the crusades is a clearly
defined thing, in no way accidental or haphazard but organi-
cally related to the whole mystique of the holy war, of which it
constitutes both one of the deepest causes and one of the
effects. It is a spirituality marked above all by devotion to the
passion. The crusader is seeking union with Christ who suffered
for mankind, and he dwells on that agony in ways that are often
very moving. It was to avenge the outrages which the saviour
underwent and which were more or less confused in the
crusader's mind with the desecration of the holy places that the
knight would set out in the cause of his Lord, and the first
popular crusade would massacre the Jews. To suffer and die in
the very place where Christ had suffered and died: such was the
crusaders' ideal, preached and grasped more or less clearly.
They were convinced that in the Holy Land there remained
some kind of presence, or at least some special influence, of
'Christ according to the flesh', and so they longed to be on the
spot themselves to make contact with that hallowed ground.

[1] *PL* 142, 611–98, *Historiae*, IV 6. One may again remark that Glaber is so
far from imagining that one could take up the sword in the service of the
church that he attributes safety from the Saracens in the Holy Land solely
to the protection of St George, whom he believed terrified the Saracens (III 7).
In the same chapter, 'De eversione templi', Glaber makes no allusion to a
possible reconquest of the Holy Land. If one wants to know everything he
says on our subject one should read his *Historiae*, IV 7, which gives various
details about the Saracen wars in Africa, about a vow made by the Christians
to our Lady and St Peter, and about the booty promised to Cluny, from
which Odilo had a ciborium made.

It could happen that the other Christian mysteries were lost
sight of, blotted out by that of Good Friday. For a long time
even the resurrection would in the popular mind take second
place to the passion.[1]

Now this type of spirituality is at the opposite pole to that of
contemporary Cluny, for the Cluniac monk concentrated above
all on the glorious mysteries. Ralph Glaber's attitude has already
been mentioned. He describes a pilgrimage to the Holy Land
which took place immediately after sacrileges committed at
Jerusalem, and yet none of the pilgrims were induced by the
memory of the cross to attempt any revenge. Indeed, the most
edifying member of the group, Lethebald, showed far more
devotion to the mount of the ascension than to Calvary. The
same author witnesses to the custom at Cluny, telling us that
the monks there did not fast between ascension and pentecost.[2]

The best representative of the Cluniac mentality, however,
is once more St Odilo in his sermons.[3] It is not merely that he
shows no sign of any special interest in the Holy Land;[4] more
significant is the fact that he consistently presents the Christian
mysteries in their glorious aspect. In his work the epiphany is
not a picturesque scene from Christ's infancy at the moment of
the redemptive incarnation, as it is for the Gothic artists; rather
it is a majestic scene, indeed a theophany, to be associated with
our Lord's baptism and the miracle at Cana.[5] The resurrection

---

[1] On all this see *BLE* (1954) 50–8.   [2] *PL* 142, 611–98, *Historiae*, III 3.

[3] *PL* 142, 991–1036. These sermons could well provide the key to the
Moissac portal or at least help us to appreciate the spirit in which it was
produced. Here, too, it is a question only of the glorious mysteries, and
Christ is portrayed with the impassibility of eternity. When the cross
appeared in the cloister it was an embellished cross, emblem of triumph and
not ignominy.

[4] The opportunity of showing such an interest might have occurred in his
sermons on the resurrection (v–vii), which, on the contrary, show no interest
in the location of the events. One knows, on the other hand, how the
crusaders identified all the places connected with the gospel and the events
of the passion. In the same way one notices the absence in all these sermons –
to my knowledge at least – of any hint of liturgical drama.

[5] Perhaps I may be permitted to refer to my paper given to the Congrès des
Sociétés savantes de Saint-Gaudens, Fédération des Pyrénées, Languedoc
et Gascogne, 1962: 'L'adoration des Mages au portail de Saint-Bertrand-
de-Comminges, sa signification théologique et spirituelle, ses parallèles'
(published in *Revue de Comminges*, 1964).

is approached less as an event than as a mystery of new creation
in the Spirit, and the same is true of the ascension and pentecost.
Above all does this spirituality show itself when Odilo is speaking of the passion: the cross is for him no shameful instrument
of torture but a symbol of triumph. In a sermon for the feast of
the finding of the cross on May 3 he compares St Helena who
discovered it to the holy women on the first Easter day.[1]

The same spirituality shines through in Odilo's other works.
His hymn to St Mayeul opens on a note of exultant joy as it
links the saint to the paschal mystery:

> On this day too Christ's light is shed
> As when, bloodspattered, from the dead
> Meek Lamb, he conquering rose. . . .
> His Easter joy we share again. . . . [2]

The acclamation known under the name of the 'Creed of Odilo'
is written in a style exuberant in praise rather than careful of
dogmatic exactitude.[3] Jotsald tells us that for Odilo Cluny was
the promised land, and he catches the spirit of Cluny as he says
it: what need is there to go seeking Christ in the Holy Land?
We are in Jerusalem already, a Jerusalem lit up with glory.[4]

It is true that we have fewer of these characteristic documents
relating to St Hugh, but there is every reason to believe that the
same spirit reigned at Cluny in his time. An indication of it is
provided by the list of feasts on which, thanks to a privilege
obtained from Pope Urban II, Hugh had the right to use
pontifical insignia: to the five great liturgical feasts are added
the epiphany, the ascension and the feast of the dedication of
his own abbey church, figure of the heavenly Jerusalem.[5]

---

[1] *Sermones*, xv, 'De sancta cruce'. See also in Odilo's *Epitaphium Ottonis*:
'crucis insignire triumphum'.

[2] *PL* 142, 961:

> Victoris Agni sanguine
> Dies sacratus hodie . . .
> Ecce paschale gaudium.

[3] *PL* 142, 1036, *Credulitas Odilonis*. This is a prayer of faith after the manner
of the Fathers, affirming their faith within the framework of the Apostle's
Creed and stressing those mysteries which were dearest to them or which
appeared to them to be the most necessary to preach.

[4] *PL* 142, 899.   [5] *PL* 151, 291, *Epist.* IX.

III. WAS MOISSAC A STARTING POINT FOR THE SPANISH CRUSADES?

Something has already been said of the relations between Cluny and the Spanish kingdoms, and it has been established that these relations were essentially spiritual. Clearly we have no right to attribute to the great Cluniac abbots some kind of secret liaison unknown to their biographers and never mentioned in their correspondence.

It would however be insufficient to confine ourselves to the evidence supplied by the actual teaching of the abbots and by the documents sent to Cluny such as the formularies employed in deeds of gift. We must examine the hypothetical possibility that the Spanish monasteries may have been more keenly aware of the holy war than was the mother house, and that the monks who lived in Spain, constantly in touch with crusaders, may not always have kept clear of compromise and may on occasions have been induced to lend support to the crusade.

Of particular interest in this matter is an episode reported by Ralph Glaber. At the time of Al-Mansur's invasion certain monks, in their anxiety for the Christian cause, owing to the dearth of combatants themselves took up arms.[1] The text is the more remarkable in that it is not content merely to state the fact but also provides us with the historian's views on the matter, and no doubt those of his heroes and his brethren. Since the monks went to their death 'not from any boastful desire to earn renown but rather from fraternal charity' they were truly martyrs. Moreover the record of a vision granted during a Mass celebrated at the altar of St Maurice, a soldier who refused to defend himself when put to death for his faith, confirms the fact. We can detect here the transition from one type of spirituality to the other: for the ideal of a martyr's death chosen in preference to a violent resistance alien to the gospel there is now substituted the ideal of resort to arms 'for the defence of one's country and the protection of the Catholic people'.

---

[1] *PL* 142, 611–98, II 9: it is even more surprising to find these monks taking up arms when one recalls that at the Councils of Puy and Toulouse the prohibition against clerks taking up arms was renewed.

This remained however an isolated incident as far as the eleventh century was concerned and until the time of St Raymond de Fitero, whose case was similar to that of the Spanish monks. The rarity of such episodes is partly due, as has already been shown, to Cluniac tradition, which did not look kindly on so wide an interpretation of the monastic vocation, but another deterrent was the Roman liturgy. Space does not allow of more than a brief reference to the introduction of the Roman liturgy into Spain at the end of the eleventh century,[1] but we should note in passing that it knows nothing of the ritual of chivalry.[2] This ritual is witness to the evolution of contemporary thinking in the face of war and military life, for it provides blessings very similar to those used in the rite of ordination to sanctify the arms and banner of the newly invested knight, and is thus an important stage in the formation of the crusading idea: the man of war is accorded a place in the church as honourable as that of the man of God. The ritual of chivalry seems to have developed in the Rhineland, but the Roman liturgy, conservative for various reasons, remained hostile to any such official recognition of the new spirituality.[2]

What line then was taken by the priory of Moissac, having as it did a foot in each camp, in the Cluniac world with its fidelity

[1] See Menendez Pidal, op. cit. 1 240, 244, 250, on the introduction of the Roman liturgy in Spain, where the Spanish Cluniacs appeared above all as agents in the process of Roman centralisation, who sometimes weakened national sentiment and substituted for the old Visigothic liturgy the Roman liturgy. In this area there was, therefore, from the eleventh century onwards, a resistance to all Cluniac influence. In Jardet, op. cit. pp. 508–9 may be seen some indications of how severely some Spanish historians have dealt with this centralising tendency of Cluny. On the question of the Cluniac introduction of a new type of script in Spain, see Menendez Pidal, op. cit. pp. 250–1.

[2] It is not possible to develop this theme here, but the reader may be referred to *BLE* (1944) 32–5 where I have drawn on the works of Andrieu and Leroquais to show that the *benedictio ensis* and the *benedictio vexilli* (the blessings of the sword and cross) are only found in the Romano-Germanic pontificals and were excluded from the Roman pontificals when there was a reaction in Rome against Germanic influence. In this respect it is significant to note that at Monte Cassino the *benedictio ensis*, used for the dubbing of a *defensor* of the monastery, came into use, it would seem, between 1022 and 1035 and was later abandoned, perhaps by Abbot Didier. Thus Monte Cassino did not favour the idea of a holy war either.

to the older monastic spirituality and in a Spanish monasticism more inclined to the ideal of the holy war? Is there any justification for speaking of Moissac as having 'Hispanicising tendencies'? Did it provide Spain with many bishops, and if so what attitude did they adopt towards the reconquest? These questions ought at least to be asked.[1]

Moissac's library, in so far as it is known to us from a twelfth-century list, does not seem to have contained much that would be relevant to the crusading idea.[2] Josephus, the 'Tripartite History' and Orosius may have fostered meditation on history, but not the kind of meditation that would lead into any epic theme of God's mighty deeds through the Franks. Other works mentioned are only those one would expect to find in any monastic library of the period.

Special consideration should however be given to Rorico, the eleventh-century author of the 'History of the Franks', whose work, being extant in a Moissac manuscript, is thought, if only for this reason, to have come from the monastery.[3] The book is a history of Gaul, unquestionably lacking in originality, that relates the reign and legend of Clovis at some length. Its interest for us is the insight it affords into the way in which men of the eleventh century regarded the distant past, for it presents Clovis as a Christian hero who fought the Visigoths precisely as heretics and describes the war as being waged in a super-natural ethos where miracles are normal.[4] But here again it must be said that these ideas occur elsewhere and are not in any special sense characteristic of Moissac, if indeed they concern the monastery at all.

A study of Moissac's liturgy as known from a hymnal of the

---

[1] It was Moissac which supplied Archbishop St Gerard to the diocese of Braga. Gerard's *dies natalis* was 5 December; the *AA SS* restricts itself to mentioning him in the index of the supplement without giving any details about him. I have been unable to consult the *Life* published in the *Portug. Monum. Hist. Scriptores* and I have had to be content with the article in *Dict. d'hist. et géog. ecclé.* IX, col. 356 on Braga. One passage in the *Life* shows that Moissac was well known in Portugal: 'beati Geraldi sanctitatis ad aures Bracharensium pervenit.'

[2] Émile Lesne, *Hist. de la propriété eccl. en France*, IV: *Les livres, 'scriptoria' et bibliothèques du commencement du VIIIe à la fin du XIe s.* ('Mémoires, et travaux . . . des Facultés cathol. de Lille', XLVI, Lille, 1938) p. 499.

[3] *PL* 139, 587, *Gesta Francorum*.   [4] Ibid. book IV.

tenth century leads to the same conclusions.[1] Nothing in its text strikes the crusading note; the saints it honours are those familiar to Benedictine devotion or locally venerated: Peter, Benedict, Saturninus, Martial, Salvius, etc.[2] The absence of holy war mystique is all the more striking when we compare these texts with Mozarabic hymns.[3] The extant Visigothic hymnal includes a composition 'For an army setting out to battle' and two others 'In time of war', all breathing the spirit of the holy war. That there were interactions between the two liturgies that flourished on either side of the Pyrenees is clear from the fact that they both give the same hymn 'For the feast of St Saturninus', yet the interactions did not result in the Benedictines of Moissac catching the spirit that sometimes prevailed in Spain.

Finally a word must be said on the art of Moissac. How far does its sculpture convey to us the feelings of the monks who lived there as regards the crusades in Spain or in the east? We should first of all rule out a work of art that has been an un-warranted intruder into the debate, the capital that is alleged to depict a procession of crusaders before the walls of Jerusalem.[4]

From a study of the whole it would appear that we are here confronted with an iconography which, far from treating

---

[1] *Analecta hymnica medii aevi*, ed. C. Blume and G. M. Dreves, ii: *Hymnarius moissiacensis, Das Hymnar der Abtei Moissac im X. Jt nach einer Hs. der Rossiana* (Leipzig, 1888).

[2] G. G. Meersseman, 'Der Hymnos Akathistos im Abendland, 1: *Akathistos-Akoluthia u. Grusshymnen*', in *Spicilegium Friburg.* ii (Freiburg, Sw. 1958) nos 16, 17, 18, pp. 153–7. The author has placed these hymns in the Marian context of the high middle ages. Dating from the tenth century, these hymns come before the influence of the Akathistos hymn, which in this sphere would merely reinforce Marian devotion in its Cluniac sense – i.e. in the direction of praise and devotion rather than towards the struggle against heresy and paganism, as happened later.

[3] In the same collection, *Analecta hymnica*, by Dreves, *Hymnodia gotica: Die mozarabischen Hymnen des alt-spanischen Ritus*, ed. C. Blume (1897). Most interesting from our point of view are nos 195, 205, 206. The hymn to St Saturninus is no. 163 (in the Moissac collection no. 89).

[4] Cap. 49 in the catalogue of Marguerite Vidal and others, *Quercy roman*, *Zodiaque* (1959) p. 133. See Rousset, op. cit. p. 8 and Émile Male, *L'art religieux du XIIe s. en France* (Paris) p. 10, who has reason to think that the Jerusalem portrayed in the cloisters of Moissac is the heavenly Jerusalem and not the city of which there was talk of conquering.

H

subjects of contemporary interest or proposing any new ideal for man, is traditional in spirit, and even archaic. A number of capitals could be cited to illustrate the point, as for example those depicting the hand of God the Father coming out of a cloud, or showing a cross, but a radiant cross studded with jewels. The ensemble of subjects is abundant in its richness and even confused and I find it impossible to discern any unifying themes, *pace* the opinion of my predecessor Mgr Saltet. What is striking, however, is the predominance of scenes drawn simply from the gospels and hence in conformity with traditional norms from the point of view of subject-matter; the question of style cannot be dealt with here. Once more it should be noted that this sculpture expresses a spirituality centred on the glorious mysteries, as for example when it juxtaposes the Cana scene with that of the epiphany or adorns the doorway with subjects from the Apocalypse.[1]

The most remarkable point, however, is that if we exclude the apostles the most typical Christian hero in this cloister is the martyr. A number of capitals attest the fact, whether it is St Peter, St Saturninus or St Fructuosus who is portrayed. We are in the climate of Odilo's preaching, or perhaps it would be truer to say in the mainstream of Cluniac spirituality deriving from Benedictine and patristic tradition, and this at a period when the crusades in the east were well under way.

Moissac, from its geographical situation looking towards the Pyrenees and Spain, might have served as a springboard for crusading thrusts, might even have been an outpost deliberately stationed there by great abbots with a taste for strategy and an awareness of the essential role this monastery could play in furthering their ideals of the holy war. It might have been, but our conclusion must be that it was not. It was simply a house of God where in seclusion from the world men devoted themselves to penance, to meditation on the gospel and to the glory of the Father.

---

[1] See Delaruelle, 'L'adoration des mages', quoted above, on the relationship between the epiphany, the baptism of Christ and the marriage feast of Cana which was established in the liturgy at this period. See Gaillard, 'Cluny et l'Espagne', pp. 155–6 for the influence of Spanish ivories on Moissac sculpture.

11 The Monastic Crisis of the Eleventh and Twelfth Centuries.[1]

JEAN LECLERCQ

The earliest documentary evidence of monasticism in the west shows it already existing in two distinct forms, urban and rural: the secluded life was led either in or near a town, or, on the other hand, deep in the country. Both forms were considered authentic, and they had in common the fundamental characteristic of the vocation of certain Christians – separation from the world, in order to seek God wholeheartedly and love him alone. In a text attributed to St Valéry of Bierzo, a Spanish ascetic of the seventh century, the two forms of monasticism are described and carefully differentiated. The author makes no secret of the fact that he considers the life of town monks more meritorious, for though they live near other men, and even right amongst them, they manage to avoid being contaminated by worldly thoughts.[2]

It depended on circumstances which of these forms would

[1] [Translated from 'La crise du monachisme aux XIe et XIIe siècles', in *Bullettino dell'Istituto Storico Italiano per il medio evo e Archivio Muratoriano*, no. 70 (Rome, 1958). Ed.]

[2] S. Valerio (*Obras*) *De monachis perfectis*, ed. R. Fernandez-Pousa (Madrid, 1942) pp. 124–8. Ought not the ambiguity of the term 'eremitic' to be recognised once and for all? At the period with which this paper is concerned expressions such as *eremus, eremita, solitudo, vita solitaria* were used in different ways, and the meaning must be determined for each particular text. These terms were used of cenobitic monasteries situated far away from urban life, of groups of hermitages such as those St Peter Damian was to organise at Fonte Avellano, of isolated hermitages like those attached to Cluny, which were praised by Peter the Venerable; of hermitages unconnected with each other or with any monastery. But in every case the vocabulary refers to a form of rural monasticism characterised by withdrawal from civilisation and by a special emphasis on a simple, poor and austere manner of life as opposed to urban monasticism in the sense described above.

predominate at a given time and in a particular place: wars
and invasions might impede their development to some extent,
but both flourished, and quite often a monastery which
originated as a rural foundation would become the nucleus of
a burg and turn into a veritable town. Take for instance St
Riquier, which at the end of the eighth century presented the
aspect of a holy city. It had three churches, five smaller chapels,
seven thousand inhabitants, of whom three hundred were
monks, a hundred scholars and a hundred and ten soldiers:
added to these were countless families of artisans, working in
the monastery precincts or on its property.[1] Experienced ad-
ministrators, who were sometimes laymen, such as Angilbert
of St Riquier, drew up juridical, and later on liturgical, codes
to cater for the needs of such vast numbers. Abbots also saw to
it that ordinals and customaries specified exactly how the
Benedictine Rule and traditions were to be applied.

The eleventh century was the golden age of customaries, and
of such powerful institutions as Cluny, Gorze, Farfa and Monte
Cassino, to mention but a few, with congregations attached to
them. Urban monasticism (including foundations near towns
and rural houses which had developed into burgs) was then at
its zenith as regards numbers, and highly productive in various
realms of culture. This period is epitomised in the names of
such abbots as Desiderius of Monte Cassino or St Mayeul and
St Hugh, abbots of Cluny at the height of its prosperity. Men
like these were reformers and organisers, and erected monasteries
and basilicas: they were masters too of the spiritual life, and
contributed to the building up of Christendom. They were in a
word, men of edification, in its original as well as its derivative
sense.

At this very time, however, critical symptoms became evident
in monasticism. A crack appeared in the edifice, with effects
that went on spreading. In the course of about a hundred years
between the middle of the eleventh century and the middle of
the twelfth the significance of this crisis was formulated with

---

[1] On St Riquier, see the interesting study by J. Hubert, 'Saint-Riquier et
le monachisme bénédictin en Gaule à l'époque carolingienne', in *Il monachesimo nell'alto medioevo e la formazione della civiltà occidentale* (Spoleto, 1957)
pp. 293–309. On monastic burgs, see E. Lesne, *Histoire de la propriété
ecclésiastique en France*, VI (Lille, 1943) pp. 414–24.

increasing lucidity and asperity. The very men, however, who saw what was wrong were, together with other men of God, instrumental in solving the problems. These were complex, and offer the historian various possible lines of investigation. Their social and economic aspects deserve more careful and perhaps more objective study than they have hitherto had. Some of the evidence belongs to the realm of literary history and has been published. It will certainly be helpful to trace the development of this crisis in the light of texts, some of which are as yet little known. We may ask ourselves: what originally caused such a crisis? What were its symptoms? And how was the growing tension eventually resolved?

I. SOURCES OF TENSION

It is difficult to say when this crisis first became apparent. New mental attitudes of any depth or import mature in silence before coming to light. But taking into account all that is revealed by monastic history of the eleventh century, one cannot help seeing that monasticism in traditional Benedictine form, however thriving, austere and beneficent it may have been, no longer satisfied the ascetic aspirations of countless generous souls. Consequently other kinds of monasticism arose, not yet institutional in character, or scarcely so; hence their great diversity. But one thing they all had in common – the predominance of the eremitic element, which had been a feature of so many western monastic foundations from the outset.

As time went on, these ventures were more often accompanied by criticism of traditional monasticism. Ardent enthusiasm nearly always seems to engender a certain amount of aggressiveness. Onslaughts came from every side: from laymen, clergy and – still more telling – from monks themselves. It was of course no new thing for monasticism to be criticised:[1] its influence was a matter of reproach, the ascendancy of its austere leaders an object of envy, and monks who fell short of the ideal standard were ruthlessly condemned. At the beginning of the eleventh

[1] See, for example, the texts studied by L. Gougaud, 'Les critiques formulées contre les premiers moines d'Occident', in *RM* XXIV (1934) 145–63.

century Bishop Adalbero of Laon with some bitterness denounced a number of abuses to Robert the Pious, king of France. Amongst others, those attributed to Cluny were not passed over in silence. They were to be seen like knights, riding through the kingdom in fine attire, going to court, visiting episcopal palaces, and even venturing as far as Rome to defend the interests of their sovereign abbot, for

> King Odilo of Cluny is my lord.[1]

Later still, satirists were even less inhibited. A poem, probably written by Serlo, a canon of Bayeux, was circulating in the district of Caen in about the year 1080. Its theme is given in the title: 'Invective against a soldier, who because he was poor, left the world and became a wealthy monk'. The text resembles other metrical compositions of Serlon of Bayeux, and describes a knight who, to put an end to his impecunious existence, left the world and embraced the religious life:

> Although turn monk the soldier may,
> The pauper gains a rich man's pay.[2]

There is admittedly a certain amount of exaggeration in these satires: ill will and envy employed humour and literary talent to good effect. The evidence adduced by them is that of outsiders, who were perhaps insensitive to the mystery of the monastic life as expressed by the author of the treatise on 'Preservation of Unity in the Church', who found mystic symbolism both in the term 'monk' and in the monastic habit: 'For the word monk has a mysterious quality, and the cowl too has a certain sacramental efficacy.'[3] But even the monks themselves were fired at times with anything but admiration for the imposing abbey buildings. Certainly few noblemen, counts or barons could boast then of such outstanding and extensive buildings as those belonging to the great abbeys. And when monks or canons resided as chaplains in palaces, their apart-

---

[1] Ed. G. A. Hückel, *Les poèmes satiriques d'Adalbéron* ('Bibliothèque de la Faculté des lettres de Paris', XIII, 1901) pp. 129–67.

[2] Ed. A. Boutemy, 'Deux poèmes inconnus de Serlon de Bayeux et une copie nouvelle de son poème contre les moines de Caen', in *Le moyen âge*, LI (1938) 254–60.

[3] *Liber de unitate ecclesiae conservanda*, ed. in *MGH Libelli*, II 278, 36–7.

ments sometimes occupied as much space as the whole of the rest of the establishment.[1] Even the pope himself, with St Peter's in Rome, could not outdo Cluny as regards the size of the building.

The voice of St Peter Damian was raised in Italy like that of some monastic prophet. For his own part, he always refused the title of abbot, and he consented to be a cardinal only for the briefest term possible: he used to refer to himself simply as 'the sinful monk'. Not even the most renowned abbots of the day escaped his castigations: he accused them of spending too much time in litigation and secular business, taking advantage of their position to evade the common observance, and caring only about acquiring more property for their monasteries. They adorned their churches with costly ornaments, so he said, added new storeys to the buildings they already had, and flanked them with the highest towers they could.[2] He quoted the example of Richard of St Vanne, venerated as a saint by the monasteries of Verdun, who because he had such a mania for building while on earth had to spend eternity climbing up scaffolding.[3]

It may be objected that this is just so much invective from a rather impassioned ascetic; then let us adduce the evidence of Joannelinus, a mild man, unusually well-balanced for his day, who never ceased recommending serenity. Born near the end of the tenth century in the neighbourhood of Ravenna, he was able for a time to enjoy real solitude in that region. But his uncle, William of Volpiano, had destined him to be the abbot reformer of a number of important monasteries; those of the Holy Trinity at Fécamp, and St Bénigne at Dijon, together with the houses dependent on them. Joannelinus generously accepted this role, but being an utterly selfless man he had a right to speak out frankly about what he saw going on around him. It was not only amongst clergy and laity that the abuses he describes were rife; he denounces two abuses prevalent amongst the monks. Like St Peter Damian, he deplores the fact that the abbots and some of the monks travel about so much, and get involved in lawsuits, their minds set on safeguarding

[1] See P. Héliot, 'Sur les résidences princières bâties en France du Xe au XIIe siècle', in *Moyen Âge*, LXI (1955) 27–61, 291–7.

[2] *Opusc.* XXI, 'De fuga dignitatum ecclesiasticarum': *PL* 145, 457–60.

[3] *Epist.* III 2: *PL* 144, 465.

their material interests: 'they are richer now than bishops'. To justify his assertion he cites outstanding examples, including even that of St Mayeul: 'But have we any right to set Mayeul before Christ?' He complains that one could hardly tell the difference between the great men of the secular world, 'kings, dukes, counts and marquises', and the abbots who cultivated their friendship. Still greater danger lay in the fact that the distinction between monks and priests had also become blurred: 'Ways and manners of clergy and people, priest and monk, are indistinguishable.'[1] Joannelinus' manner was certainly less violent than St Peter Damian's, but he too voiced a protest. Though he was longing to get back to his beloved solitude, he never actually did so: instead he accepted the office he had never wanted, and was able to teach some monks who had fled from their monastery in search of solitude that the most convincing proof of love is obedience.[2]

Leo of Ravenna, a former abbot of Nonantola, had to speak in similar vein in like circumstances.[3] But the very fact that fervent religious had to be recalled to common life in a prosperous community shows where the trouble lay. Dom Morin hit the nail on the head when he called it the 'crisis of cenobitism'.[4] This is, in fact, the crisis of prosperity. The abbeys grew richer as men of high station came to rely on them. Monastic funds were ably administered by prudent abbots, some of them saints, and this increased wealth led to the extension and embellishment of the buildings. All this provoked a reaction in favour of authentic poverty, and the only thing which could guarantee that was a return to solitude. Just as monasticism was becoming exclusively urban, the eremitic life claimed its rights, for from earliest times it also had been one of the legitimate forms of a life dedicated to God and separated from the world.

Aspirations of this sort prompted enterprises calculated to remedy the confusion of which John of Fécamp complained.

---

[1] Letter 'Tuae quidem', ed. J. Leclercq and L. P. Bonnes, *Un maître de la vie spirituelle au XIe siècle, Jean de Fécamp* (Paris, 1946) pp. 201–3.

[2] Letter to insubordinate monks, ibid. pp. 218–20.

[3] Ed. F. Ughelli, *Italia Sacra*, II (Venice, 1717) pp. 355–9.

[4] 'Rainaud l'Ermite et Yves de Chartres: un épisode de la crise du cenobitisme aux XIe–XIIe siècles', in *RB* XL (1928) 99.

'There are three orders in the world,' he had laid down with precision, echoing Gregory the Great's clearly formulated distinction; 'the first differs from the second, and the second from the third. If anyone arrogates to himself another's function, because he is not content with his own, he upsets the whole body.'[1] The situation called for the restoration of a clear distinction between priest and monk, and between both of them and the layman. In response to the former need, an increasing number of clergy claimed as their special prerogative the right to live a fervent, even austere life according to rule, with a good deal of time devoted to celebrating the divine office, but with special emphasis also on pastoral activity, that 'care of souls' which was not part of a monk's vocation. Such was the origin of many communities of priests known as 'canons regular', though as a matter of fact these two words are synonymous.

They developed successfully and were organised into congregations of monasteries during the second half of the eleventh century, and especially from the end of that century onwards. As they gradually became conscious of the specific nature of their institution, they began to assert its superiority over that of the monks. An important collection of legislative texts, drawn up for them towards the end of the eleventh century, has been preserved.[2] The prologue to this clearly defines their special dignity, which consists in combining the active with the contemplative life.[3] They are to preach, and act as pastors of the Christian people, while remaining faithful to the demands of life in the cloister. In the matter of renunciation of the world, their vocation does not differ from that of the monks; and this statement is supported by a long dissertation on the psychological aspect of 'conversion' to God. Then follows a rule of life, the last chapter of which bears the revealing title 'Distinction between the life of Canons and that of Monks'. The author states plainly that the canons' way of life surpasses that of all others, although it is less austere than that of the monks. The latter, while bound to more rigid fasting and exacting penance, are responsible for their own souls only: 'All they have to do

---

[1] Letter 'Tuae quidem', as cited in n. 1 above.
[2] Ottoboni MS. lat. 175.
[3] See J. Leclercq 'Un témoignage sur l'influence de Grégoire VII dans la réforme canoniale', in *Studi Gregoriani*, VI, for an edition of this text.

is to remain in a state of material dependence, and to live the common life under obedience.' Truth himself cries out to them: 'Whoever leaves house or brothers or father or mother or fields for my sake, will receive a hundredfold and life everlasting.' But to the disciples whom he sent out to his harvest, and whose place the canons now take in the church, the Lord says: 'You who have left all to follow me, will sit, when the day of judgement comes, judging the twelve tribes of Israel'; and again he says to them: 'You are the light of the world and the salt of the earth.'

So monks and canons, it seemed, were going their separate ways: it looked as if confusion could not arise again. However, faced with having to lay down a way of life for canons, the compiler of this collection had recourse to St Benedict, and without mentioning his name, copied out a number of pages from the Rule, and the most essential ones at that. It is true that he does quote the authority of St Gregory for them, but this subterfuge could not blind either his eyes or ours to the fact that this apparently obvious solution is really a compromise: anyone who wished to inspire the clerks regular with due appreciation for their state and set a spiritual programme before them had to draw from the 'rule for monasteries', whose wisdom had assured the prosperity of Benedictine monasticism.

The other demarcation which John of Fécamp and Peter Damian aimed at restoring was that between monks and laymen. They wished that the abbots were not so much taken up with defending their own temporal interests: they would be less wealthy, but so much the better, and they could live far away from the towns. This desire set on foot a great movement of monastic renewal which first appeared in Italy. Fundamentally it was a return to poverty and resulted in a general increase in austerity, but in many cases it also led to a longing for the solitary life. Not everyone, however, shared this eremitic tendency. St John Gaulbert, founder of Vallombrosa, wished to retain community life: it was only wealth, with its concomitant anxieties, that he rejected. He was insistent about the obligation to remain within the cloister, and never allowed anyone to set foot outside it. On hearing that a wealthy man had entered one of his monasteries and bestowed his possessions on it, he went there himself and demanded the deed of donation. In his anger he tore it up, trampled the pieces underfoot and then left the monastery, calling down God's vengeance upon it. No sooner had he left than a fire broke out and the building began to go up in flames. But John Gaulbert, so his biographer Hatto tells us, would not even turn his head to look at it.[1]

A similar protest against monastic wealth formed part of the message of those two men of God, St Romuald and St Peter Damian. As they wished to ensure complete renunciation on the part of the ascetics who drew inspiration from them, both showed a marked, though not exclusive, preference for the eremitic life. We would know little about the character and lifework of the former, were it not for the latter: in writing the life of St Romuald – his first literary work – St Peter Damian formulated his own personal programme.[2] There is no doubt that he himself was out to raise up monks, desirous of living according to St Romuald's ideal, in really lonely places far from towns or highways, and to encourage them in a life devoted to prayer and penance, lived for God alone within the narrow compass of a poor cell. St Romuald had in various places kindled enthusiasm for strictly eremitic asceticism. Some of his disciples performed heroic feats of mortification, enduring disciplines unto blood, and had worn out and lacerated their bodies by wearing iron chains and cuirasses which hampered all their movements. It remained for Peter Damian to canalise this fervour, keep some sort of check on it and organise some of these foundations. In his hermitage at Fonte Avellano, as in that of Camaldoli, where constitutions were drawn up by Prior Rodolph about the year 1085,[3] getting things organised meant consulting the Rule of St Benedict. St Peter Damian made it the code which his hermits were to consult in all cases where their own observance was compatible with it. In this way St Peter

---

[1] After Andrea of Strumi, *Vita S. Joannis Gualberti*, 47: *AA SS* July III 335.

[2] Ed. G. Tabacco, *Petri Damiani Vita Beati Romualdi* (Rome, 1957); in the notes of this valuable edition the editor suggests useful references concerning what Peter Damian said in this work and elsewhere. In *S. Pierre Damien, ermite et homme d'Église* (ed. 'Storia e letteratura', Rome, 1960) I have tried to pick out the characteristics of the work of St Romuald and St Peter Damian.

[3] Ed. Mittarelli-Costadoni, *Annales Camaldulenses* (Venice, 1755) III, cols 512–51.

Damian does belong to the Benedictine tradition. But he took care not to integrate his hermitages entirely into the pattern of that tradition: instead he instituted a new and original form of monasticism – a new Benedictine tradition, differentiated from that of the past by its eremitic trend. In his insistence on the solitary life, the discipline and other practices of mortification, his reduction of buildings to the minimum necessary for a simple, frugal life, and his refusal to be called abbot, St Peter Damian joined his powerful voice to the chorus of high-minded men protesting against monastic affluence. He still remained the friend of the great abbots of his day, Hugh of Cluny, Guy of Pomposa, Desiderius of Monte Cassino, but the example he gave did not belie his teaching. By word of mouth and through his writings he introduced a little of St Romuald's severity and something of his ideal into traditional monasticism, which he respected but did not wish to imitate.

This ascetic tendency to break away from traditional Benedictine forms developed from about 1095 onwards, especially in France. That country was swept just then by a great wave of generous vocations, many of them uninfluenced by monastic tradition. Men, and women, too, in great numbers, were eager for a life of poverty and solitude. This was the so-called 'eremitic movement' at the end of the eleventh century. It was apparent amongst certain primitive and as yet unorganised groups of canons regular, endeavouring to live together in the presence of God, ready to undertake works of charity, so long as these did not entail mixing too much with other people or settling close to any town. Some of these 'eremitic communities' – one has to designate them by that incongruous combination of words – had only a fleeting existence; others survived, and in some cases became leading houses in congregations. These then adopted the Rule of St Augustine or some other rule such as the one described above, strongly influenced by Benedictine ideas.

In contrast to these foundations there sprang up also unorganised groups of ascetics, who took the gospel for their only rule.[1] In parts of western France there were still vast tracts of

---

[1] See J. Leclercq, 'Le poème de Payen Bolotin contre les faux ermites', in *RB* LXVIII (1958) 52–86, where a bibliography is given and an attempt has been made to analyse the characteristics of this religious movement.

natural forest, and it was in such regions that this new type of
hermit appeared. Often devout, sometimes eccentric, they
caused astonishment everywhere. But sometimes what began
as admiration turned into scandal. The one thing these solitaries
had in common was their reaction against the wealth of the
monasteries and their resolve to pursue genuine poverty themselves. They practised severe fasting and prayed for long periods
on end; they worked in the forest to gain a frugal livelihood.
People who came to see them and heard them preach went
away impressed. Then some of them were tempted to go out
and preach or beg, even if this meant going into the towns and
visiting influential people. Sometimes the latter encouraged
them to come and made much of them. A number of these
hermits lived a vagabond life and became wandering preachers.
Often they had no training and no tradition. They were a cause
of disquiet to the bishops, especially as they denounced clerical
abuses. Living as they did without a rule, however, these
hermits were exposed to the very same dangers against which
they uttered their warnings. Accusations of immorality and
heresy were brought against them. At the beginning of the
twelfth century in the district around Chartres the trouble
which they stirred up came to a head: they had undermined the
reputation of monasticism, and sown nothing but seeds of
unrest in people's souls.

There is a poem by Payen Bolotin, a canon of Chartres in
the first half of the twelfth century, which deserves more
attention than it has received.[1] It is an example of the harsh
reproaches uttered against the hermits of this new variety, who
called down upon themselves in their turn many of the very
accusations which had been brought against the monks. They
claimed to be poor and were insatiable; they led a vagabond life
to satisfy their rapacity; they prowled round towns and found
a way into the courts of princes and bishops, won over influential
patrons and made the most of their favour and their gifts. They
appeared at councils, where they were sometimes accorded a
place of honour. Amid such temptations their humility and
integrity of life were exposed to dangers to which some of them
succumbed; in short, they were hypocrites. But the worst

[1] Ibid.

accusation that could be brought against them was that they belied their poverty. At the beginning of the poem Payen Bolotin sums up the case against them in lines which set the theme of the whole satire:

> Barns, stores, coffers fill with speed;
> Piled up hoards increased indeed;
> Increase cannot sate their greed.

Obviously the canon of Chartres had an axe to grind when he wrote such lines. Moreover he is unjust, for he forgets himself and lets himself be carried away by the strength of his own feelings. But at least he too plays his part in showing up the havoc wrought at the beginning of the twelfth century by this crisis in monastic life. Innovators and traditionalists, solitaries and protagonists of community life alike were bringing against one another the same accusations, and to some extent justifiably. On both sides the one thing about which all were concerned was genuine poverty: all claimed to have left the world and renounced their possessions. The original aspiration which had been at the root of all monastic life was still alive; it was only a question of how it could best be realised.

II. WORKING OUT A SOLUTION

This was a question for saints to answer rather than controversialists: a problem to be solved by action rather than by the written word. In order to understand how this crisis flared up and died down during the half-century from 1095 to 1145, we must consider some of the evidences of success in the new forms of monasticism resulting from it, and then see the reaction on the part of those following the traditional way of monastic life.

Failures there certainly were and even scandals amongst the new foundations. Many of them ceased to exist, or lost their first fervour after one generation, sometimes within a few years. But others were successful – quite remarkably so in the case of some lasting foundations outside the Benedictine tradition, to mention only Prémontré and Chartreuse, St Norbert and St Bruno. But the old Benedictine stock still showed astonishing vitality, and some founders, relying on its sap, successfully grafted onto it new branches which flourished. Though they did not join any existing congregation of monasteries, they drew inspiration from the Rule of St Benedict and from secular observances; the one difference was that they took measures against the dangers of too prosperous circumstances. In Italy, William of Vercelli lived an eremitic life with a few disciples in some poverty-stricken cottages, which later developed into the monastery of Montevergine.[1] Then too there was St John of Matera, who became the father of the congregation of Pulsano. He laid special stress on the importance of physical austerities, which he certainly practised himself. Like the early Irish monks, he would stand up to the neck in cold water to overcome sleep; like St Anthony, he wrestled with demons. Having offered his services to one of the great abbeys, he was employed there as a shepherd, but he refused to share the monks' superabundant meals. His abstinence shamed them, and they got their revenge by giving him stale bread to eat, which of course was just to his taste.[2] It may be that all these edifying details should only be taken as symbols, in spite of the fact that his biographer claims to have learnt them from John of Matera himself; but they would not have been recorded at all, had they not been regarded as significant. In that particular place, and in the life of that particular individual, as in that of many others, there was a conflict between the generosity of a solitary impelled to undertake severe penances on the one hand, and the practices accepted by the majority of monks on the other.

In France, Cadouin was founded by Gerard of Salles, Savigny by St Vitalis of Mortain, Grandmont by St Stephen of Maret, Tiron by St Bernard of Abbeville, and Fontevrault by St Robert of Arbrissel. One might mention other names, each of which would call to mind a founder of outstanding virtue, with disciples who were fervent, if not always immune from reproach. Take for instance Cîteaux, the most famous of these French foundations. Its special contribution seems to have been that of combining the new movement with a strong element of tradition. Research on the chronology of Cistercian origins has

[1] After J. de Nusco, *Vita B. Guilielmi*, ca. ll–lv, esp. nn. 23–4 in *AA SS* June v 1867, pp. 101–5.

[2] After the contemporary anonymous life, ed. in *AA SS* June v 1867, pp 36–7.

made it clear that the solidity which has ensured the permanence
of the Cistercian order is due to the unerring convictions of its
founders or 'fathers'. From the very start, two things made up
its heritage: firm organisation and a high ideal. A providential
event ensured its success: this was the arrival of St Bernard and
his companions.

Before long the youthful abbot of Clairvaux was spreading
the Cistercian ideal all around him, both by word of mouth and
with his pen. He too was unable to put forward his monastic
programme without denouncing that of others. Once more it
was wealth that he spontaneously attacked; wealth, and the
buildings resulting from it. He deplored the ostentation of
abbots who were over-fond of travelling about, dressed with
exaggerated splendour, and he inveighed against relaxations
with regard to food and clothing. But these were only secondary
matters for censure; for in the beginning of the last part of his
'Apology' he speaks out at last about what really matters: 'Let
us pass on from these details to major abuses, though these being
widespread may actually seem unimportant. I am not going to
speak about the immense height of the oratories, their immoderate length, superfluous breadth, the magnificent carvings
and remarkable paintings in them ... granted all those things
may be for the glory of God; but as a monk myself, I would like
to cross-question these monks, and ask them in the words of
a pagan poet:

What means, O priests, this gold within the holy place?[1]

The abbot of Clairvaux goes on himself to answer this quotation
from Persius, this time citing a Christian satirist, St Jerome:
'Bishops are one thing, monks another. ... We ourselves stand
apart from the crowd; for Christ's sake we have left the beautiful
things of this world, the things of value. ... And to speak
frankly, is not avarice at the bottom of all this? It is a kind of
idol worship ... we lavish money on these works of art in order
to gain more; we spend it in the hope that it will increase. ...
When they see all these costly things, people are seized with a
desire to bestow gifts on us.' In other words, employing costly

---

[1] *Apologia ad Guilelmum abbatem*, nn. 28–9: *PL* 182, 914–15; ed. J. Leclercq
and H. M. Rochais, *S. Bernardi Opera*, III (Rome, 1963) pp. 105–6.

things in the service of God was another way of begging. That was the very heart of the matter, and was not to be overlooked on account of other causes for complaint. It had to be openly stated: 'to speak frankly'. St Bernard accused the black monks of the same thing that Payen Bolotin denounced amongst the new orders, including that of Cîteaux: the accumulation of wealth, 'spending money in order to increase it'.[1]

A powerful voice like his was bound to find an echo. Other Cistercians, less gifted than he, and some less sincere, fell upon the black monks.[2] There was an element of self-sufficiency in their attitude, excused to a great extent by the fervour of their monastic convictions and their genuine austerity of life. Above all, they had implicit trust in the precautions taken by their fathers against themselves. In the *Exordium parvum* the first 'statutes of the monks of Cîteaux formerly of Molesmes' laid it down that they should never assume ownership of goods other than the fruit of their own toil, and one of the first decrees of their general chapter is headed 'On not having revenues'.[3] It was on this account that the Cistercians, by favour of the holy see, were dispensed from tithes and other taxes on revenue, to which wealthy abbeys were liable.

Such were the ideal and constitution, but what were the facts? At Clairvaux itself during St Bernard's lifetime the ruling was faithfully observed; but from the very year of his death, the cartulary reveals infractions.[4] In other places they did not even wait until 1153 before beginning to accept donations contrary to the rule. Alexander III issued a solemn warning to the general chapter of 1169. He denounced as an abuse the fact that Cistercians were accepting revenues in the same way as

[1] Ibid. The first phrase is inspired by St Jerome, *Epist.* xiv 8, ed. I. Hilberg, *CSEL* 54 (1910) 55–6.

[2] See J. Leclercq, 'Une nouvelle réponse de l'ancien monachisme aux critiques des cisterciens', in *RB* LXVII (1957) 77094, where a bibliography is given. Among the evidence of 'indirect' Cistercian attacks are the two texts edited by M.-A. Dimier, 'Un témoin tardif peu connu du conflit entre cisterciens et clunisiens', in *Petrus Venerabilis* ('Studia Anselmiana', XL, Rome, 1956) pp. 81–94 and G. Constable, 'The vision of a Cistercian novice', ibid. pp. 95–8.

[3] Ed. C. Noschitzka, in *Analecta Ordinis Cisterciensis*, VI (1950) 8 and 24.

[4] This has been established by R. Fossier, 'L'essor économique de Clairvaux', in *Bernard de Clairvaux* (Paris, 1955) p. 109.

other monks, and even specified the harm ensuing in their own
case as well as in that of others: monks and abbots were forced
into worldly contacts in order to defend their own interests.[1]
In fact from Adalbero of Laon onwards, the list of criticisms
levelled against monks anywhere remains unvaried. The pope
threatened to impose the ordinary obligation of tithes on the
Cistercians if they claimed the same revenues as other
monasteries.

In vain did voices within the Cistercian order plead in favour
of the original legislation. Bells of excessive weight could be
destroyed, useless ornamentation on buildings and furniture
removed, but no one could pull down the bell-towers or destroy
the actual buildings, which by now differed little from the old
abbeys in size. What they could do was to forbid the erection of
such buildings in the future. It was too late then to alienate
possessions which entailed responsibilities, but a series of general
chapters from 1175 onwards decreed that mills, altars and
revenues contrary to the primitive observance of poverty should
as far as possible be given up, and it was forbidden to acquire
such things for the future. The chapter of 1182 explained the
reason: 'It is evident to all that in our case when possessions
increase, scandals arise both inside and outside the monastery.
This is the sole or at any rate the principal cause of all that is
wrong.' Such was the sane and vigorous reaction of those in
authority. Others, with less weight of authority but assured of
a large public on account of their literary skill, wrote in similar
vein. Gilbert of Hoyland, abbot of Swineshead, looked back
with nostalgia on the times when 'our fathers went in search of
real solitude: they cared about holiness, not possessions. What
times! What conduct!'[2] And Conrad of Eberbach (d. 1221)
inserted into the Cistercian *Exordium magnum* the following
prophetic protest, uttered by a consecrated virgin, who passed
on to the abbot of Cîteaux the insights she had received in
prayer: 'There are three things in your order which offend
God's majesty: increase of landed property, superfluous build-

---

[1] I have published the texts of Alexander III and the general chapters in
question in 'Passage supprimé dans une épître d'Alexandre III', in *RB* LXIII
(1952) 149–51 and 'Épîtres d'Alexandre III sur les cisterciens', in *RB* LXIV
(1954) 70–82.
[2] Letter to Roger, Cistercian abbot of Byland, *PL* 184, 279.

ings, and the sensuality of the monks' voices.'[1] Historians of the chant may be left to decide what abuse underlies this last expression. Let us note that between the periods when the *Exordium parvum* and the *Exordium magnum* were composed, the very terms which St Bernard had used against the monks of Cluny began to be applied to his own order: increase of landed property and superfluous buildings. The early fathers sought out bare and lonely places, but these were now replaced by those vast monastic cities whose wealth caused Gilbert of Hoyland to exclaim: 'What times! What conduct!'[2] The Cistercian order in its turn lived through several phases of this crisis in cenobitic life.

As we have seen, this time of tension served to stir up, if not a return to their first fervour, at least a wholesome and energetic reaction in favour of the monastic ideal. The same thing happened in the case of the black monks. Attacks against them brought them a twofold advantage: they learnt both to defend and to reform themselves. To tell the truth, they were not left to defend themselves unaided. They had friends and admirers, still sufficiently impressed by them to write in their defence. Payen Bolotin was on good terms with the monasteries of Chartres, and he contrasts the vagrant life of the 'false hermits' with the austere stability of the monks, their moderate but continued penances, the holy leisure of the cloister, devoted entirely to prayer and to reading the fathers – all that unspectacular asceticism which leads to a love of silence but qualifies men to speak. Those who belittle such a life simply do not know it:

> Since they ne'er in cloisters dwell,
> Naught can they of hardships tell,
> Felt by those who know them well.

And the canon, who did know the monks, continues to describe their contemplative life:

> There they ever pray or read,
> On the fathers' writings feed –
> As from heav'n distils sweet mead –

---

[1] *Exord. magn. Cist.* v 20: *PL* 185, 1174–5.
[2] Gilbert of Hoyland, as in n. 2 above, col. 283.

> Hearts aflame with holy fire.
> Leisure that can so inspire,
> Banishes all vain desire.

He recalls their daily mortifications, their detachment vis-à-vis amenities which they might have procured for themselves but preferred to go without:

> Added lustre thence is shed:
> On choice food they might have fed;
> Freely they abstain instead.[1]

Another poet, an anonymous one, was to finish off a satire against various ways of life – including that of the innovators – with a eulogy of traditional cenobites, monks who remained genuine solitaries even in the midst of their communities:

> In sacred cloisters I can find
> Monks versed in writ right well;
> So sanctified by holy lives,
> They seem in heaven to dwell.[2]

When Hatto, bishop of Troyes, entered as a monk at Cluny in the year 1145 or 1146, the prior of the canons regular at Sens wrote him a touching letter on the value of the life there: 'Cluny provides adequate means of salvation for anyone seeking God. . . .' He congratulates Hatto on having placed himself under the jurisdiction of Peter the Venerable, whose reputation for sanctity equalled that of Odo, Mayeul, Odilo and Hugh. He especially singles out the supreme value of life at Cluny. Others might inflict corporal austerities on themselves if they so wished: 'Here at least is to be found ordered charity – love of God before all else, and mutual love amongst the brethren.'[3]

It would take too long to analyse the replies of the black monks to the attacks of the Cistercians: Peter the Venerable maintained a tone of absolute serenity;[4] Hugh of Reading was

---

[1] See p. 226 n. above. [In the original French edition of the present article these excerpts are quoted in Latin. Ed.]

[2] Ed. E. du Meril, *Poésies inedites du moyen âge* (Paris, 1854) pp. 319–25.

[3] Ed. G. Constable, 'The Letter from Peter of St John to Hatto of Troyes', in *Petrus Venerabilis* ('Studia Anselmiana', XL, Rome, 1956) pp. 38–53.

[4] *Epist.* 128: *PL* 189, 112–59.

remarkably vigorous and quite often very much to the point;[1] an anonymous writer, probably an Englishman, wrote unpretentiously and a little awkwardly, at the same time showing great directness and ardent sincerity.[2] Moreover the criticisms of some of the secular clergy in England were answered by anonymous or scarcely known Benedictines. The latter may not have been highly gifted, but there is a ring of sincerity about the verse or prose in which they express their esteem for the way of life which they professed, and in whose sanctifying efficacy they continued to believe.[3] The most explosive pamphlets – even when signed by St Bernard (his letter to Robert circulated at the same time as the 'Apology to William') – failed to shake their faith in the monastic life. They remained convinced that traditional observance, although not the only way of going to God, was still capable of satisfying the aspiration essential to all monasticism – the desire to seek God by withdrawing from the world.

Had it only served to strengthen them in this conviction, and make them more conscious of why they were really monks, the crisis in cenobitic life would have had considerable effect. But there were other results as well. Peter the Venerable organised the eremitic life at Cluny, where his predecessors had already favoured such a tradition.[4] In 1146 he promulgated decrees for the whole order emphasising austerity, the spirit of prayer and separation from the world. He decided that part of the new monastery and church should be reserved in future for monks alone, since it was essential that the religious should have a private place in which to take the discipline, practise other penances and give themselves up to long periods of prayer,

[1] Ed. A. Wilmart, 'Une riposte de l'ancien monachisme au manifeste de saint Bernard', in *RB* XLVI (1934) 296–344; on the author, see C. H. Talbot, 'The date and author of the Riposte', in *Petrus Venerabilis*, pp. 72–80.

[2] See my edition of this text, 'Nouvelle réponse de l'ancien monachisme aux critiques des cisterciens', in *RB* LXVII (1957) 77–94.

[3] See J. Leclercq and R. Foreville, who have edited or indicated several of these texts in the following articles: 'La vêture *ad succurrendum* d'après le moine Raoul', in *Analecta Monastica*, III ('Studia Anselmiana', XXXVII, Rome, 1955) pp. 158–68; and 'Un débat sur le sacerdoce des moines au XIIe siècle', ibid. IV (XLI, 1955) pp. 8–118.

[4] See J. Leclercq, 'Pierre le Vénérable et l'érémitisme clunisien', in *Petrus Venerabilis*, pp. 99–120.

just as if they were actually in the desert.[1] In this case, the increased extent of the buildings favoured the cause of eremitic life.

St Peter Damian and St Bernard scored other points as well. About 1143 Peter the Venerable sent all the priors and superiors of houses of his order a programme for reform which, it is said, was undoubtedly inspired by the 'Apology'.[2] It certainly does echo desires expressed by all sincere monks; by all those who wrote about these tensions within cenobitic life, hoping to contribute towards finding a solution. Like John of Fécamp, he wished to restore the difference between laymen and religious in matters of abstinence. Along with all the reformers, he upheld in his writings constancy in traditional austerity, unceasing prayer, work and charity – a life hidden in Christ Jesus.[3]

CONCLUSION

It is time now, by way of conclusion, to indicate the historical significance of this crisis affecting the whole of monasticism in the course of one of the centuries of its greatest prosperity. Peter the Venerable had said to Innocent II: 'In the religious life it is easier to found than to restore; to start afresh rather than to repair what has existed for a long time.'[4] Without creating anew, he himself in the Cluniac order, Suger at St Denis and others elsewhere did succeed in renewing institutions fraught with glory from the past but burdened also with wealth and the anxieties arising from it and the ensuing dangers for those who wished to live according to the gospel. If it is easier to found anew, there is more enduring achievement in maintaining what exists. By about 1145, a mere half-century after the phenomenal increase of eremitic foundations in France, many of them had already disappeared. Some of them, such as Chartreuse and

[1] Text in *PL* 189, 1023–48, esp. n. 52, col. 1040. I have analysed the character of these reform decrees in *Pierre le Vénérable* (St Wandrille, 1946) pp. 148–53.

[2] See D. Knowles, 'The Reforming Decrees of Peter the Venerable', in *Petrus Venerabilis*, p. 4. The text of the letter is in *PL* 189, 418–23.

[3] I have indicated the texts in *Pierre le Vénérable*, pp. 91–136.

[4] *Epist.* 1 23: *PL* 189, 102: also Giles Constable, *The Letters of Peter the Venerable* (Cambridge, Mass., 1967) 1 43.

Prémontré, were remarkably successful and soon firmly established. Others disappeared without leaving a trace, or else developed into large cenobitic institutions, similar to those from which they had originally broken away. Others again joined old foundations such as Cluny or some similar abbey, or else attached themselves to new ones like Prémontré or Cîteaux. St Bernard, for instance, affiliated to his order the strong congregation of Savigny, which was to prove such a heavy drag on Cistercian history in the second half of the twelfth century. During the prosperous years of Vitalis of Mortain and his immediate successors, Savigny and its daughter houses had been radiating centres of the eremitic life, places of marked austerity, solitude and poverty.[1] Later, however, they were to press their claim to tithes and revenues so insistently that Alexander III was obliged repeatedly to admonish them severely, and he insisted on these 'new houses' conforming to the statutes and obligations of the others.[2]

Within the framework of traditional monasticism, this crisis served to restore a state of prosperity, but of a prosperity that had been tested, purified and chastened. The black monks admitted that their observance had its weak points: they did their best to remedy these, but changed nothing of their tradition. They were just humbler than before. If ever they had been tempted to boast, they had lost all taste for that now. The self-esteem, amounting even to arrogance, of some of their opponents, while not robbing them of their peace, did increase their humility, and that was a great gain. In short, this protracted period of crisis tested the vitality of the monastic way of life, which, for its part, showed that it still had enough spiritual sap and sufficient reserves of charity to surmount the difficulties. The crisis had certainly borne fruit.

[1] *AA SS* Oct VIII 1866, p. 1010, n. 13 and p. 1014, n. 32.
[2] See 'Épîtres d'Alexandre III sur les cisterciens', p. 73 and 'Passage supprimé', p. 151.

Select Bibliography

The most recent summaries of the history of Christian monasticism are David Knowles, *Christian Monasticism* (London, 1969) and Dom P. Cousin, *Précis d'Histoire monastique* (Paris, 1956). Dom J. Leclercq, *The Love of Learning and the Desire for God* (New York, 1962), conveys excellently the spirit of medieval monasticism and the later critical change. The chapter on monasticism and papal reform in C. Brooke, *Europe in the Central Middle Ages, 962–1154* (London, 1964) pp. 237 ff., places Cluny in the general context of the central middle ages and so does J.-F. Lemarignier, 'Political and monastic structures in France at the end of the tenth and beginning of the eleventh centuries', in F. L. Cheyette, *Lordship and Community in Medieval Europe: Selected Readings* (New York, 1968) pp. 100–27.

To select from the monastic sources prior to the foundation of Cluny but relevant to its monasticism is an invidious task. Several references to earlier material, especially Scriptural and patristic, have been given in the footnotes of the present volume and bibliographies are included in the general works quoted above. No monastic bibliography would be complete, however, without the Rule of St Benedict (Abbot Justin McCann's translation and edition, London, 1952, has recently been reprinted), the life of St Benedict by Pope St Gregory the Great (book II of the *Dialogues*, of which an English edition was produced in 1966 at Collegeville, Minn.), and the Rule of the Master (French translation and Latin edition in *La Règle du Maître*, ed. Adalbert de Vogüé, in 'Sources Chrétiennes', ed. H. de Lubac and J. Danielou, Paris, 1964, nos. 105–7) which illuminates many concepts in the Rule of St Benedict. *Corpus Consuetudinum Monasticarum*, ed. Dom K. Hallinger, vol. 1: *Initia Consuetudines Benedictinae, Consuetudines Saeculi octavi et noni* (Sieburg, 1963) contains the main monastic legislation of the eighth and ninth centuries.

Unfortunately relatively little scholarly work on Cluny is available in English. The period from 994 to 1156 is well covered by three modern works, each containing extensive notes and bibliographies: Dom J. Hourlier, *Saint Odilon Abbé de Cluny* ('Bibliothèque de la Revue d'Histoire ecclésiastique', 40, Louvain, 1964) covers 994–1049; N. Hunt, *Cluny under St Hugh, 1049–1109* (London, 1967); *The Letters of Peter the Venerable*, ed. Giles Constable ('Harvard Historical Studies', LXXVIII, Harvard Univ. Press, Cambridge, Mass., 1967): the second volume is devoted to an excellent English introduction and comments and notes of high quality. The best summary of Cluny's history from its foundation to its demise is the article by G. de Valous, 'Cluny', in *Dictionnaire d'Histoire et de Géographie ecclésiastique*, XIII, cols 35–174.

On the question of sources, we may begin with the material and visual remains since we are now in possession of one of the most outstanding works in Cluniac scholarship, namely the complete report of the Mediaeval Academy of America's excavations at Cluny, which began in 1927 and are still continuing: *Cluny, Les Églises et la Maison du chef d'Ordre*, by Kenneth John Conant (Mâcon, 1968). This magnificent volume is a major contribution to the history of art and architecture. Thereto may be added the works of Joan Evans, *Cluniac Art of the Romanesque Period* (Cambridge, 1950) and *The Romanesque Architecture of the Order of Cluny* (Cambridge, 1938).

The main collection of literary sources, especially the lives and writings of the abbots of Cluny, have been collected in *Bibliotheca Cluniacensis*, ed. Dom M. Marrier and A. Quercatenus (Paris, 1614). Much of this material is also available in Migne's *Patrologia Latina*: *PL* 133 (Odo); *PL* 142 (Odilo, including his life of Mayeul); *PL* 159 (Hugh); *PL* 189 (Peter the Venerable, though his letters have been better edited by Giles Constable as mentioned above). John of Salerno's life of St Odo (926–44) is available in English: John of Salerno, *Life of St Odo of Cluny* and *The Life of St Gerald of Aurillac* by St Odo, trans. and ed. Dom Gerard Sitwell, O.S.B. (London, 1958). Odo's lengthy and important poem the *Occupatio* has been edited by A. Svoboda (Leipzig, 1900) and some of St Odilo's sermons have been edited by Raymond Oursel, *Les saints abbés de Cluny* ('Coll. Les écrits des saints', Namur, 1960) pp. 89–161. On the reforming decrees of Peter the Venerable, see M. D. Knowles, 'The Reforming Decrees of Peter the Venerable', in *Petrus Venerabilis* ('Studia Anselmiana', XL, Rome, 1957).

Cluny's charters are one of the richest collections of medieval documents: they have been edited by A. Bernard and A. Bruel, *Recueil des Chartes de l'Abbaye de Cluny* ('Collection de documents inédits', 18, 6 vols. Paris, 1876–1903). As yet there is no index to them. A collection of most of the papal bulls sent to Cluny was edited by P. Simon, *Bullarium Sacri Ordinis Cluniacensis* (Lyons, 1860): an extremely rare book. Some of these bulls have been edited, though incompletely, in Migne's *Patrologia* and with the Cluniac charters. The cartularies of many Cluniac monasteries have been edited; several remain to be edited: they tend to appear in the various European collections of texts, to which references are made in the books mentioned in the third paragraph of this bibliography.

Dom Bruno Albers edited fragments of three primitive Cluniac customaries and the whole of the so-called Farfa customary, now known to be Cluniac: *Consuetudines Cluniacenses Antiquiores*, ed. B. Albers (Stuttgart, 1900 and Monte Cassino, 1903–12). Further volumes of the *Corpus Consuetudinum Monasticarum*, ed. Dom Kassius Hallinger (Siegburg, 1963–   ) are to include all known early Cluniac customaries. Meanwhile, the important customaries of Bernard and Ulrich are only available in *PL* 149, 643–778 (= Ulrich, *Antiquiores Consuetudines Cluniacensis Monasterii*) and Herrgott, *Vetus Disciplina Monastica*, pp. 133–364 (=Bernard of Cluny, *Ordo Cluniacensis*). Two articles which demonstrate what insights into Cluniac history can be wrung out of the customaries by modern textual criticism are H. R. Philippeau, 'Pour l'histoire de la Coutume de Cluny', in *RM* (1954) 141–51, and K. Hallinger, 'Clunys Bräuche zur Zeit Hugos des Grossen. Prolegomena zur Neuherausgabe des Bernhard und Udalrich von Kluny', in *Zeitschrift der Savigny-Stiftung für Rechtsgeschichte, kanonistische Abteilung*, XLV (Weimar, 1959) 99–140. Here we are given a foretaste of what may be expected from the definitive editions. Dom G. Charvin is editing the visitations and Cluniac general chapters, institutions introduced later than the period with which the present volume has been concerned: *Statuts, Chapitres généraux et Visites de l'Ordre de Cluny*, with introduction and notes (Paris, 1965–   ).

The authors who have contributed to the present volume point in their footnotes to their sources and to further reading on those aspects of Cluniac monasticism about which they have written. The importance of Dr Wollasch's identification of the Marcigny necrology makes G. Schnürer's edition of it a document of great significance: 'Das Necrologium des Cluniacenser-Priorates Münchenwiler (Villars-les-Moines)', in *Collectanea Friburgensia*, n.s. x (Freiburg, Sw. 1909). Dr Wollasch's discovery is the strongest confirmation of Professor G. Tellenbach's conviction that new approaches in research would generate greater precision and would enrich our knowledge of Cluniac history. He indicates these methods and some of them are demonstrated by his disciples in *Neue Forschungen über Cluny und die Cluniacenser* (Freiburg, 1959).

Dom Kassius Hallinger, in his monumental study *Gorze–Kluny. Studien zu den monastischen Lebensreformen und Gegensätzen in Hochmittelalter* ('Studia Anselmiana', XXII–XXV, Rome, 1950), which will long remain a major work of reference, had already brought modern scholarship to bear on some of the Cluniac historical problems that previous historians had ignored. The monograph of G. Duby, *La Société aux XIe et XIIe siècles dans la région mâconnaise* (Paris, 1953) is not only an intensive study of Cluny's economy but also an important contribution to medieval economic history.

Certain works have become what may be described as classics of Cluniac history. Though in many respects superseded and needing now to be used very cautiously, no Cluniac scholar would ignore them: J. H. Pignot, *Histoire de l'Ordre de Cluny depuis la fondation de l'Abbaye jusqu'à la mort de Pierre le Vénérable, 908–1157* (3 vols, Paris, 1868); E. Sackur, *Die Cluniacenser in ihrer kirklichen und allgemeingeschichtlichen Wirksamkeit* (2 vols, Halle, 1892 and 1894); G. de Valous, *Le Monachisme clunisien des origines au XVe siècle* (2 vols, Paris, 1935); Joan Evans, *Monastic Life at Cluny 910–1157* (Oxford, 1931, recently reprinted). The reports of four twentieth-century Cluniac congresses contain a wide range of papers, diverse in subject and quality but including some valuable studies (of which three appear in this book): 'Millénaire de Cluny', in *Annales de l'Académie de Mâcon*, 3rd ser. xv (1910); *Congrès scientifique de Cluny 9–11 juillet 1949 en l'honneur des Saints Abbés Odon et Odilon* (Société des Amis de Cluny, Dijon, 1950); *Spiritualità Cluniacense. Convegni del Centro di Studi sulla Spiritualità medievale, 1958* (Todi, 1960); 'Actes du Colloque International de Moissac 3–5 mai 1963', in *Annales du*

Midi (Toulouse, 1963) LXXV, no. 64. Another volume of Cluniac essays which have already appeared elsewhere is being prepared for a German edition by Dr Richter and will appear in the series 'Wege der Forschung', CCXLI, published in Darmstadt. One may be allowed to hope that the inclusion of L. M. Smith's article 'Cluny and Gregory VII' (1911) is for historiographical reasons and not as an example of modern British scholarship: one regrets that it is not being accompanied by a translation of Dom David Knowles' review of L. M. Smith, 'Cluny in the eleventh and twelfth centuries', in the *Downside Review*, XLIX 180–2.

Other works which ought to be mentioned are J. Leclercq, 'Pour une histoire de la vie à Cluny', in *RHE* LVII (2) (1962) 385–408; ibid. (3–4) 783–812; H. V. White, 'Pontius of Cluny, the *Curia Romana*, and the end of Gregorianism in Rome', in *Church History*, XXVII (New York, 1958) 195–219; D. Knowles, *Cistercians and Cluniacs* (Oxford, 1955); J. Kritzeck, *Peter the Venerable and Islam* (Princeton, 1964); E. Werner, *Die Gesellschaftlichen Grundlagen der Klosterreform im 11. Jahrhundert* (Berlin, 1953); H. E. J. Cowdrey, *The Cluniacs and the Gregorian Reform* (Oxford, 1970).

We are still far from possessing a definitive list of Cluniac dependencies save for a few regions. The English Cluniac houses have been identified (D. Knowles and R. Neville Hadcock, *Medieval Religious Houses, England and Wales* (London, 1953) is being re-edited) and the role of these houses in English monasticism has been properly assessed by Dom David Knowles in *The Monastic Order in England* (2nd ed. Cambridge, 1963) and *The Religious Orders in England* (3 vols, Cambridge, 1948–1959). We know enough about Cluniac history in general to appreciate that no single region or district may be regarded as typical of the congregation as a whole. For references to other regional studies and lists, see the bibliographies in the works of de Valous, Hourlier and Hunt mentioned above.

The simplest way of keeping abreast of the continuing output of Cluniac studies is to consult the bulletins which appear regularly in the *Revue Bénédictine* (Maredsous), *Revue Mabillon* (Ligugé) and the *Revue d'Histoire ecclésiastique* (Louvain).

Index

This index *excludes* the names of Cluniac priors listed on pp. 178 f. and the names of Cluniac nuns of Marcigny who are indexed on pp. 183–90